REIMAGING THE PARIAH CITY

Reimaging the Pariah City

Urban development in Belfast & Detroit

WILLIAM J.V. NEILL
Department of Environmental Planning,
School of the Built Environment, Queen's University of Belfast

DIANA S. FITZSIMONS
School of the Built Environment
University of Ulster at Jordanstown

BRENDAN MURTAGH
School of Social & Community Sciences
Magee College, University of Ulster

Avebury

Aldershot • Brookfield USA • Hong Kong • Singapore • Sydney

Published by
Avebury
Ashgate Publishing Ltd
Gower House
Croft Road
Aldershot
Hants GU11 3HR
England

Ashgate Publishing Company
Old Post Road
Brookfield
Vermont 05036
USA

British Library Cataloguing in Publication Data

Neill, William J. V.
    Reimaging the Pariah City: Urban
    Development in Belfast and Detroit
    I. Title
    711.4

1 85628 480 8

Library of Congress Catalog Card Number: 95-75556

Typeset by
Textflow Services Ltd
Science Library
Lennoxvale
Malone Road
Belfast BT9 5EQ
Northern Ireland

Printed and bound by Athenæum Press Ltd.,
Gateshead, Tyne & Wear.

Contents

TABLES

FIGURES

MAPS

PHOTOGRAPHS

Preface

The last fifteen years or so have seen a major growth in the phenomenon of place marketing and the "selling of the city" which has shaped urban development agendas on both sides of the Atlantic. In turn this has spawned a considerable academic literature in which urban planning emerges as an important aspect of product development and packaging geared to city reimaging. However, for some cities the noise generated by the promotional clamour fails to screen out other signs and sounds which indicate that all is not well in the real city behind the pastel coloured shades of the advertisers' brochures and upbeat jingles. This book focuses on two cities, Belfast and Detroit, where the gap between promoted image and generally received negative urban image to outsiders has been so great that they share a common pariah status. While the problems of Belfast and Detroit are rooted in separate histories of ethnic and racial division which preclude attempts at glib comparison, nevertheless, they both throw into sharp relief, owing to the obviousness of urban cosmetic surgery, the problems associated with reimaging in more "normal" places. These include questions such as the provenance of the image chosen for promotion, the representation of local culture, opportunity costs involved in the face of other compelling needs, the concentration on reimaging obstructing any effectual remaking of the city including its economy, and the papering over, containment and concealment of real social conflict in the face of the commodification of places. And yet because of the existing very negative images of Belfast and Detroit the pressure to engage in reimaging is particularly acute.

In the context of the pervasive market driven postmodern reimaging and planning of cities, study of Belfast and Detroit can remind us that history and culture are not peripheral, academic or decorative, that the past did not start yesterday, that real history does matter, that identity involves more than designer label clothing, and that social justice cannot be left to narrow market solutions. On top of this Detroit and Belfast are interesting because they form urban crucibles which test the possibilities for resolution of racial and sectarian conflict.

The contributors to this volume, while not sharing common views on all matters discussed, nevertheless, seek to present a broad picture of the issues raised in using urban planning in particular to sell cities when "product development" is seriously out of step with "product promotion".

Chapter One provides an overview of the reimaging of cities against a background of ever more competitive urban entrepreneurialism since the 1980s. It shows the potential risks involved for places with difficult images in opting out altogether. Chapter Two casts a critical eye on urban development, image making and conflict management in Belfast since the early 1980s where the imaging of the city in 1994, in the wake of an IRA cease-fire, still remains contentious. The work of the Laganside Corporation which has spearheaded a new place vision for Belfast, if not of Belfast, is reviewed in Chapter Three. Attention then switches to Detroit where the abject failure of an image-based urban development agenda dating back to the aftermath of the 1967 urban riots is examined. The city of Detroit, the black capital of the United States, has, in the face of adversity, been more successful in reimaging itself to African-American residents than to outsiders through white elephant projects like the Detroit Renaissance Center. Chapter Five raises the question of whether a focus on the reimaging of cities, with the temptation to concentrate on the superficial, is not a distraction from a concern with remaking in a more fundamental way the economies which cities express and on which they depend. The experience presented is that of recent State-sponsored industrial policy practice in the Detroit region which has drawn on ongoing post-Fordist debates on the future of manufacturing. Its origin lies in objections to the property development led reimaging strategy in the city of Detroit. Chapter Six picks up the issue of urban inequality and poverty with reference to Belfast raising the question of the opportunity costs involved in expensive reimaging projects and the limited trickle down or ripple effects to poorer neighbourhoods. The case for more effective targeting of limited resources is presented. Chapter Seven demonstrates just how far marketing hype in Belfast can get out of synch with the brute reality of physical segregation in a divided city which remains ill at ease with itself. The final chapter takes the academic risk of a more optimistic tone and looks to how in the future the pariah cities of Detroit and Belfast can be reclaimed in the name of social justice, compromise and tolerance.

W.J.V.N.
D.S.F.
B.M.

September 1994

Acknowledgements

In addition to expressing thanks to the many individuals who gave generously of their time in interview and also provided information for this book the authors would like to record their appreciation to Carol Bardon for her painstaking proof-reading, to Lorna Goldstrom for her invaluable help with word processing and to David Houston, Dr Patrick Braniff and Billy Thompson for their kind assistance with various maps and graphics. The authors also wish to acknowledge financial support from the Publication Funds at Queen's University Belfast and the University of Ulster.

1 Planning and promotion: city reimaging in the 1980s and 1990s

Diana S. Fitzsimons

Introduction

There has been considerable academic debate about the fundamental change in the nature of urban economies over the last few decades, particularly in the developed and newly industrializing countries. This change has resulted in new forms of competition between cities at national and international levels as city leaders have sought to restructure urban economies and respond to economic trends in a more entrepreneurial and proactive way. Harvey argues that inter-urban competition amongst the post-industrial cities takes place across a number of dimensions, namely competition for position in the international division of labour, competition for position as centres of consumption, competition for control and command functions (financial and administrative powers in particular), and competition for governmental redistributions (Harvey, 1987). The resulting shift from urban managerialism to urban entrepreneurialism is regarded by Harvey, in fact, as assisting the transition of capitalism from a Fordist-Keynesian regime of capital accumulation to a regime of "flexible accumulation" (Harvey, 1989). Flexible accumulation is characterized by "time-space compression" aided by new technologies, the centralized coordination of global corporate interests, new sectors of production and new organizational forms, new markets, new patterns of consumption, more flexible labour processes and greatly intensified rates of commercial, technological and organizational innovation. It has involved a marked rise in service sector employment as industrial employment has declined and has altered the patterns of uneven development between geographical regions.

This chapter reviews the drive to restructure urban economies by creating new roles in the urban hierarchy for the post-industrial city, the characteristics of urban entrepreneuralism which have evolved and the priority given to culture and city marketing in the attraction of inward investment. Attention is specifically focused on the reimaging process, the mechanisms of place product development and place image improvement and promotion, in cities where existing place images are adverse. It is generally not capital cities but second cities, cities with a former strength rooted in a declining manufacturing base (like Barcelona, Detroit and Cleveland) or trading function (like Rotterdam) and particularily those concentrated in the now remoter industrialized regions (like Belfast, Glasgow and Newcastle-upon-Tyne) which depended on specialized economic activities, that are particularly concerned with reimaging rather than the more run-of-the-mill place promotion carried out by most major cities. Those cities formerly dependent on heavy manufacturing are widely perceived to be run down, dirty and predominantly working class, with poor urban facilities, racial problems, high unemployment rates and high crime levels. It is these cities that are undergoing some of the greatest urban transformations of the 1990s, for example Birmingham, Manchester, Philadelphia, Lille, Dortmund and Turin (Hall, 1993). The chapter evaluates the characteristics of regeneration policies adopted in order to create a favourable place image and "good business environment" and the range of criticisms that have been voiced about such strategies.

Urban entrepreneurship in the post-industrial city

Older industrialized regions, not only those in relative decline since the Second World War but also recently prosperous industrial regions such as the Black Country in Central England or the mid-west region of the USA, have in the last fifteen years faced a rapid and alarming loss of manufacturing industry so abrupt and of such a magnitude as to catch decision takers ill-prepared. Initially cities in the UK responded by seeking central government support to prop up traditional industries but, when this became unfeasible, city authorities began to consider new ways to maintain their economic position. In the USA national policies to reduce cushioning of cities from international economic forces and to force them to adapt to the major technological changes that were reshaping the economic world were fairly ruthless. The Reagan administration believed that national economic growth was the priority and that this should take precedence over the fortunes of particular urban places. The old industrial city was considered by some to be outmoded. Technological innovations and new production technologies would result in job and population shifts from the frostbelt cities of the Northeast and Northwest to the smaller sunbelt and mountain rim cities of the South and West. Private enterprise and local public leadership were to pursue urban economic development in the post-industrial cities and were to take over responsibility for making themselves attractive to private investment. Cities

2

were left to their own diminishing public and private resources while partici-
pating, as best they could, in the modern version of civic mercantilism
(Barnekov et al., 1989). Within this context central government called upon
declining urban areas "to form partnerships with their private sectors and plan
strategically to enhance their comparative advantage relative to other jurisdictions" (USHUD, 1982).

> Economic development strategies have become much more elaborate and com-
> plex. Growth cities as well as cities in decline have turned to the national market
> and scrambled to make themselves attractive to footloose private firms. All cities
> are engaged in aggressive campaigns to secure their share of national economic
> growth. . . . Entrepreneurial strategies make up the heart of the municipal agenda
> and municipal politics in the mid-1980s. Most cities have accepted the Reagan
> administration's mandate that city government cooperate with the private sector
> and compete with one another to provide a favourable climate for business (Judd
> and Ready, 1986).

Most sought to restructure by concentrating on service sector growth and the
attraction of high technology industries, with increasing emphasis being
placed on the role of the property sector in the regeneration process. Some
cities were more successful in this effort than others. In an increasingly
footloose world, not only in terms of manufacturing but also for the tertiary
sector, an understanding of what urban attributes attract inward investment
was regarded as vital. Many researchers have attempted to list the weightings
attributed by decision makers to particular urban characteristics in influencing the choice of location of branch plants of multinational corporations.
Dunning and Norman (1987), for example, found that the highest weighted
factors were those such as the suitability of the local urban image to the
company and local cultural and even linguistic characteristics, followed
closely by sets of local amenities and facilities for health, education, housing
and the like. Local financial support, land cost and availability and even local
labour were weighted much less highly that would have been expected. At a
continental scale the French government's ranking of cities (DATAR, 1989)
according to a range of indicies included: ability to attract multinational firms
and governmental agencies operating in an international market, centrality in
transport and communications networks, importance of research and development, financial institutions, international fairs and congresses, and a wide
range of cultural outputs. In Holland the Fourth National Physical Plan 1988
went somewhat further in the city ranking exercise, not only identifying the
existing competitive league of western Dutch cities within Europe but also
outlining interventionist strategies for influencing this situation through the
public planning system.

It is the relatively new stress on cultural and environmental assets in
making locational investment decisions rather than factors such as financial
incentives and land availability, and the acknowledgement by city authorities

3

of a variety of political persuasions of this change, which has resulted in the much more entrepreneurial approach to city planning in the 1980s and 1990s, not only in the USA but also in Europe. There has also been an acceptance of the need to involve private sector investment in carrying out a wide range of planning initiatives and new forms of partnership with the private sector have been developed in order for this to take place (Healey, 1991; Lawless, 1991). Development plans have reflected this change by being more market oriented and appealing to the investment and development sectors and, through emphasising the more saleable aspects of the city and supressing unfavourable characteristics or problems, being frequently overtly promotional.

> Place marketing has thus become much more than merely selling the area to attract mobile companies or tourists. It can now be viewed as a fundamental part of planning, a fundamental part of guiding the development of places in a desired fashion. It should aim to ensure that urban activities and facilities are related as closely as posible to the demands and desires of targeted customers and clients. . . . It calls for a demand-oriented approach rather than the supply-led approach of traditional urban planning. As such, it requires a more flexible approach to development plans. Above all, it requires the pro-active pursuit of the desirable rather than the reactive prevention of the undesirable (Fretter, 1993).

Policy context

The fight back of the UK's post-industrial cities in the 1980s and 1990s has to be set within the urban policy framework established by the Conservative Government post 1979. This was essentially an attempt to change the ideological climate of Britain by creating an enterprise culture and replacing state action with market forces. One key aspect of policy was "to privatise the city in line with wider attempts to market all aspects of life and create conditions for new forms of capital accumulation" (Atkinson and Moon, 1994). In this the Conservatives were very much in line with the ideological stance of the Reagan administration in the USA, which firmly believed that economic recovery for the nation would involve cities competing with each other for private investment. That this might produce uneven development – winning and losing cities – was irrelevant within the wider goal of ensuring "efficient spatial allocation of resources in the economy as a whole" (Barnekov et al., 1989). Like the Republicans, the Conservatives believed that economic growth could best be promoted if government stopped intervening to protect national, local or regional economies from inevitable economic changes. Whilst it had once been the job of planners to regulate development, it became their job to promote it. In the UK the government sought to reduce the power of local authorities, especially those of the larger cities, and to give the private sector a lead role in the urban regeneration effort. The values of urban entrepreneurialism, private sector leadership, investment in physical capital,

4

and wealth creation were to replace those of municipal provision, public intervention, investment in social capital, and the distribution of welfare. The government decided that local authorities could not lead the economic regeneration of their cities and reduced many of their traditional powers and resources. A large number of initiatives were introduced to enable the private sector to develop its position as a key actor in urban revitalization strategies.

Thus city action teams, task forces, urban development corporations, enterprise zones, freeports and city grant have all been established to encourage private sector led economic revitalization. Many of these concepts came or were sent across the Atlantic. City Grant, for example, was an idea borrowed from the USA, whereas Enterprise Zones were first used in the UK and later adopted as an economic revitalization tool by some thirty-two states in the USA. Enterprise Zones on both sides of the Atlantic were seen as a means of eliminating governmental restraints on the private sector in selected local areas. By doing so they would unleash latent entrepreneurial initiatives and economic activity. The property led focus of many of the regeneration initiatives has been primarily concerned with overcoming supply-side constraints in local urban economies, especially by streamlining of the planning system, speeding up the processes of land acquisition and assembly, and utilizing leverage planning to bring back previous unmarketable sites into the land market (Healey, 1991). This leverage model, strongly influenced by experiences from the USA, is based on the use of public sector subsidy of development on sites which would under the normal set of circumstances not appear profitable to developers because of the estimated negative gap between costs and returns. Once the first few developments are attracted by the cushioning of risk, so the theory goes, confidence in development returns increases to a point where no subsidy is required to attract further private sector investment. Time and energy in the entrepreneurial city are also spent on the shaping and projection of urban images through the built environment and the removal of aspects of the built environment which contribute towards negative images of the city (Ashworth and Voogd, 1990). Indeed as Michael Heseltine, the Conservative government minister most conspicuously concerned with the inner cities in the 1980s put it:

> We have to create a wider economic base for the regeneration process. The essence of the task is to inject quality into the environment to make it desirable in the marketplace. Improve the environment, clear out the negative values (meaning dereliction, the absence of roads and services and essential infrastructure) – then private enterprise will come in (Heseltine, 1989).

Urban leadership

The increasingly entrepreneurial style of city government in the UK is closely related to changing patterns of local leadership which have a crucial impact

5

on the way a city restructures and on the success of such restructuring. As Fainstein (1990) points out, the way cities respond to stress is determined to a large extent by their local characteristics including local leadership skills and local social composition. Thus in a time of intense inter-urban competition when the number of economic regeneration strategies available appears limited, local leadership has been one element that can improve a city's competitive position, although always within the context of locational constraints and national policies. Increasingly a partnership approach has become evident in the overall planning and coordination of the city revitalization and reimaging processes and, in England for example, a number of cities have set up city wide development committees consisting of representatives of city administration and non-elected governmental bodies, business people and local politicians to promote the city and coordinate action over regeneration. These have not developed to the same extent as the so-called "growth coalitions" of most cities in the USA, nor are they so blatantly business-led, but they are bodies comprising small groups of notable and influential individuals whose principal aim is to stimulate economic growth by making the city more attractive to private investment.

Thus in Birmingham the 1988 Highbury Initiative involved a three-day visioning exercise by key city councillors, administrators, business people and professionals who, in conjunction with invited international urban design and economic development experts, eventually came up with ideas for the city centre which later were endorsed by the Council in the form of the City Centre Strategy (Evans, 1994). In Newcastle-upon-Tyne, the Newcastle Initiative (TNI) set up by the Confederation of British Industry in 1987, is a taskforce "bringing together influential leaders from business, central and local government and the academic world", whose aim is "to bring private sector solutions to assist in the process of urban regeneration", working in partnership with the City Council, Tyne and Wear Development Corporation and the Northern Development Company (TNI, undated). In other instances non-elected officers have acted as power brokers in the process of such coalition building and city boosterism where local political power is deadlocked or dormant with respect to growth initiative (Cooke, 1989). Indeed, very often this type of alliance formation is so complex and delicate a task that the way is open for a person of imagination, tenacity and skill (such as a charismatic mayor, an astute city administrator or a high profile business leader) to put a particular stamp on the nature and direction of urban renewal, as in Baltimore and Barcelona (Harvey, 1989). As with most urban alliances incorporating the business elite, there is frequently a rejection of controversial debate associated with regeneration policies and a desire for perceived harmony in the public sphere. Local community affairs are considered to be essentially non-political and any conflict or criticism of policy is thought to create a highly unfavourable image to outsiders, an image which might well repel any prospective investor (Sadler, 1993).

The visioning process

The task perceived to be facing the post-industrial city is to mobilise public and private sector expertise and resources in order to replace a lost manufacturing role by finding a new niche for the city, be it as a service or financial centre, a trade centre, an educational centre, a tourist centre or a mixture of all these. The main problem is to develop a role that has not already been successfully fulfilled by another locality. As Fainstein (1990) points out, success in finding a new area of specialization depends on leadership groups elsewhere not imitating the same strategy. Hence, while a city's economic leadership has a certain degree of leeway in choosing new niches, it does so within a framework of a system of competing cities, and must be aware of the consequences of overcommitting public money to any single strand strategy. The sports oriented regeneration strategy of Manchester is unlikely to succeed if Birmingham launches a similar strategy, or at least one might succeed but the other not. Finding the niche or niches in the national and international economy of competing cities and projecting the right image to develop this niche are crucial in the revitalization process.

It is the dominant themes of "city centre up-grading", "image" and "promotion" that stand out in the literature of almost all cities going through the restructuring process. For example:

> In order to promote urban regeneration, it is essential that the full potential of Birmingham's assets should be realised and one of the greatest of these assets is the City Centre. To a large degree, the prosperity of the whole city will depend upon the vitality of the City Centre, which is by far the most important concentration of economic, cultural and administrative activity within the West Midlands region. It is also critical to the City Council's promotion of Birmingham as a major international City and the strengthening of its status as both the regional capital and the nation's first City outside London (Birmingham City Council, undated).

> We share a common purpose in creating an efficient infrastructure, a confident business environment, a good external image and an equitable city in which all can participate and prosper (Sheffield City Council, 1993).

> The attractiveness of the City Centre is not only important for those who live or work there but also for the image of Belfast as a whole and its ability to attract investment. In a climate of increasing competitiveness Belfast must compete with other United Kingdom and European cities for commercial and industrial investment (Department of the Environment (NI), 1994).

The reimaging process is complex, involving glossy plan preparation; public sector infrastructure investment; partnership development of flagship schemes in retailing, leisure and commercial development; an emphasis on the arts or culture; and strong marketing employed to reverse or alter existing poor

7

images of the city. Many cities have developed a check list of necessary items for altering poor place images including the provision of top-of-the-range public transport systems, modernised and accessible airports, shopping malls, business parks, theme parks, marinas, tourist sites, culture quarters, museums, concert halls, hotels, public art, highly visible environmental improvements and events on the national and international stage such as concerts, sporting events and festivals. In the remainder of this chapter many of these various elements will be discussed within four frequently overlapping themes, namely marketing and promotion, cultural strategies, flagships, and festivals and events.

Marketing and promotion

There is quite an extensive literature on place marketing, which frequently distinguishes it from the type of marketing normally carried out by the private firm trying to sell a product. City marketing has not the single overriding profit objective of the private firm but a series of related objectives. These include raising the competitive position of the city, attracting inward investment, boosting civic image and improving feelings of well-being in the resident population. Outcomes are thus difficult to measure, especially since results are often not immediate, effects may spread beyond the immediate urban area, the focus is largely on the provision of services rather than goods and the marketing caters for a potentially wide variety of groups. Another problem in terms of measurable outcomes is that many competing urban authorities are carrying out similar city marketing campaigns and may inadvertently create a situation of zero sum results. There are several features which distinguish contemporary city marketing from previous practice, in particular the manner in which the promotion of place is expressed and the adoption of targeted forms of marketing to bolster directly the process of image reconstruction. Rather than advertising per se, place promotion has sought to rebuild and reconstruct the image of the city, allied to which has been a strategy of targeting specific types of activity which both reflect and bolster the image (Paddison, 1993).

Fretter (1993) argues that a successful place marketing strategy depends on a number of factors. These comprise a shared vision developed by the community; an audit of the city's strengths and weaknesses; identification of the target customers – whether inward investors and tourists or indigenous business and the local population; an improved urban product – infrastructure, investment, training, property; knowledge about competitors; and an identification of the city's unique selling points. In relation to the latter, tradition and heritage are used to enhance the distinctive qualities of a city. In the development of urban tourism there is a premium on difference and particularity.

In a world where differences are being erased, the commodification of place is about creating distinct place-identities in the eyes of global tourists. Even in the most disadvantaged places, heritage, or the simulacrum of heritage, can be mobilized to gain competitive advantage in the race between places (Robins, 1991, p.38).

But difficult issues in this race such as who benefits from the marketing effort and the opportunity cost of the chosen reimaging strategy cannot be swept under the carpet. There are also fundamental questions as to the choice of image for the city, the types of inward investment targeted and the distribution of public expenditure in a city. Frequently a large percentage of city spending is focused on a few city centre flagship projects at the expense of spending on disadvantaged groups.

Promotion is an important but complicated element of city marketing because of the complex nature of the urban product being sold. Promotion includes advertising and public relations and is increasingly carried out in Britain by the economic development and urban tourism units of local authorities and by urban development corporations. The attempt to create a favourable image of a city and its current or new services and facilities is affected not only by the existing store of information, expectations and feelings people have about the city but also by a profusion of other influences and information sources, few of which are designed to alter consumer behaviour in any planned way. Thus most conscious promotion by city authorities is operating upon an existing information set, reinforcing existing views or endeavouring to correct what is regarded as negative or contradictory information. What gets into the popular press about a city's racial problems or joy-riding may undo all the positive promotion work carried out.

In promotional terms Newcastle-upon-Tyne's image as a tough macho working class northern city in England is to be altered to that of a liveable city, with a good quality of life and an attractive forward looking business environment (Wilkinson, 1993). Thus the advertising campaign designed for the City Council in 1990 by a leading advertising agency was primarily concerned with neutralizing unfavourable images, creating new images and reinforcing existing positive images of the city. The campaign was strongly people-centred, particularily emphasing the quality, strength and innovativeness of the people and the workforce, stressing the friendliness of the city, and projecting the image of a good quality of life with arts, education and leisure flourishing. In a similar way, at the other end of the world, the marketing of Woolongong in Australia, hit by the steel recession of the 1980s, has invoked the environment and quality of life, presenting it as a fun place to be with beautiful beaches, no pollution, sunrise over the sea and so on. Ethnic diversity is similarily celebrated and exploited in discourses on food and hedonism (Watson,1991).

Promotion is generally targeted at four groups, potential inward investors, potential tourists, the local population and the decision makers in the region.

It is usually carried out at the broadbrush level through the use of slogans and city logos, in a more targeted way through the production and dissemination of brochures, television and radio advertisements and public events and exhibitions, and in a more subtle way through the discreet lobbying of decision makers. Catchy slogans such as "Birmingham Means Business" , "I Love New York" , "Belfast is Buzzing" and "Glasgow's Alive" and simple eye-catching city logos reproduced on all promotional literature are two of the most obvious transfers of marketing know-how from private industry. Yet whilst some of these slogans have been effective and memorable, most have not. The conflict is often between the search for effectiveness of communication, which demands compression in such a slogan, and the "filtering out of distinctiveness which results from such terseness" (Ashworth and Voogd, 1994). Frequently the same can be said of city logos and the imagery of the city in the marketing literature. Barke and Harrop, for example, in an analysis of the logos of 95 industrial towns, reveal that the majority prefer traditional elements which highlight environmental or heritage characteristics. "Many local authorities are promoting similar images through their logos, another element which ill accords with the marketing strategy of stressing uniqueness and difference in order to promote places more effectively" (Barke and Harrop, 1994). The generic themes that can be identified in the marketing of cities are: emphasis on an up-beat future ("tomorrow", "growing", "new"); centrality of location ("middle of everything", "doorway to . . .", "gateway to . . ."); low rents and good quality space; good workforce; and quality of life ("liveable place", "unspoilt beauty"). This similarity in the promotion of cities, despite their intrinsic character, in order to achieve an acceptable marketing image can best be described as the "commodification" of place. This often results in the marketing of a kind of placelessness, to the extent that the content of the place promotion bears little relationship to the actual place being promoted.

Some cities are particularly difficult challenges in terms of such promotional effort because even if the "place product" is improved substantially, the place image projected is interfered with in the process of transmission. Thus the received/perceived message will usually differ to some extent from the projected place image (Ashworth and Voogd, 1990) and response changing is slow. Attracting investors to Belfast is made difficult by media pictures of burning buildings and soldiers in the streets. Another difficult city is Liverpool which, despite improvements to its facilities for metropolitan tourism, retains a poor place image, still being perceived to be strike-bound, bankrupt, run-down, wasted, hopeless and run by militant left-wingers (Madsen, 1992). The importance of networking for a city with an extremely adverse image such as Belfast cannot be overemphasized as it is only at this level that decision takers' perceptions can be dramatically changed. Here considerable attention is paid to making sure that the "right" people with the "right" contacts are employed in key positions, and that relationships with decision takers in London and potential investors from England and further afield are continually developed and maintained. One dinner party with a few key policy makers or fundholders in London or Boston can be worth more in terms of measurable outputs than an expensive advertising campaign in the main business or property journals.

Glasgow was one of the first cities in the UK to tackle, through a sustained promotional campaign, the perceived problem of its poor image as a harsh, violent and depressed industrial city in economic decline. With its traditional industries, particularily shipbuilding and mechanical engineering in terminal decline since the Second World War, the entire manufacturing base was eventually drawn into a downward spiral. Thus, in addition to population decline, the city endured a loss of some 97,000 jobs between 1971 and 1983, nearly one-fifth of the 1971 total. Although there was little hard evidence to confirm this view at the time, it was argued that Glasgow was locked into a long term economic decline in which the city's negative image was a major disincentive to potential investors. Beginning in the early 1980s the marketing of Glasgow developed as a series of proactive or responsive strategies harnessing opportunities which city marketeers read as offering potential for increasing inward investment and contributing positively to the improvement of the city's image. Surprisingly it was the Labour controlled Council which accepted that the city's image had to be changed and which showed a degree of political realism and pragmatism in adapting to Thatcherite central government policies and in harnassing as wide a range of agencies and resources as possible to assist in the economic and physical regeneration effort (McKenzie, 1990). These resources have included a considerable subsidy from the EU's European Social Fund and European Regional Development Fund. Its vigorous marketing campaign based on the Mr Man cartoon character and the slogan "Glasgow's Miles Better" was premised on a well established technique of indirect promotion used in advertising, of altering the image of a product in order to alter the pattern of its consumption. The campaign itself was subject to considerable analysis and debate because of the choice of images used to sell the city to outsiders, but on the whole it went down well with Glaswegians. One commentator described the advertising campaign thus:

> Glasgow's urban advertising strategy has muscled into a masculine discourse of publicity, of individual genius, and of the major arts. Reconsidering Glasgow's narrative, it has been conspicuously masculine, moving from the (production) hey-days of the last century to the industrial decline (with its dramatic effects on the male work force, as linked to the gritty aggression of male working-class strife) and now onward: it has almost reinvented itself through its manly narrative and through the images of this manliness. And yet the figure of Charles Rennie Mackintosh in the advertising photos looks like a woman's man with his soft bow tie and his stance to one side: after the rough production of Glasgow's *culture*, its consumption has turned out to be much more gentle-manly (Laurier, 1993).

Subsequently, more directed forms of marketing were developed, aimed at specific types of markets, tourism and service industries, in addition to a focus on hallmark events and the arts as a means of fostering the urban economy. Typically the marketing to inward service industries concentrates on the low rents compared to London, the educated workforce, low wages, labour market stability, good road, rail and air transport facilities, and the good quality of life consequent on pleasant living areas, access to the countryside, quality of education and cosmopolitan cultural facilities including concerts, ballet, opera and restaurants. The overall campaign, aimed largely at inward investors and tourists but also at the local population in an attempt to boost morale, highlighted selected urban ingredients perceived to be attractive to the private sector. These included the Victorian history of the city; its fine nineteenth and early twentieth century architecture being rehabilitated through public subsidy; environmental improvements such as the landscaping of vacant sites and the creation of new urban open spaces; flagship developments such as the Scottish Exhibition and Conference Centre built on the disused Prince's Dock; numerous new shopping and office developments in the city centre and the 1988 garden festival. Physical regeneration strategies such as these were vital to the image building campaign since the image campaign on its own would have proved hollow and short lived (Glasgow Action, 1991). However, it was the marketing of the city as a city of culture which has perhaps had the longer term impact at a national and international level (Boyle, 1989). This will be returned to in more detail later in this chapter.

Cultural strategies

Many cities intent on the reimaging process have embraced the culture-led approach to regeneration, placing much faith in the ability of culture development, both in terms of production and consumption, to improve the city's international standing, attract inward investment, create jobs, revitalize local public social life and to strengthen civic pride and identity (McNulty, 1988). The arts are thought to have a high profile, high quality label which gives the city prestige and publicity. Along with sports and special events they are considered to offer a good quality lifestyle which attracts professionals, managers and new skilled workers – the new "service class" who are important in the types of services and high technology industries which cities seek to attract (Whitt, 1988; Urry, 1990; Hendon and Shaw, 1987). In addition, there is the widely held view that culture is good and that civic life can be enhanced by its production and consumption. In fact cultural policies, closely linked with urban tourism and urban heritage concepts, have proved a fertile area for cultivating alliances between the local political system and the business community, even in Labour controlled authorities in Britain. Commercial and financial corporations have given their backing to improved cultural provision in cities, realising that sponsorship, promotion and ownership of art products and cultural activities can help firms to attract target customers, boost the public status of companies, enhance property values, provide legitimation of urban development projects and cement relationships within economic and political elites (Griffiths, 1993). Furthermore a new group of "cultural intermediaries" in certain favoured centres has created an influential pressure group for these cultural policy changes (Featherstone, 1991). EU funding for major cultural developments such as convention centres and concert halls has also influenced decision making about such public investment in a time of urban financial stress.

Culture based urban regeneration strategies include several aspects such as job creation, urban tourism and the pursuit of inward investment through the projection of a better image of the city (Karski, 1990). Major cultural projects in cities are not new but in the past, particularly in the Victorian era, civic or individual sponsorship of cultural development was regarded as an emblem of economic success in trade and manufacturing industry, whereas today city authorities are using culture to create the conditions for economic development (Griffiths, 1993).

European cities have been strongly influenced by the experiences of US cities in the 1970s and 1980s. There the desire of arts organizations for new premises and funding dovetailed with the desire of politicans to revitalize downtown areas and of developers to use arts venues, museums and leisure facilities as a means of adding value to office, housing and retail schemes in central districts (Bianchini, 1993). Many cities in the UK and also in Europe (Rotterdam, for example) were influenced in their waterfront redevelopment projects by American models like Baltimore's Harbour Place, Boston's Quincy Market and New York's South Street Seaport.

Overall, the culture led approach to city restructuring involves a fairly wide range of policy implements, including for instance the provision of cultural amenities such as art galleries, museums, and concert halls; the protection and development of architectural heritage and public open spaces; Percent for Art schemes; public art works; culture quarter development; cultural facilities in mixed use developments; and major cultural flagships as a stimulus to the private sector (Evans, 1993). Such developments are often linked with environmental improvements, enhanced civic control of the design of new buildings and public spaces, and festivals and events to create a structured urban revitalization package (Law, 1993). It is the putting together and marketing of the whole package which epitomises the reimaging process.

One can probably trace the development of British city cultural projects within urban regeneration strategies back to the Art's Council's "Urban Renaissance" initiative in the late 1980s, which itself drew on research which identified the economic importance of the arts in the UK (Myerscough, 1988). This study estimated the arts as a significant economic sector employing nearly

500,000 people with a turnover of £10 billion per annum, exceeding that of the UK motor industry, and it ranked the arts as fourth in the invisible earnings field after banking, shopping and travel. In addition the arts were identified as important to urban tourism and also to middle managers in choosing working and living environments. Thus museums, theatres, concerts and other cultural facilities were an important factor affecting the selection of the place in which to live and work for 80 per cent of those interviewed in Merseyside and 77 per cent in Glasgow, and were regarded as an important reason for enjoying working in the area by 58 per cent and 79 per cent respectively. Myerscough's conclusions were that although "cultural amenities were never an overriding consideration in the thinking of mover firms . . . they could be an important supplementary factor". Likewise, studies carried out in the USA on the economic impact of the arts pointed to roughly similar conclusions (Violette, 1982, for example). The English Tourist Board's Inner City Tourism Initiative was also very strongly supportive of the economic and urban regeneration impacts of urban tourism, and produced a document outlining examples of urban tourism initiatives throughout the world.

> Tourism can bring jobs and prosperity to inner city areas as well as helping to create an environment which is attractive to both visitor and local residents. This in turn helps to restore civic pride, promote a positive regional image and helps to attract further investment in the area (John Lee MP, English Tourist Board, undated).

Heritage

Heritage has become a strong theme in city reimaging to the extent that conservation areas and historic buildings, once regarded by the property sector as a restraint factor in the development process, have been given a substantial role in place marketing to create city identity and bolster tourism (Civic Trust/QUB, 1988). In the UK, conservation areas close to city centres are receiving particular attention and improved financing, especially when in gateway positions such as on route from the airport to the central business district. Many post-industrial cities cannot compete with the world's capital cities such as Rome, London or New York in terms of the existing building stock but they are increasingly conscious of making the most of the previously undervalued buildings they do have, with on-going programmes of stone cleaning, re-facading and flood lighting and finding sympathetic new uses for them.

The "heritage industry", so called because it involves the manufacturing of heritage and because it is expected by its proponents to replace the real industry upon which the economy depends (Hewison,1987), is indeed booming in most countries. The numbers of new museums and heritage sites have been increasing dramatically in recent years. In Britain, for example, the

14

heritage industry has provided much needed local employment and tourist revenue in areas hit by the collapse of the manufacturing economy. In the north east the 200 acre Beamish Open Air Museum attempts to recreate the region's past with a railway station, a 1930s town street, a row of miners' cottages, a colliery and a tramline. In Shropshire the Ironbridge Gorge Museum, spread over seven sites, recalls the early days of the industrial revolution. Cities have their theme museums, like Liverpool's Maritime Museum, and many smaller towns have their own equivalents, for example Dundee's Discovery Centre which re-enacts the Antarctic expeditions of Scott. Hewison criticizes this growth of the heritage industry because so many of its products are fantasies of a world that never was and because it reasserts social values that the democratic progress of the twentieth century seemed to be doing away with. The growth of nostalgia for the past is stifling the cultural development of the present.

> Yet we have no real use for this spurious past, any more than nostalgia has any use as a creative emotion. At best we turn it into a commodity, and following the changed language of the arts, justify its exploitation as a touristic resource. The result is a devaluation of significance, an impoverishment of meaning. Yet to admit that the commodity on sale is fraudulent would be deeply unsettling, especially to the salesmen (Hewison, 1987).

Urban design

Urban design, once seen as the sole responsibility of individual architects, is very gradually becoming accepted as an issue worthy of public debate and detailed control by city authorities in the interests of city reimaging. Architecture and urban design are now used in the reimaging process to create outdoor exhibits for tourists, with the construction of new landmark or trophy buildings, grand arches, and the redevelopment of waterfronts to set off spectacle buildings (Law, 1993). Indeed, an overlap between architecture and advertising can be identified in the sense that city authorities and redevelopment agencies have been drawing up design studies for their areas (LDDC, 1990b; Tibbalds et al., 1990) and commissioning individual buildings designed by well known and esteemed architects, again in order to sell the notion of the city's cultural development and international prestige. Public art works, often commissioned by city authorities, likewise seek to promote a new image of the city. Public art has been used in the reimaging of the city of Dundee in Scotland and the city of Swansea in Wales. In the latter, the redeveloped waterfront area, the Maritime Quarter, is themed by a programme of architectural enhancement features and "Stony Stories" which recall the area's past maritime-industrial heritage. Birmingham's Centenary Square has been redeveloped and unified by a well designed paving scheme, street furniture and four major sculptural elements. The most striking of these is Raymond Mason's fibreglass "Crowd Scene". Likewise in many European cities public sculptures have been used to emphasize city character. In Barcelona, for example, highly acclaimed artists have been commissioned by the city authorities to create a number of exciting and original sculptures in the city centre and particularily along the new waterfront.

But there is an on-going debate about the quality of architecture. The type of culture identifiable in the postmodern city of today can appear very intellectually elitist and raises the question of whose image is being promoted – the image chosen by the local residents or some sanitized image which fails to represent the present or past characteristics of the city. The postmodern cultural city is regarded by some as being much more image aware and culturally self-conscious than its predecessors – style and decoration are important and traditional senses of culture are decontextualized, simulated, reduplicated and continually renewed and restyled. As Crilley points out,

> ... the postmodern architecture of redevelopment – with its facadal displays, penchant for recycling imagery and theoretical rationale in semiotic theory – is fully incorporated into the ideological apparatus of place marketing, playing a major role in mediating perceptions of urban change and persuading 'us' of the virtues and cultural beneficence of speculative investments (Crilley, 1993).

Strategies in UK and European cities

Bianchini (1989) identifies three main policy models guiding the development of culture led regeneration strategies in Britain. The first is a production based strategy concerned with the development of local cultural industries (as with the Greater London Council's arts strategy of the 1980s); the second is a consumption based strategy which uses the arts to develop and enhance the tourism infrastructure (as with Glasgow's city centre strategy of the late 1980s); the third is a cultural democracy approach which emphasizes the importance of ensuring equal access and participation in public social life for all citizens. Many cities have in fact tried to develop aspects of one or more of these strands (Lim, 1993; McKellar, 1988). Birmingham's arts led revitalisation strategy contains elements of all three approaches and includes the concept of business tourism. It began with the setting up of a cross-departmental Arts, Culture and Economy (ACE) sub-committee in the City Council in the mid-1980s, out of which emanated a number of influential arts and culture reports and proposals (Birmingham City Council, 1989a,b,c and 1990). Some of the developments resulting from this thinking are Heartlands, an area based regeneration strategy, the International Convention Centre and the National Indoor Arena, a public arts programme for Centenary Square, the redevelopment of Broad Street and the founding of a Media Development Agency. Furthermore the Council subsequently helped raise the level of arts provision in the city by

Photograph 1.1 Birmingham's Centenary Square (1)

Photograph 1.2 Birmingham's Centenary Square (2)

Photograph 1.3   Rotterdam's Outdoor Museum

Photograph 1.4   Baltimore's Inner Harbour

**Photograph 1.5
Barcelona's public art
on the waterfront**

persuading the Sadler's Wells Royal Ballet and the D'Oyly Carte Opera to take up residence in Birmingham, and the city also organizes a number of top quality festivals each year. The Birmingham Convention and Visitors Bureau actively markets the area for leisure and business tourism and the Economic Development Department runs a targeted campaign to attract inward investment, which involves lifestyle promotion to attract key workers (Fretter, 1993). The proposed Brindley Place scheme adjoining the Convention Centre is eventually to include an Omnimax Cinema, a multi screen cinema, an aquarium, a festival market and 600,000 sq.ft. of offices.

Amongst other examples of cities in Europe which have been highlighted in the literature as stressing culture in their urban regeneration strategies are Bologna, Barcelona, Rotterdam, Hamburg, Bradford, Sheffield, and Glasgow, all post-industrial cities with a lost manufacturing or port function and a perceived poor image. Hamburg has used cultural policy to market the city as an international centre for tourism, conventions, fairs, media, telecommunications, high-tech industry and advanced services. The city council not only created an attractive urban design strategy and assisted the creation of an

Photograph 1.6   Barcelona – waterfront restaurant

attractive city centre shopping district but also supported prestigious cultural projects including a major festival, high art institutions and film production. Another example of arts led regeneration is Rotterdam, which suffers from an adverse image in relation to its neighbouring capital city, Amsterdam, and was regarded in the 1980s as a working class, run-down, trade oriented city with high unemployment and a high immigrant population. However, on the positive side, Rotterdam's audit of advantages/weakness revealed its pluses. These included the world's largest port, a wide variety of striking modern architecture, the dynamism of a multiracial society and a strong arts tradition from the early 1970s in terms of a resident theatre and orchestra, festivals and applied arts such as photography, film and design. Post 1987 a new policy orientation for the city was the emphasis on image and attracting inward investment through the provision of good infrastructure, electronic communication services, a reliable labour market, urban amenities, a good socio-cultural ambience and a good residential climate. The catch phrase for Rotterdam is now the "complete city", balancing the new market orientation with long running socially oriented policies. The great variety of projects over the last decade has included building new theatres and museums, a new airport, improving traffic accessibility, expanding the metro network to the suburbs, using the waterfront, building more houses in the city centre and paying more attention to urban amenities and neighbourhood design. Public/ private partnership in project development has also developed in the 1980s

20

and 1990s with a significant role given to private enterprise in enhancing the cultural life of the city.

Perhaps of all the UK cities it is Glasgow that has received the most accolades for regeneration through the development of cultural and urban tourism policies. The city's approach to culture led revitalization has been described as a mixture of measured incrementalism and opportunistic adventurism spearheaded by the coalition of the Scottish Development Agency (now superceded by the Glasgow Development Agency), Glasgow Action (a public-private partnership formed around a group of local businessmen), Glasgow District Council and Strathclyde Regional Council. Emphasis has been placed on building the city up as a service centre based on tourism, retailing, financial services and scientific research, and providing companies with regional headquarters. These were seen as the sectors which could be developed to replace lost manufacturing, and the development strategy includes a focus on hallmark events and the arts as a means of fostering the urban economy. The plan was to spruce up the city centre, develop retailing at all levels, win inward investors from financial services, government departments and high technology companies, and to exploit the city's rich cultural heritage to attract visitors. Arts tourism had been given a major boost in 1983, with the opening of the Burrell Collection and the launch of Mayfest, Glasgow's major arts festival, both of which strengthened Glasgow's already powerful infrastructure in the performing arts field, including a number of prestigious drama companies, Scottish Opera, Scottish Ballet, the Scottish National Orchestra and the BBC Symphony Orchestra. Surprisingly for other competing cities in Europe and closer to home, Glasgow was selected as European City of Culture 1990, partly because of its high level of existing cultural resources and because of its newly developed facilities such as the £30 million concert hall opened in 1990. This accolade had previously been awarded to such cities as Athens (1985), Florence (1986), Amsterdam (1987), Berlin (1988) and Paris (1989) and designation resulted in even wider publicity for the city (Wishart,1991). In terms of environmental improvement, the year saw the completion of a number of cleaning, conservation, land renewal, floodlighting and public art schemes in the city centre and the neighbouring Merchant City quarter and by the end of the year over 3800 cultural activities had been hosted. Myerclough's evaluation of the impact of the year of culture on the city concluded that:

> The initiatve generated a positive net economic return to the regional economy of £10.3m to £14.1m. Extra employment arising from Glasgow 1990 was estimated at 5,3505,580 person years" (*Financial Times*, 1992).

Culture quarters

Culture quarters or cultural districts are another aspect of arts led regeneration strategies. The concept is not new, as similar quarters naturally evolved in many

21

Photograph 1.7   Glasgow's 1990 City of Culture logo

Photograph 1.8   Publicity for Manchester's Olympic 2000 bid

of the world's great cities – London's West End or the Left Bank in Paris, for example. What is a relatively new phenomenon of the late 1980s is that they have been deliberately planned as area based urban regeneration schemes, frequently in run-down but historic inner or central city areas. The strategy is to provide centres of accommodation and work for actors, musicians, dancers, artists and media people and also the facilities such as theatres, cafés, bars and galleries where residents and tourists alike can participate in the cultural and entertainment life of the city. The trend for such quarters has clearly evolved from experience in the USA, where arts districts have usually been developed in the city centre or mid-town, for example in Boston, Dallas, Pittsburg and St Paul. The argument for a culture quarter is that a policy of clustering enables a critical mass of cultural facilities to evolve, and this in turn stimulates the private development of restaurants, pubs and speciality shopping. Although there is no empirical evidence available to support it, there is a belief that the concentration of tourism activity into one district creates a clear focus for the city and allows ease of movement from one facility to another with benefits for visitors and locals. If good public transport or safe long stay car parking is provided for tourists they are encouraged to come to the district and lengthen their stay.

In the UK culture quarters are being developed in Birmingham, Bradford, Newcastle and Sheffield and in continental Europe Rotterdam makes an interesting case study of a city developing a cultural district. This takes the form of a city centre "cultural axis", which is being consolidated and expanded, starting at the central station and running down in a zigzag towards the waterfront, which itself is undergoing major redevelopment. This axis contains a mixture of prestige cultural developments along with smaller more intimate areas of cultural production. Along its route are sculptures, a concert hall, theatres, art galleries, cafes, restaurants and a museum park. The Waterstad area of Rotterdam along the River Mass has been developed as a recreational and tourist destination with a maritime museum, an open air museum, an hotel, the National Econocentre, an Imax theatre, promenades along the river to the Old Harbour where cube shaped houses form the scenery of a harbour filled with old barges, and eventually to Tropicana, a swimming pool complex on the Maas. An office sector has been developed in this Waterstad area, primarily along the waterfront between the Inland Shipping Museum and the Leuvehaven. Housing is a mixture of public and private, with a predominance of luxury apartments occupying the sites closest to the water and the views. The preserved docks in the area, still accessible to inland waterway barges which come and go constantly, give a dynamism to the environment that is frequently missing in the redevelopment areas of many ports. The architecture of most of the main buildings in the Waterstad, as with those along most of the cultural axis, including the housing, is modern, exciting and frequently startling, exemplified by the cone-capped apartment block nicknamed "the Pencil", the public library dominated by its yellow external ducting, the Maritime museum which comprises two interlocking triangles, the De Mass

Tower, and the striking white Nedlloyd building (Pinder and Rosing, 1988). Across the river there are the early stages of the development of a major flagship project known as the Kop Van Zuid on a 125 hectare site on land formerly containing redundant port related buildings. Here an integrated residential, recreational, retail and office development is being built and old warehouses converted including the provision of an exotic festival market. A new beautifully designed bent tower bridge to connect the south bank to the city centre will shortly (1995) provide a monumental focal point for the city.

In Birmingham there has been a strong commitment to the idea of quarters or districts in and around the city centre core. A number are being developed including the Warwick Bar/Digbeth area, the Chinese Quarter, the Jewellery Quarter, the Gunsmiths' Quarter, the Aston Triangle based on the University, and the high profile Greater Convention Centre Area. The Jewellery Quarter is perhaps the most successful to date with its emphasis on jewellery manufacture, tourism and conservation. Considerable Council effort has been put into helping to develop the long established jewellery industry whilst preserving the architectural character of the most important streets and squares and upgrading the environment. Increased surface car parking provision, a new rail station in the core of the tourist part of the Jewellery Quarter and the new Jewellery Discovery Centre are expected to greatly increase the number of visitors to the quarter.

The City Council at Sheffield adopted a fairly radical cultural industries strategy in the mid 1980s which sought to create the local structures for production, distribution, employment and training in contemporary cultural forms – electronic music, film, video, broadcasting, fashion and graphic design. Part of the strategy was the creation of a cultural industries quarter in a previously rundown industrial area on the fringe of the city centre. The aims for this quarter include supporting business and social activity in the area, improving the physical environment, assisting Sheffield's development of landmark sites, and developing partnerships to make Sheffield an international city for media and cultural production and training. Funding not only comes from local government and the private sector but also from central government and Europe. Increasingly the area is providing attractions for urban tourists.

The Cultural Industries Quarter was the brainchild of the Council's Department of Employment and Economic Development and the idea has been implemented through very close working relationships with the private and voluntary sectors. The strategy centres around facilitating commercial activity through rehousing and supporting private cultural and media based companies, who all invest private finance in their accommodation and who are all given a voice in the on-going policy. At the heart of the quarter's success has been a rolling programme of refurbishment taking the area's redundant buildings and turning them into flexible new workspaces. The Cultural Industries Quarter (CIQ) now has a variety of facilities: the Leadmill,

24

Red Tape Studios, the Audio-Visual Enterprise Centre, the Workstation (54,000 square feet of lettable units in a variety of sizes) and the Sheffield Media and Exhibition Centre (Granville 1994). The CIQ is home to several recording studios, two record labels, a photographic gallery, film and video producers, graphic designers, numerous support industries and the new Northern Media School. Plans are well advanced for a £3 million art house cinema complex and for the £6 million National Centre for Popular Music (NCPM), which has been decribed in a publicity leaflet produced by the council thus:

> Alongside Sheffield Arena, Meadowhall, the Lyceum and Crucible Theatres, the untapped potential of Don Valley Stadium, as well as its sporting excellence, and the many other venues and activities that are inexorably increasing Sheffield's pulling power, this £6 million project is a further significant element in Sheffield's transformation from industrial powerhouse to leisure capital (Sheffield City Council, undated).

Likewise a second cultural district for Sheffield, in Tudor Square, is being transformed into an area concentrating on more traditional cultural provision including the Crucible Theatre, Lyceum Theatre, Rusking Crafts Gallery, a central library and other proposed facilities.

In Newcastle there has been an attempt to create a cultural district called Theatre Village in the west end of the city, an area containing secondary and tertiary shopping, warehousing, the red light district, the restored Tyne Theatre, the Pavilion Theatre, the Tyne Brewery, several museums, the Black Friars Priory and the Newcastle Arts Centre. After an unsuccessful regeneration initiative in 1988, the Westgate Trust was created to formulate and implement a strategy for Theatre Village under the umbrella of The Newcastle Initiative (TNI), a Confederation of British Industry initiative. The strategy for Theatre Village, arrived at after deliberations with the local branch of the Royal Institution of British Architects, was based on economic regeneration through property development and image regeneration through the arts. Property development, it was considered, would kick start the process, the arts developing in its wake and providing the means by which further investment and property development would follow. Major developments of tourist facilities and gateway schemes to the area were to be developed, arts production was to be supported through workshop schemes and arts training projects and there was to be investment in arts productions, specifically in the electronic media sector. The ambience of the area was to be improved through environmental upgrading, increasing public safety and the visual appearance of buildings. Despite these laudable intentions, Theatre Village is widely perceived to have been a failure, principally because of poor levels of funding, minimal staffing and administrative problems over land acquisition. Much of the little that did happen in Theatre Village in the period up until the Trust was wound up in 1991 would have happened anyway through normal market and funding mechanisms administered through government policies at national and local levels (Whyte, 1994). Smyth's conclusion is that:

> Marketing and selling innovative-local flagships depends upon first 'selling' the concept, envisioning others with the ideas and developing the policy as they feed in their ideas. Managing this process is crucial to producing an innovative set of policies that are implementable. Without this there is no 'product' to sell in the later stages, hence the flagship function fails. TNI and its subsequent vehicle, the Westgate Trust, were unsuccessful in their management efforts for the Theatre Village (Smyth, 1994).

Flagships

Flagship projects are often seen as a key element in the reimaging process. These are normally large scale, self contained, highly prestigious, consumption oriented land and property developments often with the rationale of regenerating derelict urban areas and acting as magnets for further developments. They are sometimes designed to spearhead economic development or tourism strategies and are powerful marketing tools to help localities reposition themselves and find new niches in competitive urban markets (Tavsanoglu and Healey, 1992). The flagship idea has been embraced by many city governments as a way in which to establish confidence in parts of the city with weak property markets and to encourage investors and developers to follow suit. Since urban regeneration can be unprofitable in the short term the private sector is rarely willing to take on the full burden of financing and development and very often the public sector must be the initiator, with or without private sector partners. In changing perceptions of urbanism and in creating marketable images of quality, entertainment and festivity to replace images of dereliction, emptiness and crime, flagships play an influential role. Indeed urban developments corporations in the UK, whose remit from central government is to improve specific inner city areas within a short time period (10 years or less), find flagship projects quite irresistible in image enhancement strategies. "Flagship developments perform a selling function for their location and can contribute towards the broader marketing of the city" (Smyth, 1994).

In the USA downtown retail developments have been particularly potent symbols of revival, with a number of cities such as Baltimore, Boston, New York and Toledo building festival marketplaces which feature as postmodern, upbeat, vibrant and consumerist tokens of urban renaissance and which are perceived as helping to reimage the city. Waterfronts, the former locations of defunct port related activities were particularly fertile locations for reimaging flagships. Not only could very quick results be achieved in clearing dereliction but, with public-private supply-side collaboration (grants for underpinning development along with public sector subsidy of infrastructure) in the development process, there could be the creation of a saleable product of office, leisure and residential uses. The marketing potential of blue water, postmodern architecture, city centre lifestyle and leisure has been exploited to the full.

In the UK the flagship idea was adopted in the 1980s and a publication by the Confederation of British Industry in 1988 suggested that every city should have one or more flagship projects in order to break into the cycle of inner-city decline. Many flagship projects are either wholly public sector concerns or involve the public sector in some form of subsidy. They take many forms including large scale tourism and culture related projects such as Birmingham's International Convention Centre, Glasgow's Concert Hall and Bradford's National Museum of Photography, Film and Television. Prime property developments can also be included such as Newcastle's waterfront business park, Belfast's CastleCourt Shopping Centre and Dublin's Custom House Dock development, and sometimes major refurbishment projects in run down urban districts such as the Merchant City in Glasgow and Little Germany in Bradford.

In many respects the role model for urban waterfront flagships in Europe was Baltimore, Maryland, USA. Indeed the rebuilding of 33 acres of Baltimore's commercial centre known as the Charles Center, a mixed development of offices, shops, hotels, parks and apartments completed in the early 1980s, has proved highly influential in spreading the flagship idea to city authorities throughout the developed world. Public sector involvement in funding was in terms of land acquisition and clearance, open space and infrastructure, with the private sector providing the remaining costs, whilst a quasi-public development corporation was set up to supervise the scheme's implementation. This successful scheme was followed by a more ambitious one for the 24 acre Inner Harbor Area designed to link the Charles Center with the waterfront. This scheme went ahead with the help of public funding and with the same quasi-public development corporation executing the development. The success of the flagship concept in Baltimore can be gauged by the substantial leverage of private sector investment (70 per cent of total project investment), the reversal of migration of businesses from the city centre and the creation of a new tourism industry. Among the attractions are the National Aquarium, a 150 slip marina, new hotels, a convention centre and a festival market place containing restaurants, foodstalls and boutiques. Major banks, insurance companies and services such as IBM occupy new office buildings along the shoreline. The greatest impact has been the alteration of Baltimore's image from one of industrial sprawl to that of a bright, modern city and tourist destination (Cowie, 1986), which earned it the title of "renaissance city" and put it on the front cover of *Time* magazine. In the 1990s the city has extended the project area in an easterly and westerly

27

direction with a baseball park, marina, office buildings, hotels and housing developments planned or underway.

Falk considers the way the city undertook the regeneration process, rather than the product itself (the aquarium and the festival market place), to be the key factor in the successful regeneration of the Baltimore waterfront. "This involved starting with a shared vision, creating a balance between community and commercial considerations, and involving the private sector in specific elements while retaining overall control through an agency set up for the task" (Falk, 1992).

Festivals and events

Major festivals and events, preferably on the national or international stage, also play an important part in the reimaging process. At an international level there is competition for events such as the Tall Ships Race, the Commonwealth Games, the World Cup, major conventions and world fairs, not only because of the anticipated spin-off effects in terms of visitor spending but because of the hype given to the winning city by the international media. At the national level the annual arts' years for bidding cities, e.g. Birmingham's 1992 Year of Music and Manchester's 1994 Year of Drama, major annual city festivals such as the Edinburgh Festival, pop concerts, and even sporting fixtures such as city marathons can form an important element of a city's marketing programme. Sporting events draw a particularly high level of popular interest, crossing all ages and social classes, and attract high levels of media interest. Thus Sheffield attracted much attention through its successful bid for the World Student Games held in 1991, Cardiff and Edinburgh have hosted the Commonwealth Games, several cities have constructed indoor arenas for international indoor sporting fixtures, and even successful football teams have been used in marketing urban tourism in Liverpool and Manchester.

Sport generally can have a major influence on a city's economic restructuring programme. In the USA, for example, Indianapolis's regeneration strategy of the 1980s included downtown rejuvenation, infrastructure improvement, tourism and world class sport. The city spent $168 million on major sporting facilities such as a natatoriun and velodrome, a sports dome, a regatta course, a soccer complex and a skating rink, adding to the sports developments of the 1970s. The results appear to have been rewarding, with a high number of national and international sporting meetings taking place each year, the relocation to the city of a number of headquarters of sports organisations, and the further attraction of many non-sporting companies. As Law points out, however, it is difficult to evaluate the extent to which these firms have moved to the city because of the impact of sports, either in enhancing lifestyle or changing image (Law, 1993).

Photograph 1.9   Manchester's metro – major transportation
investment as a component of reimaging

Photograph 1.10   Manchester's airport – undergoing major
investment

Manchester City Council has targeted sport as one of the key features of its reimaging campaign along with major transportation investment (the light rail metro and the airport) and environmental improvements to the city centre, and although it was clearly disappointed when in September 1993 it failed to win the bidding for the millennium Olympic Games, there have been a number of positive outcomes from the bidding process. The bid managed to attract essential government support of around £80 million of which most has been spent on the development of sport related facilities or essential infrastructure, and the city marketing spin-off appears to have been well worthwhile (Kitchen, 1993). Indeed, the national and international attention focused on Manchester in the period leading up to the decision to award the Games to Sydney is perceived by city officials as having been a valuable marketing exercise in its own right helping to establish it as Britain's second city in the eyes of UK decision takers. The Olympic related flagship investments completed or underway include the grant subsidised redevelopment of the 14 acre Victoria Station site at the northern gateway to the city centre by a consortium of public and private sector partners. Phase 1 of the new development, involving a 16,000 seater indoor arena and car parking is to be completed in 1995. Phase 2 will involve a vast City Room spanning the rail tracks and above this 22 floors of offices surmounted by a 12 storey hotel. There is also to be a metro station. At the main 150 acre Eastlands site, about two miles from the city centre, environmental improvements have been carried out and the City Council and their development partners remain committed to the construction of a 60-80,000 seat national stadium, possibly with government support through the Millenium Fund. Part of the overall scheme for the area includes the construction of a combined train and metro station with the provision of new or re-opened track. Close to the stadium site, Britain's first indoor velodrome costing £9 million has been recently completed, assisted by a substantial City Grant. Finally a mixed use housing/commercial development scheme is planned for the Ashton Canal Corridor, the site intended for the Olympic Village if the 2000 Olympic bid had been successful. So the momentum of the Olympic Bid has not been allowed to subside and the city has now set its sights on hosting the 2002 Commonwealth Games. City officials are confident that if Manchester is successful in securing the Commonwealth Games then the city would make an attempt at the Olympic bid for 2004.

For the actual winners of such Olympic bids the spin-off in terms of improved infrastructure, improved image, civic pride and city marketing can be phenomenal. Also there is now a level of profitability not experienced by host cities prior to the 1980s. Barcelona, venue for the 1992 Olympics, in which 172 countries took part and to which 600,000 visitors were attracted, is a very good case in point although city authorities stress that much of the groundwork for the property development boom began in the early 1980s with an unleashing of entrepreneurial fervour so long suppressed by Franco. Winning the Olympic games, however, acted as a catalyst for and provided much needed regional and national funding for major infrastructural projects (sports, housing, transport and communications) to be completed over a short time scale and helped to put the city on the map as a quality tourist venue in Europe (Sanchez, 1992; Law, 1993; Buchanan, 1992; Riera and Keogh, 1995). Indeed, the city and regional governments have been zealously involved in marketing the city as a European growth pole since Spain entered the European Union and this has been made easier by the successful transformation of Barcelona's infrastructure to accommodate the Olympic Games. Moreover the efficiency with which the Games were organised helped to reinforce the perceptions of investors and businessmen in Europe that the Catalan people are hard working and reliable.

The types of work undertaken in Barcelona in the years and months leading up to the Games included the provision of major open spaces for public use, sometimes involving the removal of buildings, underground car parking, paving at various levels to define routes for pedestrians and traffic and the creation of a variety of urban sculptures. The Olympic Village, built for the Games and since sold for private housing, now connects the city to the sea where formerly industrial land, redundant warehouses and railway tracks existed. The waterfront also now contains a park, harbour and marina and large stretches of new beaches with protective breakwaters plus two large tower blocks, identical in dimension but different in design. One of these has been converted into a hotel by a Japanese Company and the other is not yet fully let as offices. Although temporarily shelved by recessionary pressures in the early 1990s the regeneration momentum along the city's waterfront is now being continued through the development of the Maremagnum Project, comprising a World Trade Centre, Imax Theatre, acquarium, festival shopping and marina spaces, all linked to the city's main street, 'La Ramblas', by a floating pedestrian bridge across the harbour. Many of the sporting facilities for the Olympics were situated at Montjuic, the hill that dominates the southwest corner of the city, where already some sporting facilities set in a landscaped park existed. One thing that marks the regeneration of Barcelona is the high design standards imposed with the use of architectural competitions for most important buildings and the wholeness of the urban fabric retained, not fragmented as in many cities. Chains of new plazas and parks link the city areas together with the public realm retained as an important element of the city structure. "So it is appropriate that this transformation of the city has been driven by a sense of social purpose, by the needs of the future rather than by the short-term imperatives of the Games" (Rogers and Fisher, 1992).

31

Just as the Olympics have been used by cities internationally to assist in the reimaging process and attract inward investment, so too were the biennial UK garden festivals of the 1980s intended to change perceptions of formerly derelict sites and to improve the host city's image. To date there have been five garden festivals – at Liverpool, Stoke-on-Trent, Gateshead, Glasgow and Ebbw Vale. The basic idea is that a large tract of land suffering from neglect or complete dereliction in a city is developed over a short time period (two to three years) as a horticultural garden and landscape event lasting several months from late spring to early autumn and involving indoor and outdoor exhibits, nature trails, informal walks, sculptures, catering and festival events such as bands, clowns and puppet shows. Garden exhibits are contributed by countries from around the world and from organizations within the UK. After the event is over the land is marketed for permanent uses such as housing, industry or parks. The example of German International Horticultural Exhibitions (IGAs) and Bundesgardenschaus (BGSs) led decision takers and city marketeers to hope that the garden festivals would have further regenerative effects such as forcing the completion of other private sector projects that would otherwise not happen.

Initially in the UK, garden festivals were lauded for restoring local confidence in run down parts of the city and boosting tourist numbers. As Beaumont proclaimed in relation to the Liverpool Garden Festival 1984:

> speedy reclamation work followed by ambitious development of a complex event with world-wide support has, together with events such as the Tall Ships Race and the refurbishment of the Albert Dock complex, already given a significant boost to a battered city. No longer is there a static image of despair and dereliction but one which has begun to change and has continued to do so throughout the period of the Festival. It is essential thereafter to maintain the catalytic action which the Festival was intended to inspire (Beaumont, 1985).

The reality has not been quite so positive, however, with many of the festivals having made a small loss, met by the local council or the Development Corporation as in the case of Liverpool. It would appear that any long term environmental and economic benefits resulting from garden festivals could have been achieved anyway without such an event if the government had allocated the same funds without the impetus of a festival (Law, 1993). The average cost of the investment in garden festivals has been approximately £40 million each. It has been questioned whether greater permanent benefit would not have been achieved if this investment had been spread more widely in the cities concerned through the use of Derelict Land Grant. The Department of the Environment commissioned study (PA Cambridge Economic Consultants, 1990) of garden festivals in the UK found that they may not have been powerful instruments in isolation but were a useful additional element in a regional strategy. To date no plans have been made for any further major garden festivals and this would seem to speak for itself.

Evaluation

The intention in this chapter has been to describe the range of city reimaging strategies that have been used in the UK and elsewhere in the 1980s and early 1990s, and to outline the benefits that these strategies are considered by the marketeers to have had in terms of place marketing, confidence building and the attraction of private sector investment and urban tourism. But the voices of caution and outright condemnation of some of these initiatives have been increasingly heard, not only from commentators from the left. The deep recession in the UK from the late 1980s to 1993 and the weak recovery thereafter have shown up some of the weaknesses of over dependence on property led regeneration and have brought to light the increasing urban poverty experienced in most cities, despite the hype and the image-makers' activities. Indeed, in response to a growing concern that existing policies are not making the intended impact on the inner city problem one can identify a slight shift in Conservative Government thinking in the direction of increasing local government and local community involvement in regeneration initiatives (City Challenge, for example) and a shift in local government thinking towards a more balanced urban regeneration policy including a greater concern for social as well as image issues.

> By the early 1990s, the onset of the longest and deepest recession in post-1945 British history forced the government to acknowledge that the private sector and the associated trickle-down mechanism could not be relied upon to rejuvenate urban areas and solve urban problems. This led to a new emphasis on public-private partnerships, in which a more compliant local government was to be allowed to participate so long as it made the correct noises regarding the role of the private sector (Atkinson and Moon, 1994).

Looking back over the reimaging strategies of the last ten years a number of key criticisms of reimaging emerge, not only of the principle of reimaging itself as a cornerstone of urban policy but also of the different elements in practice. It has been claimed that city authorities, even those supposedly of a socialist leaning, have followed the reimaging path lemming-like without any analysis or critique of alternative policies (Sadler, 1993). Why was this so? It may be that it is as important politically to be seen to be doing something about the inner city problem as to critically examine the problem itself. Thus the rhetorical power of reimaging, of spectacular redevelopment, should not be underestimated in political terms.

It should therefore be of little surprise if the expenditure on inner city regeneration turns out to be a risible fraction of that necessary to have a major impact on the level of urban immiseration as long as it can still produce the sort of photogenic spectacle so clearly embodied in Birmingham's super-prix or Phoenix's grand prix, Boston and New York's marathons or Liverpool's Tall Ships Race. This line of argument does not demand an exercise in conspiracy theory sociology, or even a belief in premeditated state malice, only an acceptance of the realities of the world of policy formulation in which both issues and policy prescriptions are not structured solely by empirical reality. The spectacle of inner-city regeneration offers a powerful medium for a political commitment to a strategy based on what is superficially market led growth (Keith and Rogers, 1991).

The emphasis on creating the right climate and the right image for private sector investment confidence has also come under fire because it failed to understand the demand side of the development equation.

What we have seen in the application of marketing concepts to the city during the 1980s is largely an effort to help unblock the supply side. In other words, the hype has been applied in a general way with little or no understanding of the demand side. While it hit certain targets, it has largely failed to meet demand because it has soon been seen to make exaggerated claims and create unrealistic expectations. . . . The resultant supply-side emphasis helped fuel the oversupply of development in the property market. Development decisions, including those for some flagships, were made on the basis of false confidence. This was a long way short of the marketing principle of creating and satisfying a customer . . . real demand cannot be created because that is a broader economic issue; however, effective demand can be identified through innovation, latent market need, persuasion, product substitution and trade-offs (Smyth, 1994).

Central to much of the criticism is the question of whether reimaging strategies have been achieving the goals intended, namely inward investment, urban tourism, improved lifestyles, economic growth, the wholesome post-industrial city. The opportunity costs of the expenditure on reimaging strategies have also been highlighted and the perceived failure of such spending to impact on the lives of those worst off in society. The types of images chosen in place marketing cities and the types of culture chosen in culture led regeneration have also been strongly attacked by commentators, particularly those on the left.

At the broadest level the wisdom of dependence on the service sector, the sine qua non of most city restructuring policies, has come under attack in the 1990s in the wake of the severe recession. Some argue that whilst globalization may have enhanced the importance of financing, informational and control functions, it has also enlarged the number of competitors in the tertiary sector, and this sector is not immune from instability caused by occasional crises in the world financial markets. Hence many cities which emphasized service sector growth in the 1980s are now seeking a more balanced approach to

34

economic restructuring. Glasgow's Director of Planning has elucidated this changing approach thus:

> Glasgow should not simply be viewed as a post-industrial city whose future is tied to commerce and tourism. A heavy reliance is already placed on the service sector but it is not strong enough to provide the stable economic platform necessary for the next century. In spite of its long-term decline, manufacturing industry (some 60,000 jobs) remains a much more important employer than the arts and cultural industries (15,000 jobs) and tourism (20,000 jobs) . . . Whilst service industry will remain significant, particularly in the City Centre, modern manufacturing industry is a better secondary employment generator than any other economic activity (Rae, 1991).

In Glasgow the emphasis on reimaging the city for inward investors and urban tourists is being rethought. "Evidently Glasgow is not yet renascent: it is still in labour" (Reed, 1993). Relocation of either public sector or private industry from the South East of England has not occurred in the way anticipated. In reality privatization has reduced the role of government generated relocations, whilst private companies throughout the UK have been cautious about major relocations and expansion plans. Recently developed offices in the city centre, particularily in secondary locations, have not sold or let as anticipated by the developers (Morrison, 1994). Likewise unemployment has never dropped below 14 per cent even in the economic upturn years, whilst manufacturing has continued to decline so that it now employs only 16 per cent of the workforce, and Glasgow still has some of the worst peripheral housing estates in the UK, in areas such as Easterhouse, Drumchapel, Castlemilk and Pollock. The mood in Glasgow is now one of consolidating past achievements rather than launching any new re imaging packages, and the Labour leader of the council has stated that the city no longer needs spectacular events (*Financial Times* 1992). Nevertheless image and tourist potential do enter into the thinking behind Glasgow's winning bid for the 1999 City of Architecture and Design, though the publicity material is perceptibly more community oriented than it would have been five years ago.

Cities with the greatest potential for the future have been identified as those with a diverse manufacturing and services economy concentrated in high value industries, an educated and skilled workforce, a strong research, design and educational infrastructure, excellent communication links within the international urban network and cultural and environmental assets that can attract and retain qualified and mobile labour (Parkinson et al., 1991). When accompanied by adequate infrastructure, a diverse economic base may not only protect the local population from the extremes of recession and external decision making, but also help to attract and retain inward investment. Cities thus need to evaluate their spending plans carefully before committing an unrealistic proportion to reimaging strategies targeted at the attraction of inward service sector employment, especially if this is at the expense of initiatives such as employment training and education that will also support a modern diverse economy.

The question of the extent of economic trickle-down from expensive flagship projects and the image gap between the flagship schemes and the nearby neglected inner city residential areas has also been extensively debated. Some argue that although cultural or leisure flagship projects do frequently result in improvements to local economies in terms of increased tourism and the spawning of consumer service industries nearby, as well as providing the much needed imagery for city promotion activities, many are not well integrated into the urban fabric. Wilkinson (1992) maintains that flagships represent a marketing tool, a form of branding device aimed at boosting a city's image, but that they in reality create urban fragments which float free from the rest of the distressed urban area. Flagship development intended to boost the regenerative potential of a depressed area is, she argues, an approach concerned with superimposing fragments on the city rather than with the comprehensive planning of urban areas. When the recession of the 1990s ripped away the spectral image of a vigorous and thriving market place in the post-industrial cities of Britain, it revealed a situation in which, although small parts of the city had experienced flagship style developments, the vast majority of run-down areas, and the people living in them, had not benefitted (Atkinson and Moon, 1994).

Many commentators have discussed whether or not the developments of Baltimore's downtown and waterfront have improved the quality of life for the working class people of the city, and whether or not the jobs created have gone to local people (Levine, 1987; De Jong, 1991; Falk, 1986; Giloth, 1992). The conclusion is generally negative. Downtown/waterfront development has benefited the city's developers, increased tourism and improved citizens' sense of belonging, but it masks, behind the glitter, accelerating urban problems in a highly segregated city with high unemployment, poor schools and crime. An opposing view is held by Frieden (1990) who considers that in general the benefits of major public projects have spread beyond the new downtowns and the cleaned-up waterfronts. The revival of city centres as places to do business has, he contends, created a variety of jobs for people of many educational levels, including average city residents and members of minority groups.

More specifically there are arguments about the opportunity costs of the high levels of expenditure on reimaging in particular cities. Many argue that reimaging strategies employed by post-industrial cities have absorbed large proportions of public resources and shifted attention away from the worsening of the quality of life for many residents. Dangschat (1994) points out that the city of Hamburg recovered very quickly from its deep economic crises of the 1980s, benefiting from the Single Market and German unification and investing much in improvements to the city's attractions. However the

36

'boomtown' represented by some first class hotels, a system of ten shopping malls and a huge mass of office buildings is in stark contrast to a growing housing problem for the city's poor and the neglect of peripheral areas. Indeed, increasing social polarisation in the city is seen by some local decision makers as a necessary part of the 'successful' transformation of the city region economy.

Discussing Birmingham, Loftman also highlights social polarisation, concluding:

> Within the current planning policy framework the City Council, in its determination to create a new image for Birmingham and secure its economic regeneration through 'prestige projects' such as the Convention Centre development, is likely to exacerbate poverty in and the social polarisation of the City (Loftman, 1990).

Indeed, in order to pay for the building of the megaprojects in Birmingham in the 1980s and 1990s – the £180 million Convention Centre, the 13,000 seat indoor athletics arena, the £30 million symphony hall and other prestige developments such as the environmental upgrading of Centenary Square (£3 million), it now appears that £123 million was taken from Birmingham City Council's housing budget and that spending on school buildings fell by 60 per cent. In addition little trickle-down impact was subsequently felt from the new projects by local people because any jobs that were created were few, low-paid and menial. In the case of the Birmingham International Convention Centre, an optimistic estimate of its likely impact was made at the planning stage but a study undertaken since it was opened argues that traditional impact analysis ignores the employment foregone through the cost of financing the debt on the capital expended (Loftman and Nevin, 1992). More jobs might have been created in Birmingham had the funds been used on education and housing, another responsibility of the city council. "Most notoriously of all, the council took more and more from the budget for education, leaving Birmingham with some of the worst schools in the country" (Cohen, 1994).

The counter argument is that many of these cultural projects in the city centre of Birmingham were funded by new money, not existing money, so that there was little element of opportunity cost. European Union funding, it is argued by city officials, has been a key factor in the types of regeneration projects favoured by the city (the Convention Centre, for example) and this could not have been assigned to alternative social policies. The City Council worked hard to have the city declared an Assisted Area in 1984 and subsequently took a proactive stance in securing EU funding for urban regeneration securing the first Integrated Development Operation approved in 1988. The additional funds, it can be argued, were a due reward for effort by the Council and the results of increased tourism have benefitted the whole city population.

> A key feature of . . . the approach was the way in which it [the council] began to look towards the EC Commission as a potential source of funding for economic regeneration leading to a shift from a predominantly national view to an increasingly international perspective on the city's economic problems and their solution (Martin and Pearce, 1992).

City officials believe that flagship investments like the International Convention Centre, in conjunction with less costly investments by the City Council on environmental improvements to the surrounding area such as repaving, art works, pedestrianization and floodlighting, have had an impact in attracting relocations such as the Trustee Savings Bank, which now occupies a headquarters building close to Centenary Square. Likewise the view is taken that the one and a half million pounds of private property investment in the city centre since 1989 is greater than would have been achieved without the reimaging strategy. Today, however, responding to the claims that city reimaging strategies have been skewed in favour of capital owning interests rather than the interests of the poor, a new left wing Labour leader of the City Council has pledged that the future priorities will be housing, education and social services, not tourists, theatre-goers and conventions (Cohen, 1994).

Not only are the initial capital costs of reimaging flagship projects such as concert halls, convention centres and garden festivals a source of deep concern but it is also contended that the cost of maintaining them constitutes a long term drain on public finances and yet few independent assessments are made of the extent to which such schemes have attained their stated objectives (Bianchini et al., 1992). It is difficult not only to predict or measure direct economic costs and benefits associated with large scale state sponsored projects and to trace indirect costs and benefits, but also to measure the impact of developments in terms of social, environmental and urban design criteria.

The substance of the imagery used to alter perceptions of different places has also come under considerable analysis and criticism. Harvey goes further to the left than most commentators by arguing that the aim of urban regeneration strategies in the 1980s was to mobilize "every aesthetic power of illusion and image . . . to mask the intensifying class, racial and ethnic polarisations going on underneath" (Harvey, 1989b). Thus the city of the 1980s and 1990s is viewed by some as an urban spectacle, a city of fun, games, glitter and fleeting experiences which hides unrelenting decline and tenacious inequalities (Beauregard, 1993). Discussing American cities he argues that the promise of reinvestment in and renaissance of cities temporarily pushed to one side consciousness of the poverty and decline endemic in these cities, but the problems of the poor highlighted in the 1970s did not go away; rather this class was pushed into neigbourhoods away from those gentrified by the new middle classes. The lot of the poor was further diminished in the so-called boom decade with a rising destitution in what has become known as the underclass.

Wealth and poverty were not only inextricably linked, with the poor frequently serving the rich in return for low wages, poor housing, inadequate health care, and poor quality education, but the exchange was terribly unequal in the gentrifying cities of the eighties. In fact, for the poor it was always and everyplace a bad deal (Beauregard, 1993).

Others agree that city councils which seek to promote a dream image of their city not only ignore the social consequences of focusing on private sector needs and perceptions, but can actually make matters worse for poor people (Hambleton, 1991). New developments designed with reimaging in mind, especially the glamorized flagship projects and their promotional imagery, are in bad taste when juxtaposed with areas of intense poverty. Malone (1993), for example, argues that the imagery of Dublin's major flagship development at Custom House Dock (a partly completed office, leisure, retailing development on an eleven hectare site between the city centre and a redundant area of docklands) consists of three strands, each of which contrasts with the realities of the surrounding inner city areas. There is the festival imagery generated by the American architects, that is the imagery of striped umbrellas, garden furniture and reproduction capstans. There is the high-tech, "life in the fast lane" imagery promoting the International Financial Services Centre to international business and capital. Thirdly there is the imagery which sells Ireland as a place where the quality of life is desirable – that is Ireland as a land of golfers, anglers and yachtsmen. None of this sits very happily with the realities of inner city life in close proximity to Customs House Dock, where crime and poverty are high, housing conditions appalling and job expectations from the new development minimal.

So not only is there deep concern about the substance of the images sold by the post-industrial city but there is also concern about its sameness, that serial copying of the sport, heritage, culture and tourism type of theme can result in oversupply of similar facilities within a country (economically unsound) and can crush the essential character of particular places (culturally unsound).

How many successful convention centres, sports stadia, disney-worlds, harbour places and spectacular shopping malls can there be? Success is often-short lived or rendered moot by competing or alternative innovations arising elsewhere. Over-investment in everything from shopping malls to cultural facilities makes the values embedded in urban space highly vulnerable to devaluation (Harvey, 1987).

Festive retailing may work for the first cities that revitalise their waterfronts using this formula, but impulse-buying tourists can support only so many stores selling brass ships' furnishings and Irish shawls. Research parks have spurred developments in Cambridge, England, and Charlotte, North Carolina, but they are predestined to languish in most places (Fainstein, 1990).

This leads to the fear that internationally cities are losing their separate cultural identities. As Holcomb states:

Photograph 1.11   Financial Services Centre, Custom House Dock, Dublin

Photograph 1.12   Model of Custom House Dock Development, Dublin

40

The packaged image reflects the aesthetic tastes of the postmodern society, with its eclectic conformity, its fragmented palimpsest of past times and distant spaces, its commodified ethnic culture and sanitised classlessness. The city is rebuilt to conform to this increasingly international aesthetic so that, although the beer is better in Glasgow, the chablis and the spider plants are indistinguishable from those in both Cleveland and Pittsburg (Holcomb, 1993).

Belfast, for example, in reimaging itself as if it is a normal British post-industrial city and in welcoming the American styles of waterfront postmodernist development, including Baltimore style festival shopping, risks losing its own identity as a remarkably complete Victorian city with overtones of Ulster-Irishness. In the rush to produce an image of neutrality and normality for the city we seem to have forgotten that much of attractiveness of the city is because of its unique cultural identity. Although a city culturally divided is a difficult one to reflect in logos and slogans, in open space design and in building styles, the challenge must be faced.

Likewise the imagery of the type of post-modern architecture and urban design frequently associated with private sector led regeneration in reimaging cities, especially their waterfronts, has been fiercely attacked. The creation of spectacle without any sense of locality is widely condemned. As Francis Tibbalds, past president of the Royal Town Planning Institute in the UK, succunctly put it:

If you want to see what, left to its own devices, the private sector produces, one need look no further than the Isle of Dogs in London's Docklands. The British Government's flagship of Enterprise Culture Development and the urban design challenge of the century adds up to little more than market-led opportunistic chaos – an architectural circus – with a sprinkling of post-modern gimmicks, frenzied construction of the ghastly megalumps of Canary Wharf and a fairground train to get you there. It is a disappointment to residents and workers. There was a necessary step between balance sheet and building, that got missed in the rush. It is called 'urban design' (Tibbalds, 1992).

In a postmodern world of "pastiche and nostalgia what we increasingly consume are signs and representations which are accepted in a spirit of spectacle" (Urry, 1990). Thus postmodern tendencies in architecture show the reintroduction of decoration, the mixing of styles and a playful pop art simulation of commodities (Featherstone, 1991). The postmodern city has become a centre of consumption, play and entertainment, saturated with signs and images to the extent that anything can become represented, thematized and made an object of interest, an object of the tourist gaze.

As for the culture chosen in culture led reimaging strategies it has also come under intense fire, not least because the culture chosen often reflects the imagemakers' view of the city's characteristics rather than reflecting the

41

intellectual, spiritual or aesthetic needs of the majority of citizens (Bianchini, 1991). Too often the culture industry creates its own sanitized environments which have very little to offer the "lived practices" of local communities (Lim, 1993). In Belfast, although the events sponsored by the city's promotional public-private partnership, Positively Belfast, have been well supported, some 400,000 having visited the Tall Ships Race in 1991, there is the nagging doubt that ordinary working class people cannot feel a strong cultural identity with events which are dominated by elitist middle class sports and art forms such as golf, power boat racing, ballooning and opera. Indeed, because of the need to project images conducive to inward investment, most cultural projects tend to take the form of prestige art events that cater to a select audience in city centres and can lead to disaffection in more community based arts organisations on the periphery. Yet the promised jobs brought by cultural industries and cultural consumption are largely low paid and very often not available to the most needy sectors of the population. Thus the expected trickle-down effects of a cultural policy can be limited and there is little substantial evidence to show that much inward investment has directly resulted from the cultural investments. According to David Harvey prestige art led regeneration projects function as a "carnival mask that diverts and entertains, leaving the social problems that lie behind the mask unseen and uncared for" (Harvey, 1989).

In Glasgow, as discussed earlier, the culture led strategy has been under fire for some time, criticisms evolving around the issues of the real as opposed to the manufactured identity of the city and the use being made of culture – instrumental and economistic, rather than a value in its own right. James Kelman, for example, suggested that the 1990 City of Culture celebrations were an assault on the real cultural life of the city and the application of the city of culture concept derived from intellectual poverty, moral bankrupcy and political cowardice. McLay, another left wing activist, described the Year of Culture as having "more to do with power politics than culture: more to do with millionaire developers than art" (McLay, 1990). Wishart, on the other hand, responds with fervour that the policies pursued have resulted in a very real transformation of the city, despite its continuing housing problems.

> Would it have been more ideologically sound to leave the scars of industrial decline as ugly, mocking symbols of the heyday of heavy engineering, rather than landscape the gap sites? Were the near derelict warehouses morally more aceptable to the socialist soul than the bright new apartments? (Wishart, 1993).

She goes on to argue that those on the left should involve themselves in helping to fashion the future of the city rather than constantly re-examining the city's historical navel. Such issues are common to much of the debate about the reimaging process in other post-industrial cities in the UK.

Difficult cities

In conclusion then my own view is that despite the many criticisms of image enhancement strategies in urban regeneration increasing inter-urban competition means that second cities cannot afford to opt out of the reimaging game altogether. However the reimaging should be balanced with a wide range of policies aimed at social as well as economic regeneration. Concern must be expressed that cities are more or less following similar patterns of reimaging without sufficient research having been carried out into the success of such initiatives increasing economic prosperity and its distribution. Some studies have been made of place boosting advertising campaigns and these suggest that the confidence of local investors is enhanced by changing images (e.g. Burgess and Wood, 1988) but the extent to which a revitalised image has contributed to economic success is difficult to assess where there is such a plethora of other initiatives working together in a given locality. There is some recent evidence of the durability of Glasgow's poor external image as a place in which to live, despite the lengthy reimaging campaign, the garden festival and the Year of Culture. It would appear that hallmark events combined with an advertising campaign may influence specific aspects of a city's image which may in turn influence the decision to visit the city but may leave unaffected the overall image of the city and particularly its more negative aspects. Surveys of white collar households in the southeast of England taken at the start and end of Glasgow's year as European City of Culture showed that despite substantial increases in those feeling that Glasgow was rapidly changing for the better (34–49 per cent) barely 10 per cent "would be happy to live and work" in Glasgow (Paddison, 1993).

Therefore reimaging strategies should be carefully thought out by city authorities or the urban growth coalitions, whichever take the lead role, and there should be caution in relation to over-promising and under-delivering. If the reality jars with the image presented then visitors and entrepreneurs attracted by the promotion will become cynical. If image campaigns are to result in sustainable and sharable benefits, they must be both credible and backed up by substance. Furthermore, image marketing strategies must relate more successfully to urban regeneration strategies and investment programmes if they are to reposition older industrial cities effectively. Care should be taken in initially carrying out an audit of the city's strengths and weakness so that the strengths can be built on and the weaknesses overcome or diluted. This audit should pinpoint the characteristics of the city which make it different from other cities in the region or the country and these should be emphasised and developed in improving the product to be marketed, i.e. the city. As Ashworth and Voogd (1990) argue, place images only exist through their difference from other place images so a no-win situation can arise if all cities in a region embark on similar schemes. Liverpool, Newcastle, Manchester and Glasgow, for example, must each find a different image to emphasize and develop rather than emitting a cliched version of a post-industrial culture conscious and heritage filled urban playground. Unfortunately it is the cliched model that many of the most "difficult" cities have been deliberately following.

References

Ashworth, G.J. and Voogd, H. (1990), *Selling the City: Marketing Approaches in Public Sector Urban Planning*, Belhaven Press, London.

Ashworth, G.J. and Voogd, H. (1994), 'Marketing and Place Promotion' in Gold, J.R. and Ward, S.V. (eds), *Place promotion. The Use of Publicity and Marketing to Sell Towns and Regions*, Wiley, Chichester.

Atkinson, R. and Moon, G. (1994), *Urban Policy in Britain. The City, the State and the Market,* Macmillan Press, London.

Barke, M. and Harrop, K. (1994), 'Selling the Industrial Town: identity, image and illusion' in Gold, J.R. and Ward, S.V. (eds), *Place promotion. The Use of Publicity and Marketing to Sell Towns and Regions*, Wiley, Chichester.

Barnekov, T., Boyle, R. and Rich, D. (1989), *Privatism and Urban Policy in Britain and the United States*, Oxford University Press, Oxford.

Bassett, K. (1993), 'Urban cultural strategies and urban renaissance : a case study and critique', *Environment and Planning A,* vol. 25, pp.1773-1788.

Beaumont, R. (1985), 'Garden festivals as a means of urban regeneration', in *New Partnerships in Urban Regeneration*, Ninth INTA International Conference Glasgow, Den Haag, The Netherlands.

Beauregard, R.A. (1993), *Voices of Decline*, Blackwell, Oxford.

Bianchini, F., Fisher, M., Montgomery, J. and Warpole, K. (1988), *City Centres City Cultures*, Centre for Local Economic Strategies, Manchester.

Bianchini, F. (1989), *Urban Renaissance? The Arts and the Urban Regeneration Process in 1980s Britain*, Working Paper No 7, Liverpool John Moores University, Liverpool.

Bianchini, F. (1991), 'Alternative Cities', *Marxism Today,* June, pp. 36–38.

Bianchini, F. and Schwengel, H. (1991), 'Re-imaging the city', in Corner, J. and Harvey, S. (eds), *Enterprise and Heritage: Cross-currents of National Culture*, Routledge, London.

Bianchini, F., Dawson, J. and Evans, R. (1992), 'Flagship projects in urban regeneration' in Tavsanoglu, S. and Healey, P. (eds), *Rebuilding the City: Property-led Urban Regeneration*, Spon, London.

Bianchini, F. (1993), 'Remaking European Cities: the role of cultural policies' in Bianchini, F. and Parkinson, M. (eds), *Cultural Policy and Urban Regeneration*, Manchester University Press, Manchester.

Birmingham City Council (undated), *City Centre Strategy*, Department of Planning and Architecture, p.2.

Birmingham City Council, (1989a), *Heritage Development Plan.*

Birmingham City Council, (1989b), *Economic Impact of the Arts.*

Birmingham City Council, (1989c), *Towards a Cultural Strategy.*

Birmingham City Council, (1990), *An Arts Strategy for Birmingham.*

Boogarts, I. (1990), *A new urban planning tool kit: are investments in the arts and culture new tools for revitalising the city*, paper presented at the 6th International Conference on Cultural Economics, UMEA, Sweden, June.

Boyle, R. (1989), 'Private sector urban regeneration: the Scottish experience' in Parkinson, M., Foley, B. and Judd, D. (ed), *Regenerating the Cities – the UK Crises and the US Experience*, Manchester University Press, Manchester.

Boyle, M. and Hughes, G. (1991) 'The politics of the representations of 'the real': discourses from the Left on Glasgow's role as European City of Culture, 1990', *Area,* vol. 23, no. 3, pp. 217-228.

Buchanan, P. (1992), 'Barcelona, a city regenerated', *Architectural Review*, vol. 121, no.1146, pp. 11–15.

Burgess, J. and Wood, P. (1988), 'Decoding Docklands: place advertising and decision-making strategies of small firms' in Eyles, J and Smith, D. (eds), *Qualitative methods in Human Geography*, Polity Press, Cambridge.

Chaney, D. (1990), 'Dystopia in Gateshead: The Metrocentre as a cultural form', *Theory, Culture and Society,* vol. 7, no. 4, pp. 49–68.

Cheshire, P.C.(1990), 'Explaining the recent performance of the European Community's major urban regions', *Urban Studies*, vol. 27, pp. 311-333.

Civic Trust/Queens University Belfast (1988), *Conservation in Belfast*, Belfast.

Cohen, N. (1994), 'Rattled of Symphony Hall', *The Independent*, 9 March 1994, p. 19.

Colenutt, B. (1993), 'After the Urban Development Corporations? Development elites or people based regeneration' in Imrie, B. and Thomas, H. (eds), *British Urban Policy and the Urban Development Corporations*, Paul Chapman, London.

Confederation of British Industry (1987), *Initiatives beyond charity*, CBI, London.

Cooke, P.(1989), 'Municipal enterprise, growth coalitions and social justice', *Local Economy*, vol.3, no.3, pp. 191–200.

Cowie, H. (1986), 'Partnerships in US cities', *Public Finance and Accountancy*, 14 November, pp. 7–9.

Crilley, D. (1993), 'Architecture as Advertising: Constructing the Image of Redevelopment' in Kearns, G. and Philo, C. (eds), *Selling places. The City as Cultural Capital, Past and Present*, Pergamon Press, Oxford.

Dalby, S. (1991), 'Going it alone', *Financial Times*, October 18, p. 22.

Dangschat, J.S. (1994), 'Concentration of Poverty in the Landscapes of Boomtown Hamburg: The Creation of a New Urban Underclass?', *Urban Studies*, vol. 31, no. 7, pp. 1133–1147.

DATAR (1989), *Les Villes Europeenes*, La Documentation Francaise, Paris.

De Jong, M.W. (1991), 'Revitalizing the urban core: waterfront development in Baltimore, Maryland' in Fox-Przeworski, J., Goddard, J. and De Jong, M. (eds), *Urban Regeneration in a Changing Economy*, Clarendon Press, Oxford.

Department of the Environment for Northern Ireland (1994), *Belfast City Centre. Vision for the Future.* p.8, HMSO, Belfast.

Dunning, J.H. and Norman, G. (1987), 'Locational choice of offices of international companies', *Environment and Planning A,* vol. 19, pp. 613–631.

Esser, J. and Hirsch, J. (1989), 'The crises of fordism and the dimensions of a 'postfordist' regional and urban structure', *International Journal of Urban and Regional Research*, vol. 13, no. 3, pp. 417–437.

Evans, G. (1993), *An Urban renaissance? The role of the arts in urban regeneration: a survey of local authorities in Greater London*, University of London Press, London.

Evans, R. (1994), 'Birmingham' in Harding, A., Dawson, J., Evans, R. and Parkinson, M. (eds), *European Cities Towards 2000*, Manchester University Press, Manchester.

Falk, N. (1986), 'Baltimore and Lowell: two American approaches', *Built Environment*, vol. 13, no. 4, pp. 145–152.

Falk, N. (1992), 'British Experience in Regenerating Urban Docklands' in Hoyle, B. and Pinder D. (eds), *European Port Cities in Transition*, Belhaven Press, London.

Fainstein, S. (1990), 'The Changing World Economy and Urban Restructuring', in Parkinson, M. and Judd, D. (eds), *Leadership and Urban Regeneration*, Sage, London.

Featherstone, M. (1991), *Consumer Culture and Postmodernism*, Sage, London.

Financial Times (1992), 'Glasgow', pp.13–15, 25 June.

Fretter, A. (1993), 'Place Marketing: A Local Authority Perspective' in Kearns, G. and Philo, C. (eds), *Selling places. The City as Cultural Capital, Past and Present*, Pergamon Press, Oxford.

Frieden, B. (1990), 'City centres transformed: planners as developers', *Journal of the American Planning Association*, vol. 56, part 4, pp. 423–428.

Getz, D. (1991), *Festivals, Special Events and Tourism*, Van Nostrand Reinhold, New York.

Giloth, R. (1992), 'Beyond common sense: the Baltimore renaissance', *Local Economy*, vol. 4, no. 4, pp. 290–297.

Glasgow Action (1991), *Towards a Great European City*, Glasgow.

Granville, D. (1994), 'From Cutlery to Culture', *Planning Week*, vol. 2, no. 44, pp. 16–17.

Griffiths, R. (1993), 'The Politics of Cultural Policy in Urban Regeneration Strategies', *Policy and Politics*, vol. 21, pp. 39-46.

Hall, P. (1993), 'Forces Shaping Urban Europe', *Urban Studies*, vol. 30, no. 6, pp. 883–898.

Hall, T.R. (1992), *Art and Image: Public Art as Symbol in Urban Regeneration*, School of Geography Working Paper Series, no. 61, University of Birmingham.

Hambleton, R. (1991), 'American Dreams, Urban realities', *The Planner*, vol. 77, no. 23, pp. 6–9.

Harvey, D. (1987), 'Flexible accumulation through urbanisation: reflections on postmodernism in the American City', *Antipode*, vol. 19, no. 3, pp. 260–286.

Harvey, D. (1989a), 'From managerialism to entrepreneurialism: the transformation in urban governance in late capitalism', *Geografiska Annaler*, vol. 71B, no. 1, pp. 3–17.

Harvey, D. (1989b), 'Down Towns', *Marxism Today*, January.

Healey, P. (1991), 'Urban regeneration and the development industry', *Regional Studies*, vol. 25, no. 2, pp. 97–110.

Hendon, W. and Shaw, D. (1987), 'The arts and urban development', in Gappert, G. (ed), *The Future of Winter Cities*, Sage.

Heseltine M. (1989), *Sunday Times*, 18 June.

Holcomb, B. (1993), 'Revisioning Place: De- and Re- constructing the Image of the Industrial City' in Kearns, G. and Philo, C. (eds), *Selling Places*, Pergamon Press, Oxford.

Imrie, R. and Thomas, H. (1993), 'The limits of property-led regeneration', *Environment and Planning C: Government and Policy*, vol. 11, pp. 87–102.

Judd, D.R. and Ready, R.L. (1986), 'Entrepreneurial Cities and the New Politics of

Economic Development' in Peterson, G.E. and Lewis C.W. (eds), *Reagan and the Cities*, Urban Institute Press, Washington DC.

Karski, A. (1990), 'Urban Tourism – A Key to Urban Regeneration?', *The Planner*, 6 April, pp. 15–17.

Keith, M. and Rogers, A. (1992), 'Hollow promises? Policy, theory and practice in the inner city' in Keith, M. and Rogers, A., *Hollow Promises. Rhetoric and Reality in the Inner City*, Mansell Publishing Limited, London

Keens, W., Owens, P., Salvadori, D. and Williams, J. (eds) (1989), *Arts and the Changing City: An Agenda for Urban Regeneration*, British American Arts Association, New york.

Kitchen, T. (1993), 'The Manchester Olympic Bid and Urban Regeneration', *Town and Country Planning School Report of Proceedings*, pp.34–38, Royal Town Planning Institute, London.

Laurie, E. (1993), 'Tackintosh: Glasgow's Supplementary Gloss' in Kearns, G. and Philo, C. (eds), *Selling places. The City as Cultural Capital, Past and Present*, Pergamon Press, Oxford.

Law, C. (1993), *Urban Tourism : Attracting Visitors to Large Cities*, Mansell Publishing Limited, New York and London.

Lawless, P. (1991), 'Urban policy in the Thatcher decade: English inner city policy', *Environment and Planning C: Government and Policy*, vol. 9, pp. 15–30.

Levine, M. (1987), 'Downtown redevelopment as an urban growth strategy: a critical appraisal of the Baltimore renaissance', *Journal of Urban Affairs*, vol. 9, no. 2, pp. 103–23.

Lim, H. (1993), 'Cultural strategies for revitalising the city: a review and evaluation', *Regional Studies*, vol. 27, no. 6, pp. 589–594.

Loftman, P. (1990), *A Tale of Two Cities: Birmingham the Convention and Unequal City. The International Convention Centre and Disadvantaged Groups*, research paper no. 6, Built Environment Development Centre, Birmingham Polytechnic, Birmingham.

Loftman, P. and Nevin, B. (1994), 'Prestige Project Developments: Economic renaissance or Economic Myth? A Case Study of Birmingham', *Local Economy*, vol. 8, no. 4, pp. 307–325.

Madsen, H. (1992), 'Place-marketing in Liverpool: a review', *International Journal of Urban and Regional Research*, vol. 16, no. 4, December, pp. 633–640.

Malone, P. (1993), 'The difficulties of assessment: a case study of the Custom House Docks, Dublin', in White, K.N. et al. (eds), *Urban Waterside Regeneration Problems and Prospects*, Ellis Horwood, Chichester.

Martin, S. and Pearce, G. (1992), 'The Internationalization of Local Authority Economic Development Strategies: Birmingham in the 1990s', *Regional Studies*, vol. 26, pp. 499–509.

McKellar, S. (1988), 'The Enterprise of Culture', *Local Work*, part 8, pp. 14–17.

McKenzie, G. (1990), '"Glasgow's Miles Better" – A study of a decade of change in political approaches to policy making', *Local Government Policy Making*, vol. 16, no. 4, March, pp. 23–31.

McLay, F. (1990), 'Glasgow 1990: the shameless endorsement of greed' in McKay, F., (ed), *Workers City: the reckoning*, Clydeside Press, Glasgow.

McNulty, R. (1988), 'What are the arts worth?', *Town and Country Planning*, vol. 57, no. 10, October.

Morrison, N. (1994), 'The Role of Planning in the Redevelopment Process of Glasgow's City Centre', *Planning Practice and Research*, vol. 9, no. 1, pp. 31–41.

Myerscough, J. (1988), *The Economic Importance of the Arts in Great Britain and Regional Studies in Glasgow, Ipswich and Liverpool*, Policy Studies Institute, London.

Neill, W.J.V. (1993), 'Physical Planning and Image Enhancement: Recent developments in Belfast', *International Journal of Urban and Regional Research*, vol. 17, no. 4, pp. 595–609.

PA Cambridge Economic Consultants (1990), *An Evaluation of Garden Festivals*, HMSO, London.

Paddison, R. (1993), 'City marketing, image reconstruction and urban regeneration', *Urban Studies*, vol. 30, no. 2, pp. 339–350.

Parkinson, M., Bianchini, F., Dawson, J., Evans, R. and Harding, A. (1991), *Urbanisation and the functions of cities in the European Community*, Commission of the European Community, DGXVI.

Parkinson, M. and Judd, D. (1990), 'Urban leadership and Regeneration' in Parkinson, M. and Judd, D. (eds), *Leadership and Urban Regeneration*, vol. 37, Urban Affairs Annual Reviews, Sage, London.

Pinder, D. and Rosing, K.E. (1988), 'Public policy and planning of the Rotterdam waterfront: a tale of two cities' in Hoyle, B.S., Pinder, D.A. and Husain, M.S. (eds), *Revitalising the Waterfront*, Belhaven Press, London and New York.

Rae, J.H. (1991), *City Planning Aims For The Next Decade*, p.2, May, Glasgow City Council.

Reed, P. (1993), 'The Post-industrial City?' in Reed, P. (ed), *Glasgow. The Forming of the City*, Edinburgh University Press Ltd., Edinburgh.

Riera, P. and Keogh, G. (1995), 'Barcelona', in Berry, J. and McGreal, S. (eds), *European Cities, Planning Systems and Property Markets*, Spon, London.

Robins, K. (1991), 'Tradition and translation: national culture in its global context' in Corner, J. and Harvey, S. (eds), *Enterprise and heritage. Crosscurrents of National Culture*, Routledge, London.

Rogers, R. and Fisher, M. (1992), *A New London*, Penguin Books, London.

Sanchez, J.E. (1992), 'Societal responses to changes in the production system: the case of Barcelona metropolitan region', *Urban Studies*, vol. 29, no. 6, pp. 949–964.

Sheffield City Council (1993), *Sheffield Economic Development Plan 1993–1994*, Department of Employment and Economic Development.

Smyth, H. (1994), *Marketing the City. The role of flagship developments in urban regeneration*, Spon, London.

Tavsanoglu, S. and Healey, P. (eds)(1992), *Rebuilding the City: Property-Led Urban Regeneration*, Spon, London.

TNI, (u.d.), *The Newcastle Initiative*, Newcastle-upon-Tyne.

Tibbalds, F. (1992), *People Friendly Towns – Public Environment in Towns and Cities*, Longman, London.

Tibbalds, Colbourne, Karski and Williams (1990), *City of Birmingham, City Centre Design Strategy*, Birmingham Urban Design Studies, April.

Tickell, A. and Dicken, P. (1993), 'The role of inward investment promotion in economic development strategies: the case of Northern England', *Local Economy*, vol 8, no 3, pp. 197–208.

Urry, J. (1990), *The Tourist Gaze*, Sage, London.

USHUD (US Department of Housing and Urban Development) (1982), *The President's 1982 National Urban Policy Report*, HUD S-702–1, Washington, DC.

Violette, C. and Taggu, R. (eds) (1982), *Issues in Supporting the Arts*, Washington.

Watson, S. (1991), 'Gilding the Smokestacks: the new symbolic representations of deindustrialised regions', *Environment and Planning D: Society and Space*, vol 9, pp. 59–70.

Whitt, J.A. (1988), 'The role of the arts in urban competition and growth' in Cummings, S. (ed), *Business Elites and Urban Development: Case Studies and Critical Perspectives*, State University of New York Press, Albany.

Whyte, H. (1994), *Marketing the City: The Role of flagship developments in urban regeneration*, Spon, London

Wilkinson, S. (1992), 'Towards a new city? A case study of image-improvement initiatives in Newcastle upon Tyne' in Tavsanoglu, S. and Healey, P. (eds), *Rebuilding the City: Property-Led Urban Regeneration*, Spon, London.

Wishart, R. (1991), 'Fashioning the Future: Glasgow' in Fisher, M and Owen V. (eds) *Whose Cities?*, Penguin, London.

Zukin, S. (1988), *Loft Living. Culture and Capital in Urban Change*, Radius, New York.

2 Lipstick on the gorilla? Conflict management, urban development and image making in Belfast.*

William J.V. Neill

Introduction

It is difficult to pick up an airline in-flight magazine these days without encountering ever new examples of cities seeking to project an attractive image to potential inward investors and tourists. This chapter considers the special circumstances of this process in Belfast in particular through the mobilization of physical planning to reimage the city thereby dovetailing economic development and conflict management objectives into one strategy (Greer and Neill, 1990). After some comments on the importance of image marketing to localities generally the history of recent image based urban planning in Belfast is reviewed and the process of this policy formulation within the local state presented. Couched within an internal conflict view of the "Northern Ireland problem" this normalisation strategy is then assessed with particular regard to its limits given its class based impact and implications for the British Unionist and Irish Nationalist sectarian division.

Localities and rationales for reimaging

There is considerable debate on the degree to which regional economies can be masters of their own destiny in the present period of economic restructuring. Amin and Robbins (1990, p. 29) stress the "body of work which views

---

* This is a revised version of an article which appeared in the International Journal of Urban and Regional Research, vol. 17, no. 4, 1993. Reprinted with permission.

contemporary transformations as a threat to localities as they become fragmented, integrated into, and subjugated by international forces beyond their control and victims of more intensified inter regional competition". However, other writers place more stress on local proactivity. Harvey points to the irony that it is because of the collapse of spatial barriers that the uniqueness of geographical circumstance matters more than ever before. He points to the changing role of spatiality in contemporary society:

> If capitalists become increasingly sensitive to the spatially differentiated qualities of which the world's geography is composed, then it is possible for the people and powers that command those spaces, to alter them in such a way as to be more, rather than less, attractive to highly mobile capital . . . . The qualities of space stand thereby to be emphasised in the midst of increasing abstractions of space. The active production of places with special qualities becomes an important stake in spatial competition between localities, cities, regions and nations . . . [cities strive] to forge a distinctive image and to create an atmosphere of place and tradition that will act as a lure to both capital and people (Harvey, 1989, pp. 294–5).

A recent study of local economic development in Britain points out that "the relationship between the different scales [in the political economy] is not simply a one-way street with localities the mere recipients of fortune or fate from above. Rather localities are actively involved in their own transformation, though not necessarily as masters of their own destiny" (Cooke, 1989, p. 296). Image mobilisation is identified as a key component in this economic proactivity of localities (Cooke, 1990, pp. 119–133). Reimaging as an aspect of place marketing in the United Kingdom emphasises quality of life, liveability, and soft infrastructural aspects of locality, ideas often being drawn from Europe through the filter of American consultancy firms (Bianchini and Schwengel, 1990). Occurring in a range of political and institutional contexts and with a strong focus on tourism and the attraction of private investment, the general twin themes of the urban image makers are first the triad of heritage, culture and the arts and second explicit space related concerns with the nature and quality of the built environment. The promotion of flagship or prestige projects, the nurturing of "cultural quarters" in cities, upgrading of the public realm in general and a concern with architectural quality are all aspects of the latter.

Examples of reimaging in UK cities through the mobilisation of the arts and cultural industries, local heritage and physical renewal centred on the city centre are not hard to find. Newcastle-upon-Tyne boasts image building initiatives with marketing and product development blending in the appointment of a major international advertising agency to create "a strong positive image for the city" projecting ongoing environmental improvements, the regeneration of Theatre Village, Chinatown and Quayside areas, the promotion of culture in the city and the hosting of important events with additional tourist spin-off (Payne, 1991). Glasgow as European Cultural Capital following on from the city's Glasgow's Miles Better Campaign deliberately used image building via the arts to sell the city's investment potential. Since this was combined with major physical redevelopment of the central area including a new concert hall even one of the strategy's critics was forced to admit that "certainly there has been a significant improvement in the general image of the city" (Hambleton, 1990, p. 71). Even Liverpool recently described as "stuck in the past, in a time-warp of Beatlemania and class solidarity" (*Economist*, 1989) has in the Albert Dock development taken on board the possibilities inherent in arts led inner city development (Wishart, 1991, p. 49). Birmingham, with a recently failed Olympic bid put down in part to a poor cultural image (Mulgan, 1989, p. 270), now has a new vision for the city incorporated in current plans. The intent is to improve the image of the central area while strengthening the special character of its various quarters of which the Jewellery Quarter is the most famous. An important part of the revitalization of the city centre, which includes plans to pull down concrete developments of the 1960s such as the notorious Bull Ring shopping centre, is the carefully designed Centenary Square. This includes the new Birmingham Symphony Hall and International Convention Centre. The Square with its new Hyatt Hotel is adorned with specially commissioned public works of art. (*Planner*, 1991). Such prestigious and costly projects are intended as "loss leaders" which it is hoped will generate private investment and act as a catalyst in establishing Birmingham as Britain's second city (Dalby, 1991). "Birmingham – City 2000", a private sector led initiative in partnership with the city council has been formed explicitly to promote Birmingham's image as a business centre of international standing. In Manchester the recent opening of a street running light rail rapid transit system is the latest in a series of image building initiatives in a city which, after an aggressive although ultimately unsuccessful campaign to host the Olympic Games in the year 2000, has been nominated as City of Drama in 1994. A new concert hall is due to open soon to provide a fitting home for the city's famous Hallé Orchestra. Bradford and Halifax, whose image many in Belfast would be content to settle for, have been recently referred to as "twin centres of a startling cultural renaissance". Bradford's National Museum of Film and Photography is the second most visited attraction in the North (Bastable, 1990). Halifax's image promotion strategy has included the reported destruction of all postcards on sale showing a smoky 1930s view of Halifax, the sandblasting of grime off the town's stone buildings, the restoration of original Victorian shop front designs, the subsidisation of the Northern Ballet to move from Manchester to Halifax and the building of a "Eureka" museum which will give children experience in scientific experiments (*Economist*, 1991).

Reaction to reimaging amongst the left in Britain is mixed. There are the dangers of the over commodification of places, a consumption rather than production centred approach to economic regeneration and the possibility of the "co-existence within the same city of small 'islands of regeneration' with growing social polarisation and injustice" (Bianchini and Schwengel, 1990,

p. 10). The nostalgia laden nature of the heritage arm of the British reimaging process is well documented (Hewison, 1987). In Birmingham, a number of Labour Party councillors have resigned objecting to the opportunity costs involved in the creation of "white elephants" (Dalby, 1991). The cost of attracting the Northern Ballet to Halifax caused a large swing against Labour in the local elections of 1991 (*Economist*, 1991). However, a significant body of opinion on the left sees reimaging as potentially progressive. Cultural industries can give a fillip to local employment and equally importantly the reinvigoration of the public realm, especially in the shared civic space of city centres, can be a refreshing check on the privatism still prevalent in urban policy (Bianchini et al, 1988; Fisher and Owen, 1991; Rogers and Fisher, 1992). Mulgan (1989) in arguing for urban cultural policies which promote integration and conviviality presented as a warning the urban nightmare of the film *Blade Runner* as a possible future where the city reflects a sharp division between core and peripheral workers.

Image and planning in Belfast: the policy

Given the centralised nature of the local state in Northern Ireland the context is one of strong hands-on political direction of planning. With local government bereft of physical planning and other powers as a penalty for past sectarian practices, the Department of the Environment for Northern Ireland is virtually a monopoly employer of planners who are accountable upwards through a tier of administrators to central government ministers. The nature of this policy process which involves the mobilisation of strategy from the top is explored in the following section. Focus here is on planning strategy itself in Belfast, the central plank of which in recent years has been the cultivation of a neutral and normal city centre. Economic planning and political management of the Troubles dovetail in ways which make the reimaging process in Belfast distinctly different from that in any other UK city. The main means have been the promotion of a critical mass of physical development spearheaded by flagship and prestige projects and the toleration and at other times outright promotion of a market led postmodernist design aesthetic which for all its incongruities carries neutral symbolism intended to create images and spaces which dilute the backward looking symbolism evident in the present. This use of planning as a strategy of normalisation and economic promotion to influence perceptions of both locals and outsiders can be set in the context of the following periodisation of government policy towards Belfast city centre since the early 1970s:

a. Defensive policy of the 1970s
b. Encouragement of tentative recovery, 1980-84
c. Active promotion and planning, 1985-94

Defensive policy of the 1970s

Between 1970 and 1975 an IRA bombing campaign destroyed around 300 establishments in Belfast city centre and over a quarter of total retail floorspace (S. Brown, 1985). Radical defensive security measures ensued including the

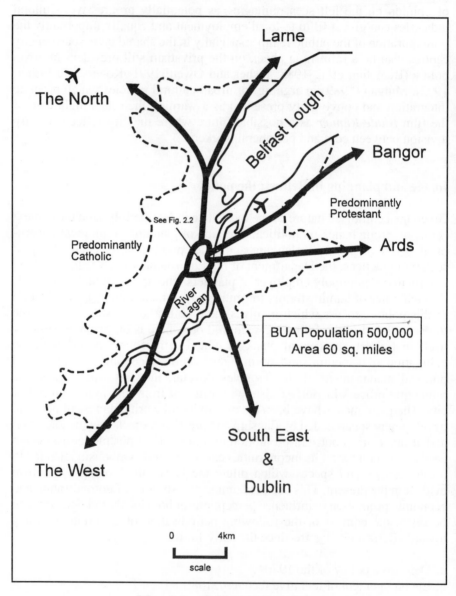

Map 2.1   Belfast Urban Area

"ring of steel" security cordon at entrances to the city centre where pedestrians and vehicles were searched. The government's Review of Transportation Strategy in 1978 recommended the construction of a high grade motorway link running to the North and West of the city centre and canyoned through part of its length. This road, while achieving urban transportation objectives, also acts virtually as a moat, cutting off the city centre from the Catholic and Protestant housing areas of the Falls and Shankill. The spreading of riots emanating within these areas into the city centre has been made extremely difficult, if not impossible, since the construction of this 'Westlink'. Where the road forms a flyover, or is at ground level, pedestrian access to the city centre is easier, but heavily fortified police bases guard such entrance points, almost like bastions in medieval walled towns. (Logan, 1988).

The seeds of future policy can be detected in a nine point package "to spell the rebirth of Belfast" announced by the Labour Government Secretary of State, Roy Mason, in 1978. This included the setting up of a working party to "examine how sparkle can be brought back into city centre night life", the "stepping up of schemes to spruce up the city and give it a brighter look" and the employment of consultants to explore the possibilities of government partnership with private developers to redevelop centre city sites. At that time the site currently occupied by the CastleCourt downtown shopping centre was identified as a key location. More government jobs were promised for the city centre and the report of a River Lagan Working Party was announced with "extensive possibilities ... to beautify and enrich central Belfast". Mason looked forward to the spread of "oases" through the central area and "the creation of a new Belfast of which all its citizens can be proud" (Northern Ireland Information Service, (NIIS), 1978). Already in 1975 the Arts Council of Northern Ireland, assisted by a government grant, had bought for restoration the architecturally distinctive Grand Opera House which had been closed following falling audience figures and bomb damage. Its re-opening in 1980 was generally seen as symbolic of a return of some semblance of normality to downtown Belfast.

Encouragement of tentative recovery, 1980-84

The recovery of Belfast city centre in the early 1980s can be attributed to a number of factors not least of which was a change in IRA strategy away from commercial bombing towards attacks on the security forces and other state personnel (S. Brown, 1985). This, as Brown points out, led to a relaxation of town centre security restrictions. Environmental improvements in Belfast were coming on stream including extensive pedestrianisation which made a virtue of a security necessity. City centre traders introduced late night shopping one evening per week and generous Urban Development Grant aid was made available by government for investment in the physical fabric of their businesses. In early 1985 the boast was that almost 140 new eating establishments had opened mainly around the city centre, demonstrating that people were coming back to the city (Simpson, 1985). A government sponsored seminar in October 1983 convened by Chris Patten, the new Conservative minister responsible for the environment, explored with retailers, the City Council and potential investors ways of orchestrating the emerging change in central Belfast's fortunes (ibid, 1985). The result was the Belfast Urban Area Plan initiative which got underway in 1985.

Active promotion and planning, 1985-94

This period includes the major initiative of the new Belfast Urban Area Plan itself and in 1991 a significant increase in the government's stake in the promotion of the normality of Belfast with celebratory events and a new city centre local plan based almost exclusively on image. The coincidence of the signing of the Anglo-Irish Agreement in 1985 with the start of a new plan for Belfast is symbolic. The former represented an awareness by the British government that it was in for a long haul and that movement towards an internal settlement in Northern Ireland could be achieved only with the involvement of others. Crisis management had now been replaced by a concerted strategy in which the mobilisation of economic and physical development in both urban and rural areas had been identified as a key to resolving the problem. Improvement in the quality of life of people living in Northern Ireland was considered the precondition for greater equality and democracy, and for the achievement of the elusive internal settlement. This hands-on approach to development has been facilitated by the untrammelled powers held by central government, and has been endorsed not only by the Irish Government but also by the European Community through its Structural Funds, and the United States of America, Canada and New Zealand, through the creation of the International Fund for Ireland.

Belfast led the way. The attention of Chris Patten was drawn to the relationship between physical planning and economic development and importantly to the role that both could play in the management of the political process in Belfast and indeed Northern Ireland as a whole (Greer and Neill, 1990). The planning strategy in Belfast since the mid 1980s has been to incorporate physical planning directly into the overall process of political management of the Troubles using development in a proactive manner. In 1985 a "heart transplant" was deemed necessary for Belfast city centre, an image which drew on urban renaissance experience in America and appealed to local business interests. This conjunction of political and private business interests allowed a mood of optimism to be quickly generated. Infrastructure investments and environmental improvements continued apace giving the impression of considerable activity. The slogan "Belfast is Buzzing" was coined at the same time as the new Belfast Urban Area Plan was instigated, thus making an image link between what was envisaged and what was already deemed to be

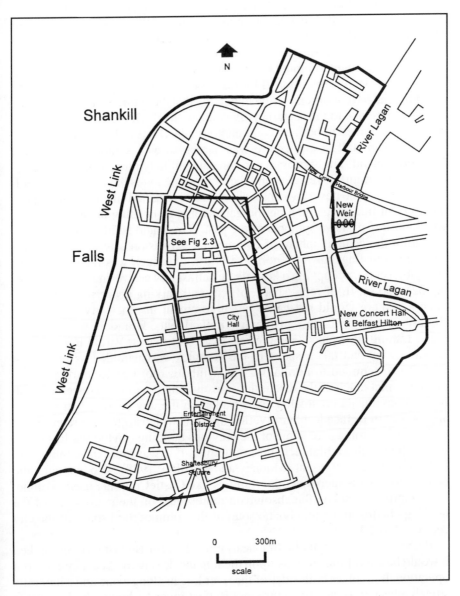

Map 2.2   Belfast City Centre & Environs

happening. The key symbols of the new plan for Belfast were normality, neutrality and consent. The year 2001 was chosen as the horizon period of the plan as if to correlate the rate of change envisaged for Belfast with the lure of the millennium itself. Final adoption in December 1989 produced a designer plan, on high quality paper, with clear uncluttered text and state of the art graphics. A suite of positive images of newly built or planned developments was projected, counterpointed by anaemic toned panoramas of the city as it is today. This selective rendition of Belfast tapped into the pride of people about the industrial past of the city while indicating that the future would be brighter, and any reference to the sectarian divisions with which the city is riven, was studiously avoided in both text and photographs (DoE (NI), 1990).

In the plan Belfast city centre was harnessed as a symbol for a normal Northern Ireland. The appearance in force, in publicly pump primed developments, of the multiple retailers and their corporate logos has come to symbolise normality. The new city centre shops are marshalled like icons to oppose the array of images painted on the gable walls of housing areas in the city, which portray divisive symbols of the past. (Greer and Neill, 1990).

Within the general sphere of commercial expansion a few projects were singled out as flagships of a normal Belfast. One such was the CastleCourt shopping centre, occupying a key site in Belfast city centre and accommodating 325,000 sq. ft. of retail space, offices and parking space for 1,500 cars. Such a venture would not cause much comment in other city centres, but Belfast was one of the last city centres in the United Kingdom to construct a major trading showpiece, and the fact that Debenhams, Virgin Records and Laura Ashley had taken space in the complex was heralded as proof that Belfast had returned to normality. The symbolism of CastleCourt is underpinned in that much of the discussion surrounding it was less concerned with its possible impact on smaller scale traders in the city centre, than with the appearance of its facade. Conservation interests which argued for retention of the Victorian frontage of some of the previous buildings on the site lost out to those who felt that a hightech, postmodernist style was more in keeping with Belfast's economic revival (Mooney and Gaffikin, 1988). The iconographic battle in Belfast is such that opportunities like CastleCourt are used to dilute, if not entirely dissolve, the absolutism represented on the gable walls of the housing ghettos in the relativistic soup of the commodified space of the city centre (Map 2.3).

If CastleCourt is symbolic of a heart transplant for Belfast city centre then it would be appropriate to look upon the Laganside scheme as a major arterial operation. It involves both sides of the river Lagan along a one and a half mile stretch adjacent to the city centre and Belfast inner harbour. The Laganside project taps into the maritime tradition of Belfast, and is aimed at transforming the presently neglected waterfront area by a series of interconnecting schemes for commercial, retail, light industrial, recreation and leisure uses. The whole project echoes experience in the United States and closer to home that of

Photograph 2.1   CastleCourt: Belfast's retail flagship
© Kevin Cooper, Photoline

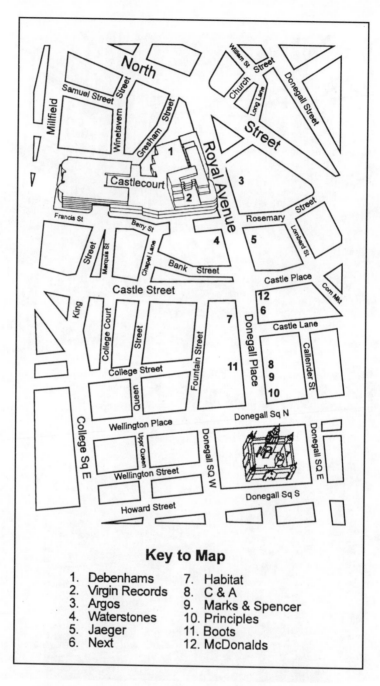

Key to Map

1. Debenhams
2. Virgin Records
3. Argos
4. Waterstones
5. Jaeger
6. Next
7. Habitat
8. C & A
9. Marks & Spencer
10. Principles
11. Boots
12. McDonalds

Map 2.3   The Neutral Zone: multiple retailers on
Belfast's main shopping thoroughfare.

London, Merseyside and Salford, with Government commitment being expressed in the formation of a Development Corporation with powers to promote the potential opportunities. As with CastleCourt, the type of project embodied in Laganside has come late to Belfast, and again image is central. Creative Image and Future Image advertising and public relation companies working with the Laganside Corporation have extended an invitation through brochures, concept plans and development briefs to leave behind sectarian space and to identify with a new neutral symbolic terrain in the "anywhere" of post-modernist space. Indeed artists' impressions of the future pivotal Laganside sixteen acre flagship Laganbank project which will bestow on Belfast a new international Hilton hotel, conference centre and concert hall, lead one to question if some of the design concepts are not leftovers from Euro Disney. The developer for the Laganbank site chosen by government is a local company with the Baltimore-based Enterprise International Development Company, a subsidiary of the Rouse Corporation, having been involved in the early stages. Work started on the £100 million project in 1992 with a completion date of 1996. Public subsidy will underpin Laganside developments largely in the form of infrastructure and environmental improvements. A dramatic new Lagan Weir on which construction has recently been completed cost £14 million and a new cross-harbour road and rail bridge due for completion in 1995 will cost £65 million. However, other forms of government support, such as office uptake for Laganside developments, is not ruled out (Shiells, 1991). In addition the innocuously named Waterfront Concert Hall, which in 1994 is taking shape on Belfast's new skyline, will cost Belfast City Council £29 million with potential annual losses of £1.5 million (Purdy, 1994).

A review of the Belfast city centre commercial property market in 1991 noted a shift in development focus from retailing to offices since 1989. The Northern Ireland Industrial Development Board (the main economic development agency) is actively promoting Belfast as a centre for back office activities. However, with tenants such as the Department of Health and Social Services (DHSS), Inland Revenue and Royal Mail lined up for office buildings about to come on stream the review concluded that: ". . . there is strong dependency upon public sector agencies as potential occupiers, with major companies in the private sector seemingly yet to be convinced that Belfast city centre provides a desirable office location" (Berry and McGreal, 1991).

The year 1991 was a major image promotion year for Northern Ireland in general and Belfast in particular. The Northern Ireland Department of Economic Development having unsurprisingly identified "image" as the Province's major tourist marketing handicap in 1989 (DED (NI), 1989), set the framework for a new indicative plan produced by the Northern Ireland Tourist Board in 1990 including the major theme of city tourism in Belfast (NITB, 1990) and followed this by a near doubling of the budget of the tourist promotional agency in 1991 (Jones, 1991). October 1991 saw publication by the Department of the Environment for Northern Ireland of a preliminary statement on the production of a Belfast City Centre Local Plan (DOE (NI), 1991), the final form of which was published in 1994. The central aim is to "improve the world-wide image of the city centre" by among other things "creating a number of memorable places, buildings and events and providing high quality shopping, leisure and tourist facilities to make the city an international centre". In particular the plan will seek to "provide a heart for the city which is unique and distinctive and which for both residents and visitors epitomises the character and identity of Belfast". LDR International, which has experience of urban revitalisation, especially in the United States, was appointed to advise on urban design.

Finally, running throughout 1991 in Belfast was a festival of events, coordinated by a government assembled "Belfast 1991" board of directors and with administrative support provided by the Belfast Development Office (BDO), the promotional development arm of the Department of the Environment for the city. Sponsorship from government and private sources supported urban events intended, in the words of the Belfast 1991 Chairman, to provide "a glimpse of what the future might be all about" by projecting "an image for the people" and injecting "a new sense of community pride". A secondary intention was to enhance Belfast's image abroad (Oswald, 1991). The highlight of the Belfast 1991 celebrations was the visit of the Tall Ships Race to Belfast in July. Commenting in a letter to the *Belfast Telegraph* in August on his interpretation of what was undoubtedly a popular cross cultural urban spectacle, the Minister of the Environment, Richard Needham could not resist an air of triumphalism:

> So what lessons can we draw from the tall ships carnival? What does it all mean to those on Short Strand, Springfield Road, Sandy Row or the Shankill [Catholic and Protestant inner city areas]. First, it means, we all belong to the same City, we can all share in the success of our City and be proud of our differing but complementing traditions and cultures . . . .. Of course there was a ghost at the feast. The men of violence and their apologists have not gone away but even they must now begin to realise how hopeless is their campaign, how useless their attempts to divide through violence and control through intimidation. The people of Belfast have given their answer to that in their tens and hundreds of thousands (Needham, 1991).

The BDO in subsequent summers, under the banner of a "Positively Belfast" campaign, has brought amongst other events, powerboat Grand Prix racing and a balloon carnival to the city contrasting with the less neutral and traditional Protestant 12 July celebrations.

Aspects of policy formulation

As a prelude to considering the class and sectarian implications of government reimaging strategy in Belfast this section considers three major aspects of policy formulation which have a bearing on this. These are, first, what has recently been called the "structural bind" within which the Irish nationalist and unionist communities are caught in Northern Ireland (Ruane and Todd, 1991); second, the centralized nature of British direct rule in the city which facilitates privileged access to political power whilst simultaneously leading to the exclusion of many from the policy debate; third, Conservative government economic policy in Belfast,which, whilst exhibiting a degree of local pragmatism, has been imported from Britain where in turn it has been influenced by an American model of urban regeneration with a property led bias. These constraints will be outlined in turn followed in the next section by a consideration of their effects and the class and sectarian problems which they engender or fail to address.

A structural bind

Traditional Irish marxism argues that the Northern Ireland state is irreformable (e.g. Collins, 1985; Rowthorn and Wayne, 1989; Munck, 1992). Advocates of this position, whilst they might disagree on the exact reasons for the British presence in Northern Ireland, would incline to the view that the effect of British imperialist involvement is to shore up the Protestant position, thus underpinning working class sectarian disunity. However, an alternative position accepts that the separate identity of the northern Protestants is not just grounded in material concerns but has deep historic roots, and recognises that while a colonial situation can be ended by the departure of the imperial power, an ethnic conflict may remain as long as the two groups exist (Whyte, 1991, p.179). In the words of two academic authors who are identified with the revisionist position "the problem of the involvement of the British State in Northern Ireland lies not in its existence but in its specific forms" (Bew and Patterson, 1985, p.144). Two clashing cultural identities lie at the core of the problem, engaged in a conflict which is subject to a structural bind where, as Ruane and Todd argue, the fundamental interests of one community can be secured only at the expense of the fundamental interests of the other. Northern Protestants believing that membership of the United Kingdom is a condition of their survival as a community are prone to see full equality for nationalists, especially cultural equality, as a threat to their security since defences against Irish unity would be removed. The communities' fundamental interests (for unionists security and for nationalists equality) are thus incompatible within Northern Ireland as it is presently structured, a possible solution not lying within the power of the people of Northern Ireland to reach alone, but requiring a reordering of relationships within and between the British and Irish states (Ruane and Todd, 1991). This reordering of relationships is taking some time to achieve. In the wake of a disappointing breakdown of inter-party political talks on Northern Ireland's future, May 1993 saw publication of the recommendations of an independently organized "citizens' inquiry" on possible ways forward, chaired by Norwegian human rights lawyer Torkel Opsahl. One important recommendation was stated as follows:

> So far, the law and authorities in Northern Ireland and the British government, while accepting expressions of Irish identity and the right to work by peaceful means for Irish unity, have only tolerated such expressions of and aspirations towards nationalism. Their exercise has never been granted any form of recognition in domestic law . . ..

> 'Parity of esteem' between the two communities should not only be an ideal. It ought to be given legal approval, promoted and protected, in various ways which should be considered. Such recognition could be made operational at the highest level by an Act of Parliament (Pollack, 1993, pp. 112-13).

It is then added almost as an afterthought:

> It should be stressed that if this parity of esteem is to be achieved, the legal recognition of Irish nationalism should not mean the diminution of 'Britishness' for unionists (ibid., p.113).

In the Downing Street Declaration of December 1993, which has led eventually to the announcement by the IRA of a "complete cessation of military operations" on 31 August 1994, the British and Irish governments are trying to walk an uncertain tightrope between these positions. Article four of the joint declaration seeks agreement based on " full respect for the rights and identities of both traditions in Ireland."

Concentration of power

Since 1972 Northern Ireland has been governed directly from London with a Secretary of State of cabinet rank assisted by several junior ministers. The junior English political appointee responsible for the Department of the Environment (NI) portfolio has been described by one senior civil servant as also the "Minister of Belfast" (Morrison, 1990, p. 32). In the face of this centralised power the elected Belfast City Council has only the right to be consulted on physical planning matters. The Department of the Environment, in the absence of local democracy and political accountability, makes final decisions. The pivotal agency within the Department of the Environment responsible for the planning of Belfast is the Belfast Development Office. This is in effect an extension of central British administration to the local Belfast scene (Scott, 1980, pp. 45-6). With a budget of around £15 million per annum and a staff of around fifty civil servants the BDO has been described as follows:

It has administrative responsibility for strategic planning including the preparation of the Belfast Urban Area Plan 1986-2001. The functions of the BDO also include evolving the policy for the development and redevelopment of the city and where necessary creating the legislative framework for the implementation of that policy. In addition the BDO services the various co-ordinating groups that bring together government Ministers and their officials (both administrative and professional) with representatives of Belfast City Council, Statutory Boards, Trade Unions, the Chamber of Commerce, the CBI, retailers, banks and the professional institutions (Murtagh, 1992, p. 97).

Policy formulation by the BDO exhibits the following characteristics. First, it operates through direct political appointments to statutory authorities, most notably the Laganside Corporation for which the BDO has oversight responsibility. The Corporation is chaired by the Duke of Abercorn and includes other paternalistic notables deemed to have an acceptable interest in Belfast's future. Second, senior officials in the BDO attuned to the market philosophy of government ministers give privileged power access to property interests in the development of the city. Developers in addition to having the ear of the Minister have their interests liberally represented in the many informal plans and steering groups which make up the hidden planning in the city. In such non statutory planning the BDO favours closed styles of interest mediation and has total discretion over the level of public consultation, participation and even knowledge of a plan's existence (Murtagh, 1992, p. 254). In the formulation of the present statutory strategic plan for the city privileged economic interests (multiple retailers, major developers, volume housebuilders) had their views ascertained both directly in negotiation and indirectly through consultants' reports. (Gaffikin et al. 1991, p. 424). Third, policy debate is restricted simply because the Department of the Environment is virtually a monopoly employer of physical planners and others possessing such expertise. Those not employed directly by government are likely to be working in private practice which is largely dependent on government work. The fact that the departments dealing with planning issues in both of Northern Ireland's universities are dependent on the DoE for research funds and consequently cannot always afford the luxury of a critical position tends to close the circle completely with the planners' local professional institution (the Northern Ireland Branch of the Royal Town Planning Institute) fearful of biting the hand that feeds it (Mooney and Gaffikin, 1988, p. 65). In addition, given the upbeat way in which many planning developments have been announced by government in Belfast criticism could be interpreted as tacit support for terrorism thus further adding to policy closure.

Urban privatism

Belfast has been a testing ground for Conservative government urban economic ideas since 1979. These have been shaped in particular by the United

States model of urban regeneration with its reliance on privatism (Barnekov et al., 1989). Unlike in Britain, local democracy, left wing or otherwise, has not been an impediment. Albeit against a background of greater public investment especially for housing programmes in a pragmatic approach to conflict management, urban economic policy has exhibited a reliance on privatisation and private- sector-led solutions, a property-focused approach to economic development and a faith in trickle-down economics.

Class and sectarianism: is planning really so neutral?

Given the property-led focus of government economic strategy in Belfast and the favoured access to power enjoyed by such interests, policy can hardly be regarded as neutral in class terms. In the face of some of the worst inner city urban unemployment rates in Western Europe (Rolston and Tomlinson, 1988) it is arguable that, in a very weak regional economy, the main benefici- aries of Belfast's reimaging have been a relatively prosperous middle class whose income is substantially underpinned with high public spending and who enjoy lower housing costs than in any other part of the United Kingdom (Hendry et al., 1991). Highly paid civil servants, lawyers and consultants are the tip of an iceberg of people who are benefiting economically from the management of the Troubles and who can afford to eat, drink, shop and socialize in the new city centre facilities. However, the inability of this strategy to deliver a qualitative change in the unemployment situation in West Belfast, the ideological cockpit of struggle between Sinn Fein and the British government, puts a serious class impediment on the possibility of mobilizing consent behind a policy of planning for neutrality. Although there have been government initiatives targeted at Belfast areas of special disad- vantage, they are unlikely to be enough. The violence of the late 1980s in West Belfast raised the profile of the area and put urban deprivation firmly onto the urban management agenda (Murtagh, 1992, p. 270). With a budget now running at around £22.5 million per annum, a Making Belfast Work (MBW) programme targeted at inner city poverty areas dates back to 1988 and will continue until 1997. The money is spent on school equipment, local health care facilities, environmental improvement schemes, job clubs and adult education. A recent academic evaluation of MBW concludes that "no significant in-roads into the lack of jobs and long-term unemployment in the disadvantaged areas" have been made (Birrell et al., 1993, p. 51). Also coordinated by the BDO, nine Belfast Action Teams consisting of small groups of civil servants each with an annual budget of £0.5 million work on community projects in the MBW neighbourhoods primarily in the North and West of the City (Murtagh, 1992, p. 270). In addition, with strengthened fair employment legislation, government sees Belfast city centre as a neutral location conducive to mixed workforces. However, leaving aside important factors such as the quality of part-time and poorly paid jobs in city centre retailing and the marginality of MBW resources in relation to the scale of the problem involved, the main difficulty with reimaging is its property led focus. This tends to be skin deep with too little understanding that, while it is important, it can be only part of the soft infrastructure in a wider supportive institutional environment which invests in people. The Department of Economic Development in Northern Ireland, operating in the context of what has been called "a mendicant entrepreneurial culture" (Teague, 1994, p. 289), has increasingly reflected a narrow Conservative government focus on market competitiveness, individual entrepreneurialism and efficiency in individual firms (DED (NI), 1990). In Belfast, urban regeneration focused on expansion of the retail economy of the city and latterly public pump primed office developments, while perhaps generating an air of optimism in certain quarters, also raises questions of sustainability. The spectre of oversupply in the commerical property sector has been the subject of comment for some time (Berry and McGreal, 1991). In 1994, the signs are that retail expansion in Belfast city centre may have reached a plateau with rental growth fairly static and few significant new names moving into the core (Valuation and Lands Agency, 1994). Sadly in fact, one famous old name, the Anderson and McAuley department store in Belfast which dates back to Victorian times, has closed its doors, unable to compete with CastleCourt. Belfast office rentals in 1994 have also remained static for the second year in succession with 12 per cent of total office stock vacant (Morton, 1994). At best Belfast city centre with its icons of prosperity may continue to be dramatically counterposed with the economic hardship of numerous areas of the rest of the city where many inhabitants will be able to do no more than gaze at the spectacle of the rejuvenated city centre. It is doubtful if a recent proposal for a new Univerity of Ulster campus straddling the 'peace line' between Protestant and Catholic West Belfast will change this. The rhetoric of a costly educational image laden flagship development may, however, obscure wider questions regarding limited direct job creation in West Belfast and the high opportunity costs (£98 million) involved in the face of more pressing basic, higher and vocational educational needs in the area.

A policy of city centre neutrality has more than just class based problems in mobilizing consent. Sectarian relations subject to a structural bind also impose major limits on the possible. Quite simply the city centre in sectarian terms is not neutral. For a considerable time after 1987 and the signing of the Anglo-Irish Agreement, at the instigation of unionist councillors a 'Belfast Says No' banner was draped across the front of the City Hall which continues daily to fly the Union Jack. Inside the council chamber, chairmanships of committees are shared out between the unionist parties to the exclusion of nationalists including Sinn Fein, the second largest party on the council. However, following several court decisions Sinn Fein, with 24 per cent of first preference votes in Belfast local council elections in May 1993, can no longer be excluded from council committees, will no longer be banned from civic functions and will have access to all documentation. Nevertheless, such moves towards 'parity of esteem' have some considerable way to go and are likely to be interpreted by unionists as a threat to their security, forcing Irish unity closer. Thorny issues raised recently by the Sinn Fein leader on Belfast City Council questioning the ethos of City Hall include the ban on the Irish language; the singing of the British national anthem at certain council meetings; a royal toast before all civic functions; the absence of any paintings, statues or other memorabilia which reflect the Irish nationalist tradition; the installation of special windows to honour the British army, Royal Ulster Constabulary and Royal Irish Regiment; the failure to recognise sporting achievements by the city's Gaelic sportsmen and women and the absence in the 106 years since the position was created of a nationalist mayor (Maskey, 1994). A recent statement by a former Unionist Lord Mayor of Belfast, objecting to 'parity of esteem' and to a recasting of the ethos of the state to incorporate political, symbolic and administrative expression of nationalist identity, is an indication of the practical road to peace still to be travelled in Belfast (R. Empey, 1994). In addition Belfast as a whole continues to be symbol-laden. The cranes of Harland and Wolff undoubtedly symbolise to many a predominantly Protestant shipyard, the Belfast City Hall itself is read by a visiting French academic as signifying turn-of-the-century Protestant self-assertion (Goldring, 1991, pp. 33–4) and the parliament buildings at Stormont opened in 1932 have been described as "the outward and visible proof of the permanence of our institutions; that for all time we (Protestants) are bound indissolubly to the British crown" (H. Pollock, quoted Bardon, 1982, p. 225). Likewise it would hardly be surprising if official statues and street names, where Prince Albert and Queen Victoria are liberally represented, made for differential symbolic idenitification with the public realm. While bilingual street names written in both English and Irish will soon become lawful in Belfast and Northern Ireland the erection of such signs remains controversial with unionists.

On top of this, the right to march and protest in the city centre has long been selectively managed by the security forces. Thus republican/nationalist protests and marches have been confined to Catholic West Belfast while Orange marches, official British commemorations of war dead and acceptable peace marches are allowed in the city centre. Where marching is one form of 'possessing' territory in Northern Ireland, the fact that the Orange Order in particular is supported by the police in triumphally marching through the city centre and through Catholic areas nearby in a form of psychological warfare shows how far a policy of normalisation and neutrality has still to go. On 8 August 1993 for the first time a large-scale republican march was allowed through Belfast city centre with Gerry Adams, leader of Sinn Fein, telling crowds : "This is not a triumphalist gathering. It is you people claiming what is yours, the right to your city, your City Hall" (Grattan, 1993).

Indeed it can be argued that perhaps too much concentration on superficially reimaging the city in the eyes of both Belfast residents and potential tourists and investors has been a distraction from dealing with real and deeply felt ethnic antagonisms. Postmodernist consumerist imagery can offer at best distraction rather than more acceptable substitute identities. It risks being lipstick on the gorilla. At times in Belfast the hype of image making combines elements of denial and farce. For example, while in 1991 the Northern Ireland Tourist Board boasted its best year ever in terms of visitors to the Province since the start of the Troubles (Brien, 1991), this sat uncomfortably with widespread press reports that a significant number of tourists were actually attracted by the abnormality of Northern Ireland's urban centres rather than the image of pastoral tranquillity projected by the Tourist Board (Thornton, 1991; Sharrock, 1991; Moore, 1991). In May 1992 the Northern Ireland Tourist Board, to public astonishment, actually announced that there could well be a niche market in attracting the gaze of the curious 'terror tourist' (Magee and McGuckin, 1992). As one journalist has after all suggested, the macho prestige of holidaying in a real live, but generally safe for bystanders, war, threatens to turn Belfast into a terrorism theme park (Margolis, 1993). A serious proposal in 1994 to construct a half-size replica of the Belfast built *Titanic* to float as a restaurant on the river Lagan adds an element of macabre nostalgia to Belfast's reimaging (Cowan, 1994). However, the ultimate example of urban reimaging as farce must be reserved for a gala ball, hosted by Belfast's Lord Mayor and the former US Defence Secretary Casper Weinberger among others, at Belfast's City Hall on 13 January 1992. With the prize for the city being a promotional feature in the US business journal *Forbes Magazine* (Malcolm Forbes Jr also hosted the event) star guests included still exiled Romanian Royals flown in from Geneva. Apologies for non attendance were read out for Ronald and Nancy Reagan, Elizabeth Taylor and Roger Smyth, chairman of General Motors. The majority of the VIPs stayed overnight at an upmarket hotel in Belfast's richest suburbs and flew out the next morning. The fact that a multitude of buildings around the City Hall were boarded up following a massive IRA bomb attack on the city centre just a week previously only added to the sense of unreality.

Policy which has tried to paper over conflict is also creating blandness in the built environment. This has been touched on already. While the city centre is certainly more convivial than it was fifteen years ago, postmodernist aesthetics in Belfast seek to induce historical amnesia, a considerable task in this part of Ireland. Cooke, while recognising that postmodernist architecture is all too prone to market driven incomprehensibility and illiterate pastiche, points out that on the progressive side "post-modern architecture seeks to restore identity to local cultures swamped hitherto by the austere universalism of modernist aesthetics. Local sensitivity, the use of vernacular forms and the reinterpretation of the past in ways which give local meaning to the present are part of that project" (Cooke, 1990, pp. 114-5). However, in Belfast, in the words of the Professor of Architecture in the university, it is only "post-modern cliches" which are found at every turn in the town (Woolley, 1991). Such bland postmodern developments take precedence over conservation interests in a city for so long starved of new investment. On top of this, international urban design consultants threaten to extend pastiche from individual buildings to the public realm generally. As George Melly has said of present English postmodernist architecture: "It is the cultural and visible sign of an inner and spiritual state, a proof we are not well" (Melly, 1989). While the serial reproduction of architectural design is all too common in the United Kingdom, in Belfast this comment strikes deeper resonances. A postmodernist consumerist kaleidoscope of images floats uncomfortably on top of the brutalism of terrorist-proof buildings and the symbolism of the past. It is a condition of visual schizophrenia (Photograph 2.2).

Photograph 2.2   Lipstick on the gorilla: a sentry post in Belfast city centre

Conclusion

Because of class and sectarian based limiting factors planning for neutrality in Belfast has had inherent weaknesses as a strategy of conflict management. Fragile modest gains that the policy of normalization may have engendered were shattered between 1991 and 1993 with a renewed Provisional IRA bombing campaign against the city centre. On two occasions this severely damaged the Grand Opera House, the most symbolic expression of the city's return to normality. At times the security response, with checks on vehicles entering the city centre, gave the impression of a city under siege.

The constraints within which urban planning will continue to operate in reimaging Belfast stay considerable. What Cooke refers to as the "Janus-faced character" of the making of identities, "keeping one foot securely in the past while placing the other in the uncertainties of the future (being) actively produced" is more problematic in Belfast than elsewhere (Cooke, 1990, p. xii). Protestants in the city are likely to fear identity with anything Irish

Photograph 2.3   Loyalist wall mural in East Belfast

(Ferguson, 1990, p. 44) or as another Northern Protestant commentator puts it "the northern protestant has no ready access to an Irish identity of any very developed kind" (T. Brown, 1991, p. 77). The new Irish state from the 1920s onwards projected, not least in symbols, statues and general iconography, an exclusivist Irish identity (O. Tuathaigh, 1991, p. 58). While this may now be declining in the Republic "the spirit of the Nationalist cultural project of 1916 is still alive in Northern Ireland" (Aughey, quoted in Longley, 1991, p. 102). Hence parts of Catholic West Belfast can appear as quite separate cognitive realms with wall murals the most obvious outward manifestation of an alternative loyalty which is trapped within a structural bind. Cultural equality is impossible within present constitutional arrangements which simply cannot accommodate the conflicting identities lying behind clashes of iconography in Belfast. In this situation consumer distraction which puts an image gloss over all too obvious ethnic division is no substitute for identity. While in the longer term a cognitive picture of the city is needed which can draw broad identification urban planning cannot get too far ahead of local political accommodation. On this front the prospects are now, in September 1994, more favourable than for some time. The formation in 1990 of the Northern Ireland Community Relations Council offers, perhaps, some signposts for a way forward. A significant impetus for this came from the Institute of Irish Studies at Queen's University of Belfast along with other academics and people in the arts concerned with the exploration of cultural diversity in Northern Ireland. Core funding for the Council, a non statutory limited company, is provided by government with significant sponsorship for conferences and publications provided by the International Fund for Ireland. Exploring the idea that "varieties of Irishness can be complementary rather than competing" (Foster, 1989) the project strives for a new definition of Irishness which does not exclude varieties of Britishness as part of "creative cultural diversity". Given the "attachment to place and respect for local identity" which is basic to the cultural traditions initiative (Hawthorne, 1990, p. 22) it is to be hoped that engagement is forthcoming with what cultural diversity could mean for urban planning in Belfast. While there is the danger of moving prematurely to such concrete matters of policy, there is also the risk of having the debate too narrowly confined within an arts based liberal intelligentsia. A recent urban design study for Birmingham calls for a physical environment which is "uniquely Birmingham not just a collection of inappropriate trans-Atlantic copies or anonymous tired solutions that can be seen anywhere" (Tibbalds and Karski, 1990, p. 2). Agreement is needed on urban design and on a role for public art in Belfast which reflects the city's cross community cultural heritage. While recognition that public art can be something other than affirmatory will not be easy, Belfast deserves better than a public realm which reflects the lowest common denominator. In the longer term, but hopefully the medium term, Belfast needs to be reimagined, not superficially reimaged.

References

Amin, A. and Robins, K. (1990), 'The re-emergence of regional economies? The mythical geography of flexible accumulation', *Environment and Planning D: Society and Space,* vol. 8, pp.7-34.

Aughey, Arthur (1991), quoted in Longley, Edna (ed.), *Culture in Ireland – Division or Diversity?* Institute of Irish Studies, Queen's University of Belfast, p. 102.

Bardon, J. (1982), *Belfast – an illustrated history,* Blackstaff Press, Belfast.

Barnekov, T., Boyle, R. and Rich D. (1989), *Privatism and Urban Policy in Britain and the United States,* Oxford University Press.

Bastable, Jonathan (1990), '101 Points North', *Sunday Times, 6* May , pp.34-35.

Berry, Jim and McGreal, Stanley, (1991), 'Regeneration Game', *Estates Gazette,* 12 October , pp.99-102.

Bew, Paul and Patterson, Henry (1985), *The British State and the Ulster Crisis,* Verso, London.

Bianchini, Franco et al., (1988), *City Centres, City Cultures,* Centre for Local Economic Strategies, Manchester.

Bianchini, Franco and Schwengel, H. (1990), 'Re-imagining the City', unpublished paper.

Birell, D. and Wilson, C., (1993), 'Making Belfast Work : An Evaluation of an Urban Strategy,' *Administration,* vol. 41, no. 1, Spring, pp.40-56.

Brien, Linda (1991), 'Ulster enjoys all-time high tourist figures', *Belfast Telegraph,* 10 September.

Brown, Stephen (1985), 'Central Belfast's shopping centre', *Estates Gazette,* 19 October, pp.256-258.

Brown, Terence (1991), 'British Ireland' in Longley, Edna (ed.), *Culture in Ireland – Division or Diversity?,* Institute of Irish Studies, Queen's University of Belfast. pp.72-83.

Collins, Martin (ed.) (1985), *Ireland After Britain,* Pluto Press, London.

Cooke, Philip (ed.) (1989), *Localities: The Changing Face of Urban Britain,* Unwin Hyman, London.

Cooke, Philip (1990), *Back to the Future: Modernity, Postmodernity and Locality,* Unwin Hyman, London.

Cowan, Rosie (1994), 'Lagan plan for a mini replica of the Titanic', *Belfast Telegraph,* 26 August.

Dalby, Stewart (1991), 'Going it alone', *Financial Times,* 18 October.

Department of Economic Development for Northern Ireland (1989), *Tourism in Northern Ireland – A view to the future,* Belfast.

Department of Economic Development for Northern Ireland (1990), *Competing in the 1990s,* Belfast.

Department of the Environment for Northern Ireland (1990), 'Belfast Urban Area Plan 2001', HMSO, Belfast.

Department of the Environment for Northern Ireland (1991), 'Belfast City Centre Local Plan 2005 – Preliminary Statement', Belfast.

Economist (1989), 'Liverpool – Believing in Yesterday', 12 August.

Economist (1991), 'Halifax: Farewell dark, Satanic mills', 17 August.

Empey, Reg (1994), 'Mind the Language or you'll cause confusion', *Belfast Telegraph,* 17 August.

Ferguson, Raymond (1990), 'Locality and Political Tradition' in Crozier, Maurna (ed.),. *Cultural Traditions in Northern Ireland – Varieties of Britishness,* Institute of Irish Studies, Queen's University of Belfast, pp.40-45.

Fisher, Mark and Owen, Ursula (1991), *Whose Cities?* Penguin, Harmondsworth.

Foster, Roy (1989), 'Varieties of Irishness', in Crozier, Maurna (ed.), *Cultural Traditions in Northern Ireland – Varieties of Britishness,* Institute of Irish Studies, Queen's University of Belfast.

Gaffikin, F., Mooney, S. and Morrissey, M. (1991), 'Planning for a change in Belfast: The urban economy, urban regeneration and the Belfast Urban Area Plan 1988', *Town Planning Review,* vol. 62, no. 4.

Goldring, Maurice (1991), *Belfast – From Loyalty to Rebellion,* Lawrence and Wishart, London.

Grattan, G. (1993), 'Nationalists claim right to city – SF',. *Belfast Telegraph,* 9 August.

Greer, J.V. and Neill, W.J.V., (1990), 'The Plan as Symbol: A Case Study of Belfast', paper delivered at a conference entitled: Planning Theory : Prospects for the 1990s, Oxford Polytechnic, 2-5 April.

Hambleton, R. (1990), *Urban government in the 1990s: lessons from the USA,* Occasional Paper 35, School for Advanced Urban Studies, Bristol.

Harvey, David (1989), *The Condition of Postmodernity – an Enquiry into the origins of cultural change,* Basil Blackwell, Oxford.

Hawthorne, James (1990), in Crozier, Maurna (ed.), *Cultural Traditions in Northern Ireland – Varieties of Britishness.* Institute of Irish Studies, Queen's University of Belfast, pp.20-22.

Hendry, J., McDonagh, P. and Neill, W.J.V. (1991), 'House Price Change and Private Sector Housebuilding in Northern Ireland', *Housing Review,* vol. 40, no. 6, pp. 121-2.

Hewison, Robert (1987), *The Heritage Industry: Britain in a Climate of Decline,* Methuen, London.

Jones, Gwyneth (1991), 'Cash Boost for Tourism Industry', *Belfast Telegraph,* 30 November.

Logan, S.J. (1988), 'Planning for Neutrality'. unpublished BSc dissertation in the Department of Architecture and Planning, Queen's University of Belfast.

Magee, K. and McGuckin, O. (1992), 'Troubles may be Tourist draw', *Belfast Telegraph,* 27 May.

Margolis, J. (1993), 'Belfast lures tourists on the terror trail with a pocket guide to the troubles', *Sunday Times,* 8 August.

Maskey, Alex (1994), 'Different but equal', *Fortnight,* no. 327, April.

Melly, George (1989), *Rum Bum and Concertina,* Weidenfield and Nicholson, London.

Mooney, S. and Gaffikin, F. (1988), *Reshaping Space and Society: A Critical Review of the Belfast Urban Area Plan 2001,* Belfast Centre for the Unemployed.

Moore, John (1991), 'Sinn Fein launches Belfast 'terror tours'', *Sunday Times,* 29 September.

Morrison, B. (1990), ' Making Belfast Work' *Planner,* vol. 76, no. 49, pp. 32-5.

Morton, Robin (1994), 'Office Rents in doldrums', *Belfast Telegraph,* 23 August.

Mulgan, Geoff (1989), 'The Changing of the City' in Hall, Stuart and Jacques, Martin, (eds) *New Times,* Lawrence and Wishart, London, pp. 262-278.

Munck, Ronnie (1992), 'The New Marxist 'Revisionism' in Ireland', *Capital and Class*, no. 46, pp.95-110.

Murtagh, B. (1992), 'A comparison of two land use planning organizations in Belfast', unpublished PhD thesis, Department of Architecture and Planning, Queen's University of Belfast.

Needham, R. (1991), 'Gods smile on Belfast', letter to *Belfast Telegraph*, 8 August.

Northern Ireland Information Service (NIIS) (1978), '9 point package to spell the rebirth of Belfast,' Belfast.

Northern Ireland Tourist Board (NITB) (1990), *Tourism in Northern Ireland – an indicative plan*, Belfast.

O Tuathaigh, G. (1991), 'The Irish-Ireland idea: rationale and relevance', in Longley, Edna (ed.), *Culture in Ireland – division or diversity?* Institute of Irish Studies, Queen's University, Belfast.

Oswald, Ivor (1991), quoted in Foy, Marie, 'Belfast 1991', B*elfast Telegraph*, 28 December.

Payne, Phil (1991) 'Economic Development Strategy, Focus on Newcastle', supplement to *Planner*, 7 June.

Planner (1991), 'Birmingham's Broad Street Redevelopment wins the Jubilee Cup', 13 December.pp. v – vi.

Pollack, Andy (ed.) (1993), *A Citizens' Inquiry: The Opsahl Report on Northern Ireland*, Lilliput Press, Dublin.

Purdy, Martina (1994), 'Showpiece that may become a white elephant', *Belfast Telegraph*, 16 August.

Rogers, Richard and Fisher, Mark (1992), *A New London*, Penguin, Harmondsworth

Rolston, B. and Tomlinson, M. (1988), *Unemployment in West Belfast: The Obair Report*, Beyond the Pale Publications, Belfast.

Rowthorne, B. and Wayne, N. (1988), *Northern Ireland: the Political Economy of Conflict*, Polity Press, Cambridge.

Ruane, J. and Todd, J. (1991), '"Why can't you get along with each other?": Culture, structure and the Northern Ireland conflict', ch. 3 in Hughes, E. (ed.), *Culture and Politics in Northern Ireland*, Open University Press, Milton Keynes.

Scott, N. (1980), 'Corporate Planning: Its relevance in the Northern Ireland Context', unpublished MSc thesis, Department of Town and Country Planning, Queen's University of Belfast.

Sharrock, David (1991), 'Belfast offers safer haven for tourists', *Guardian*, 7 September.

Shiells, Keith (1991), 'A source of opportunity', *Estates Gazette*, 12 October, pp.103-105.

Simpson, Billy (1985), 'Belfast – the great revival', *Belfast Telegraph*, 13 May .

Teague, Paul (1994), 'Government Structures and Economic Performance : The Case of Northern Ireland', *International Journal of Urban and Regional Research*, vol. 18, no. 2, pp. 275-292.

Thornton, Chris (1991), 'Trouble spot trail draws 'revolutionary tourists''. *Irish News*, 5 October.

Tibbalds, Colbourne, Karski and Williams (1990), 'City of Birmingham, City Centre Design Strategy'.

Valuation and Lands Agency (1994), *The Belfast Retail Market*, HMSO, Belfast.

Whyte, John (1991), *Interpreting Northern Ireland,* Clarendon Press, Oxford.

Wishart, R. (1991), 'Fashioning the future : Glasgow' in Fisher, Mark and Owen, Ursula, *Whose Cities*, Penguin, Harmondsworth.

Woolley, Tom (1991), 'Where is Architecture in Northern Ireland Going?' *Royal Society of Ulster Architects Yearbook*, pp. 91-92.

3 Spearheading a new place vision: the Laganside Corporation

Diana S Fitzsimons

Introduction

The reimaging of the city of Belfast in Northern Ireland makes a very interesting case study as image makers face a particularly difficult task of changing perceptions, not only of a fairly typical former industrial city in a UK context but also of a city of sectarian division, violence and hatred as presented in the news media; a city in which a large minority perceive themselves to be Ulster-Irish and the majority perceive themselves to be Ulster-British (Whyte, 1990), with different religious affiliations, different educational provision below tertiary level and residential segregation in working class areas. In the 1970s, when the terrorist activity in the city centre was at its height, the government's main planning efforts were targeted at the city's housing and transportation problems but since the 1980s attention has been turned on the city centre (Morrison, 1990). A relatively small group of civil servants drew up a series of policy initiatives modelled to some extent on the types of strategies being implemented in other large cities in the UK, including Urban Development Grant which is similar to City Grant in England but adapted to meet broader criteria. Three areas of the city centre were considered as priorities for focused and sustained effort, namely: the central shopping core; Northside, an historic but rundown mixed use area to the north of the central business district; and Laganside, a neglected area running along the banks of the River Lagan in close proximity to the city centre.

It was within the context of lessening terrorist activity in the city centre of Belfast from the early 1980s and a subsequent boom in commercial developments that the government commitment to urban regeneration became realizable. Partnership arrangements, such as the Belfast City Centre Partnership and the Belfast Coordinating Committee were set up to ensure coordination of policy output from various government departments and the City Council, and cooperation with private sector commercial interests. The regeneration effort, particularly the attraction of inward investment, was seen to be greatly dependent on changing adverse perceptions of the city through the development of an attractive and prosperous city centre and improving the gateways to the city. To this end public sector monies were expended on environmental improvements and grant subsidy for refurbishment and new development in the city centre by the private sector. In retrospect these policies can be firmly located within the context of broader Thatcherite policies being implemented throughout the UK, both by Conservative and right of centre Labour local governments. Not to attempt to reimage the city and attract footloose service sector employment and property development when other similar northern post-industrial cities such as Manchester and Glasgow were doing so would have been regarded as fatalistic. There was also, to a certain extent, a form of growth consensus within the city, led by the civil servant elite but involving the key elements of the middle classes and the property professionals, including financiers, agents, developers, the press, and the business and academic elites. With the constitutional issue dominating party political structures in Northern Ireland, normal left-right politics do not exist and thus there was little public debate about the need to change the image of Belfast and to attract inward investment. Over a decade of conflict in the city and often exaggerated press coverage of the effects of violence had left much of the middle class population enthusiastic to embrace any initiative which would upgrade the city and alter perceptions of it in the outside world. Criticisms or doubts about the reimaging policy or even questioning of its declared success were perceived to be ill-founded, disloyal, and damaging to business confidence. Sadler (1993) identified a similar situation in the North-East of England where, because there was perceived to be no alternative policy to place marketing, "even to question the basis of proclaimed success was somehow damaging to it".

Perhaps one of the most notable elements of the reimaging process in Belfast was the setting up of the Laganside Corporation to implement plans for the rejuvenation of lands along a one and a half mile stretch of the River Lagan. The area had a limited residential population (900), a larger working population (1500), several viable industries, a number of listed buildings, offices, law courts, a bus station, a park, indoor leisure facilities and some commercial development, but largely consisted of vacant or underutilised land and buildings including an old gasworks site and much temporary surface carparking. The whole idea developed from what were perceived to be positive experiences in other waterfront cities in the UK and further afield – cities like Swansea, Cardiff, Dundee, Salford and London (Docklands) and it was hoped that Laganside could become the symbol of the way forward in the Province and provide a pleasing and positive environment close to the city centre. A senior group of civil servants visited the eastern seaboard cities of the United States and were impressed with the turnaround in the fortunes of waterfront areas such as Baltimore and Boston and the impact this was having on urban tourism and external image. Thus the first stage was the commissioning of a concept plan by a consortium of consultants including Building Design Partnership which has a Belfast office and Shepherd, Epstein and Hunter which had a close involvement with the redevelopment of the Salford waterfront beside Manchester.

The Laganside concept

The stylish and pictorial concept plan, published with the endorsement of the Department of the Environment for Northern Ireland in 1987, identified 120 acres considered to have potential for development within the 300 acre Laganside area. Its cleverly designed front cover, high quality graphics, photographs and artists' impressions marked it out as a new form of consultancy report in the planning field in the Province. The message was that of a new and exciting vision for the future, with a foreword written by the Minister of the Economy, Richard Needham, whose Westminster constituency was in Wiltshire, England. Needham, who became known as "Minister for Belfast" so great was his enthusiasm for the city's regeneration efforts, stated fervently:

> Belfast's vibrancy and friendliness have always been evident to those who knew the City well. Its many fine buildings, particularly near the River Lagan, are visual reward for those who take the trouble to explore. Its beautiful setting between the Antrim and Castlereagh hills is a surprise and delight to those visiting for the first time. But to people who have never been to Belfast their image of the place is often far-removed from the reality. This study of Laganside was commissioned by my Department as a contribution to the Belfast Urban Area Plan. It describes the potential which exists to transform completely the environmental quality of a vital part of the City, and by this means to help transform perceptions of Belfast at an international level (Building Design Partnership et al, 1987).

The "concept plan", as it was called since it was not prescriptive and had no statutory footing, outlined fairly detailed proposals for each of eight development sites ranging in size from 2.5 to 47 acres, most in some form of public ownership, the three main landowners being the City Council, the Department of the Environment and the Harbour Commissioners. Land uses proposed included retailing, offices, residential, leisure and civic uses and the plan stressed the importance of a common urban waterside theme in all the developments: a maritime character, three to five storey buildings and the development of urban squares using street furniture, artifacts, paving and materials to echo the waterfront theme. The diagrams were indicative of the layout, scale, massing and appearance which the consultants felt was appropriate for Laganside. Given the timing of this plan, all these themes can be traced back to areas in Britain such as Salford, Swansea and Dundee undergoing similar waterfront revivals. The plan also highlighted the importance of Laganside to the development of the city's urban tourism strategy and suggested provision of amenities such as a concert hall, hotel, garden exhibition, tourist gateway centre and maritime museum. Likewise it stressed the recreational potential of the area – for canoeing, power boat racing and yachting, for indoor and outdoor sports, and for informal recreation such as walking along the riverfront. The development of open spaces, new embankments, urban parks and sculptures was recommended. In terms of infrastructure the major investments identified were a cross-harbour road and rail bridge (already a government commitment), a river weir, and new embankments and walkways, the new weir being considered essential to alter the perceptions of the riverfront as a muddy, smelly and derelict environment unsuitable for leisure, residential or commercial development. The plan set out a timetable for implementing the schemes and an estimate of likely funding, and outlined a number of possible implementation structures, floating the ideas of an Urban Development Corporation along the lines of the early English UDCs, a specially formed Trust involving a partnership between the public and private sectors, or implementation using the existing powers of the Department of the Environment and the Harbour Commissioners. The report concluded that the objectives of the plan could be best achieved through the formation of a unitary authority, for which new legislation would be required.

The Laganside Corporation

In 1987 a company limited by guarantee, Laganside Ltd., was set up to progress the proposals prior to the establishment of the Laganside Corporation by statute in May 1989 (and incidentally prior also to the approval of the statutory Belfast Urban Area Plan 2001 also in 1989), mainly because it was seen to be vital to avoid any delays in getting the development ball rolling. The permanent staff remained much the same when the Corporation was finally in place, expanding eventually to twenty-eight. The Corporation, a non-elected body with an anticipated life of fifteen years, has a nine person Board including city councillors, representatives of the main public sector landowners and local business people, the chairman being the aristocratic, but Northern Ireland domiciled, Duke of Abercorn whose family has a previous association with this part of Belfast. The chief executive, George Mackey, a local businessman who has proved himself in a number of previous roles in public office including some years as chief executive of Northern Ireland's Local Enterprise Development Unit, presides over a technical team of surveyors, planners and marketing experts. As a List 1 public company the

Corporation has the right to seek funding and hold monies from different sources including the European Union, although its main source of funding is the Department of the Environment for Northern Ireland. Like most other UDCs in the UK the objective given by statute to the Laganside Corporation is "to secure the regeneration of the designated area", and this is to be brought about by "bringing land and buildings into effective use, encouraging public and private investment and the development of existing and new industry and commerce, by creating an attractive environment and by ensuring that housing, social, recreational and cultural facilities are available to encourage people to live and work in the area" (DoE (NI), 1989). In practice, as with the other UDCs, the stress is very much on property led regeneration, considerable emphasis being placed on quickly realised and highly visible results such as flagship projects that will materially improve the local environment and its image, so that social regeneration inevitably takes a much lower priority.

The Corporation appears to have substantial powers including acquisition of land and property through vesting by the Department of the Environment, carrying out building and other operations, and carrying out any relevant undertaking necessary to achieve its objectives, but it is very much subject to the overall control of the Department of the Environment for Northern Ireland and the Department of Finance and Personnel. Critically it does not have planning powers and was initially encouraged to work with existing public sector landowners in site development rather than seeking to acquire such lands. This has, at times, proved to be the source of some difficulties and delays since these landowners have differing agendas and priorities.

The government decision to set up such a Corporation, rather than using the Department of the Environment's already very extensive powers to implement the scheme appears not to have been universally approved of within government circles at that time. It was foreseen that there would be considerable additional funding required for staffing, premises and operating costs and that this skewing of expenditure towards Laganside would undermine funding for, and government commitment to, other initiatives underway or planned for the city. There may also have been doubts as to whether the population of the city could support such a large office/commercial sector close to the city centre without its having an adverse impact on the Central Business District (CBD). It could be argued that the main reasons for setting up the Development Corporation were to do with the then current fashion in urban regeneration policy and the greater image impact which a separate high profile agency would have. Thus the civil servants who led the thinking on the city's urban regeneration effort were determined that the city would not miss out on any policies which might help at least keep up with the recovery anticipated for other competing urban areas in the UK, particularly those on the so-called "Atlantic rim" such as Liverpool, Manchester and Glasgow. Already many of the property led regeneration initiatives from England had been copied – enterprise zones, a freeport and urban development grant to name but a few, and it was considered that Belfast could ill afford to fall behind in the cutthroat arena of inter-urban competition for central government and European Community spending and the attraction of inward investment. Also crucial to the argument in favour of the UDC approach rather than a central or local government approach was the fact that an Urban Development Corporation was likely to be more palatable to the development and investment industries. It would be regarded as single-minded and unlikely to be distracted by competing priorities or overtly political considerations and would be perceived as having a more entrepreneurial, flexible and thrusting approach to urban regeneration. Spending on glossy advertising campaigns, firework displays, a Chinese circus, champagne receptions for developers and so on would have been quite out of the question for an existing Northern Ireland government department. Thus image enhancement was a very important element in the decision to create a separate entity to implement the Department's proposals for the riverfront.

The timing of the setting up of the Laganside Corporation was also crucial, since the image of UDCs in the UK was at that time still relatively untarnished, the highly critical reports by the House of Commons Employment Committee and the National Audit Office not being published until 1989 and 1993 respectively. In the rest of the UK Urban Development Corporations had emerged in the 1980s as a central plank of the Government's urban policy and had begun to be allocated an increasing proportion of central government funding for the regeneration process (Imrie and Thomas, 1993). So despite the initial resistance in England from Labour-controlled urban authorities, many eventually accepted or even lobbied for these non-elected bodies in their area because it was clear that otherwise very little governmental funding for regeneration would be forthcoming. Thus between 1981 and 1993 thirteen UDCs were set up throughout England and Wales, varying substantially in their size and the nature of the perceived regeneration problem.It was not until the latter years of the 1980s that much criticism was levelled at Urban Development Corporations, (particularly London Docklands DC), for their lack of democracy, their property-led approach to urban regeneration, their overly-cooperative stance towards private sector developers, their lack of strategic thinking, their disregard for the needs of local people and the disadvantaged, and for the quality of design of the new developments implemented (Tibbalds, 1992; Middleton, 1991; Colenutt, 1991; Brownill, 1991; Church, 1990; National Audit Office, 1993). It is interesting to note that the Department of the Environment for Northern Ireland was keen to disassociate the newly formed Corporation from the aims and style of the London Docklands DC with which it was compared by objectors at the public inquiry into the Belfast Urban Area Plan 2001.

Just as in dockland developments elsewhere in the UK, public investment would be employed in the creation of an infrastructure which, it was hoped, would be found attractive by the private sector. It was wrong to make a direct comparison with London Docklands, the reality in Belfast would take account of economic and geographical circumstances which were entirely different. Since many of the sites were in public ownership there would be opportunity to oversee and influence their development to ensure that the end result was in the widest public interest (DoE representative reported in Guckian and Hawthorne, 1989 p.307).

To understand the role of the Laganside Corporation within the overall framework of planning in Belfast involves further explanation. The planning system in Northern Ireland is essentially based on the system in operation in England and Wales but with the one crucial difference that planning is a central government function rather than a local government function. The Department responsible for planning is the Department of the Environment for Northern Ireland (DoE(NI)) which is headed by the Minister for the Environment. The Town and Country Planning Service of the DoE (NI) is organized on the basis of six divisional offices and two sub-offices located throughout the Province including one in Belfast, plus a headquarters office. As in the rest of the UK all development requires planning permission and the decision on planning applications is made with reference to the development plan and any other material considerations. The DoE (NI) plays a somewhat unique role, exercising executive control over planning and at the same time seeking actively to promote development and investment opportunities in the property sector through the operation of a variety of mechanisms (Berry and McGreal, 1993). Conversely the twenty six local authorities, including Belfast City Council, have very limited powers and in relation to planning, housing and roads, for example, are simply consulted by the relevant government departments. Thus in the Belfast situation it made little difference to the City Council whether an Urban Development Corporation was set up or not as the Council had very little power to influence planning or regeneration, all local authorities in Northern Ireland having lost their planning powers in 1973. However, when the Laganside Corporation was set up two places were reserved on the Board for councillors, even though not in the capacity as representatives of the City Council, in a gesture towards the participation of the citizenry of Belfast in decisions relating to such a key part of the city. In many ways the setting up of the separately funded Corporation made little difference to the Department of the Environment either since the Department retained its planning powers for the designated area, unlike the local planning authorities in England. To some extent the setting up of an Urban Development Corporation was merely a means to attract EC and other funding which could not come directly to the Department of the Environment and yet its aims and policies remained firmly controlled by the Department, most directly through its linkages with the DoE's Belfast Development Office (BDO). In addition, the vast majority of the government-appointed professional personnel, apart from the Chairman himself, were also from the existing public sector and brought with them knowledge of and good working relationships with government departments and governmental bodies including the Planning Service of the DoE, the Northern Ireland Tourist Board, the Northern Ireland Housing Executive and the Department of Economic Development.

The statutory planning framework

The Belfast Urban Area Plan 2001 (DoE, 1989) is the statutory development plan for the city and the broadbrush elements of the 1987 consultants' proposals to rejuvenate the Laganside Area were subsequently incorporated into it, with Laganside and the proposals for the Cross Harbour Road and Rail Bridge described in the plan as "perhaps the single greatest challenge and development opportunity for developers, public and private, during the plan period". Included in the stated objectives for Laganside are strengthening of links with the city centre, the development of a variety of land uses to create a new and visually exciting waterfront, job creation, conservation of historic areas, improvement of water quality, improved public accessibility, the promotion of cultural and recreational activities along the river, and the strengthening of the city's tourism industry through river and waterfront developments. The four detailed policies relate to: the development of riverside lands; the development of the waterfront as a major landscape feature; the improvement of the water quality and amenity of the river; and the requirement that the design of new development reflect an urban waterfront character.

> The Lagan could be made much more attractive and become a major asset to Belfast. Few other cities have such beautiful scenery as found in the Lagan Valley Regional Park, which penetrates right into the south of the City and within two miles of the City Hall. There are, however, parts of the Lagan in the industrial City which are dismal and unsightly. There are also significant areas on both banks with scope for development schemes which will attract investment, allow waterside communities to become established, promote leisure use, encourage business activity and enable provision of interpretive facilities of interest to resident and visitor (DoE (NI), 1989 p.96).

Surprisingly little attention was given to the Laganside proposals at the public inquiry into the plan, possibly because of the relatively few people living in the area or because of the broadbrush nature of the proposals included in the plan, presumably deliberately in order to leave the way free for a flexible response by the implementing authority to any changes in market circumstances. Community Technical Aid, a publicly funded organisation located in Belfast whose role is to assist community groups with planning and housing problems in the Province, coordinated the community response throughout

84

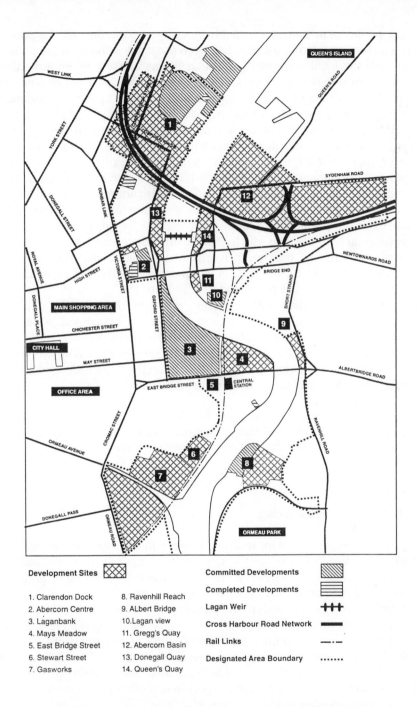

Development Sites

1. Clarendon Dock
2. Abercorn Centre
3. Laganbank
4. Mays Meadow
5. East Bridge Street
6. Stewart Street
7. Gasworks
8. Ravenhill Reach
9. ALbert Bridge
10. Lagan view
11. Gregg's Quay
12. Abercorn Basin
13. Donegall Quay
14. Queen's Quay

Committed Developments

Completed Developments

Lagan Weir

Cross Harbour Road Network

Rail Links

Designated Area Boundary

Map 3.1   Laganside boundary and development sites

Belfast to the plan and at the public inquiry argued that the Laganside proposals incorporated in the plan had been prepared without proper consultation with the local community and that it was unlikely to improve their economic development prospects. It was also argued that what was needed was public rather than private housing and that the plan gave no guarantees regarding the employment of local people. The Planning Appeals Commission (PAC), an independent body with similar functions to the Planning Inspectorate in England, in recommending to the DoE in the subsequent inquiry report that all the Laganside policies be confirmed without any alteration, was enthusiastically supportive of the whole idea. It emphasized the importance of the Laganside area to the wider community of Belfast, not just to local residents, and concluded that a successful development "must inevitably make a significant impact on the residential, employment and environmental lives of those who live in the immediate area". This faith in the economic principle of trickle-down was widespread at that time and was frequently expressed by the UK government to justify the early UDCs' emphasis on property led regeneration (Coulson, 1993). The PAC actually went further than dealing with the issues raised by objectors, by outlining what it considered important common features of successful waterfront regeneration schemes elsewhere, namely effective public-private sector partnerships, central and accessible locations, pleasant water based environments and a wide diversity of activities, concluding that the Laganside area had the essential bases for such successful regeneration.

> The challenges are manifest, not least in our view, the obvious need for inward investment, but given the sensitive approach which the site merits, we feel confident that Laganside can play a pivotal role in the future of Belfast (Guckian and Hawthorne, 1989).

Marketing as image making

How then is image important to the development of Laganside and to what extent is Laganside crucial to the reimaging of the city in a national and international context? To examine possible answers to these questions one can look at several aspects of the Corporation's work, particularly its marketing activities and its approach to the planning of the area.

Taking marketing first of all, it is important to see the marketing activities of the Corporation within the wider context of the marketing of the city as a whole, because there is a very striking overlap of activity. To sell Laganside has involved selling the city as a good place also. Surprisingly, perhaps, the City Council has not, as one would expect in any other city in the UK, taken a lead in the marketing of the city to outside investors, tourists and residents, mainly because it has had since 1973 very few real powers and also because of its unwillingness to cooperate with government for a number of years after the Anglo-Irish Agreement was signed. Indeed it has been largely through the work of the Northern Ireland Departments of the Environment and Economic Development, as well as the Northern Ireland Tourist Board, that strategies for reimaging the city and its environs have been designed and implemented. Although there has been no official policy statement about reimaging the city, efforts to do so can be traced back to the mid-1980s when senior civil servants were concerned about Belfast's poor image and the fact that no statutory agency was addressing the problem. The BDO was thus charged with the job of promoting the city nationally and internationally and with pulling together the marketing efforts of various statutory bodies whose marketing was primarily geared towards the Province as a whole. The Tourist Board's role is to market the whole Province as a holiday destination and within that there is a place for urban tourism in the city of Belfast; the Industrial Development Board's role is to attract job creating inward investment to the Province, with large scale service sector employment most likely to be located in the capital city; and the BDO's role is specifically to market the city to inward investors, visitors and local residents. It is within this policy context that the Laganside Corporation can be seen as a crucial element in the strategy to alter outside perceptions of the city as well as improving the self confidence of the citizens of the urban area as a whole.

Marketing by the Belfast Development Office

The BDO's marketing effort outside the Province has been mainly targeted at property professionals and retailers and it has increasingly been aided in this activity by representatives of the private sector, particularly property professionals. The simple message is that Belfast is no different from any other British city, including the hard sell to property professionals and investors that the returns on property development and investment are above the average for other British cities. This is supported by well-researched property data which show that the office sector has outperformed other office centres in Great Britain, such as Edinburgh, Liverpool, Leeds and Manchester since 1980 (Laganside Corporation, 1993). To overcome fear of property destruction strong emphasis is placed on the fact that the property market is cushioned from the troubles because of complete government compensation for any losses incurred as a result of terrorist bombing. BDO's outreach effort involves staffing property and trade exhibitions in the UK and further afield (Hong Kong and France, for example) and the inreach involves encouraging relevant people to come to Belfast – retailers, property developers and investors, financiers, academics, politicians and journalists, where they are given great hospitality and guided tours. In addition considerable effort is made to attract conferences especially those related to property, planning and housing, with recent success despite the continuing violence. Much of the positive work is carried out through personal contacts and networking which are regarded as very important in actually overcoming prejudice against the city. Often, if individuals can be persuaded to come to the city they are so enchanted with the warmth of welcome and the continued optimism of the people that they become in turn missionaries for the city.

In terms of its wider marketing effort the BDO has for a number of years supported the arts activities of various organizations in the city, such as the very successful annual Belfast Festival at Queen's which attracts artists from around the world for a three week period in the autumn. This policy was pursued despite the absence of any published arts strategy for the city. Such a strategy has recently been presented by the City Council in the form of a discussion document which identifies as one of its five policy statements:

> The City Council recognises the importance of the arts in enhancing the image of Belfast, and in effecting economic development in the City. It will work to maximise the benefits in these areas through investment in the arts (Belfast City Council, 1994b).

Another element of the marketing effort is the encouragement of city pride amongst the citizens themselves and to this end a small group representing government and business, called Positively Belfast, was set up in 1991 with the aim of organizing several events each year which would catch the imagination of the citizens of the city, bring them together despite their differences and also attract positive media coverage. Thus there have been several hallmark events such as the Tall Ships Race in 1991, hot air ballooning in 1992 and 1993, the Irish Senior Masters Golf Tournament each year, power boat racing in 1993 and 1994, and a concert and laser firework show in 1993. These events are supported by the private sector, are free of charge to the public and take place in perceived "neutral" territory in the divided city. The major events have been given Sky television coverage throughout the world and thus present a new image of quality of life and normality in the city.

Marketing by the Laganside Corporation

The Corporation's Marketing Department has a strategy aimed at each of the identified target audiences – potential investors, the general public in Belfast, local decision takers and local communities in the area. The maintenance of confidence in the regeneration effort by all these sectors is perceived to be vital to the success of the strategy – a confidence which could be severely dented by terrorist activity, by failure to get high quality development on the ground at an early stage and by any antagonism from local communities. The staff and premises themselves are an integral if unselfconscious part of the marketing effort. There is a largely home-grown, attractive, youngish, cheerful and courteous staff, well presented and radiating professional competence and confidence in the product. The premises are a tastefully and expensively refurbished Georgian listed building, Clarendon Building, right on the edge of the docks and close to the Harbour Commissioners' Offices. The quality of the craftsmanship and the design of the refurbishment has attracted several architectural awards and the airy open plan interior, views of the waterfront, and the fine meeting room sporting furniture intended for the *Titanic* but not ready for her maiden journey, all exude capability, heritage, good taste and a non-bureaucratic attitude towards the development industry. The logo chosen, based on a swan and bollard in pale blue and white, is strictly adhered to on all development briefs, advertisements and other documentation. Criticisms have been levelled at this logo: that it insipid; that it uses the waterfront theme without any reference to the place that is Belfast and that it seeks to create the impression that the Laganside is no different from any other waterfront regeneration area in the UK, be it Bristol, Swansea or Southhampton.

Photograph 3.1   Laganside logo

Officials of the Corporation argue, however, that there was no hidden agenda in designing the logo – it was designed by an individual in the consultancy firm, Future Images Limited, and endorsed by the Board without extensive debate. Very large freestanding information panels have been erected at intervals throughout the area to describe briefly what is planned for each particular site. The common background colour is pale blue, presumably to denote the waterfront theme, whilst the word Laganside and sometimes the European Union logo are also evident. The sign on the river to explain the dredging and riverbank works funded by the EU, for example, has large cartoon style red, orange and yellow fish with bubbles coming from their mouths, to give the impression of a high level of water quality. Altogether these large panel advertisements are cheerful and optimistic, telling the people of Belfast that all is well with the development and that things are underway. One of the Citybus buses is also painted pale blue and white and sports the Laganside logo.

**Photograph 3.2
Free standing
information panel –
Laganside**

The attraction of inward investment, mainly offices, was given number one priority by the Corporation at the outset, and it was acknowledged that it was the poor image of Northern Ireland that discouraged inward investment and tourism in the Province. In collaboration with the Industrial Development Board there are selective advertising in the property and business press, occasional direct mail shots, attendance at property business shows and editorial coverage in the business columns of national newspapers. Initially the stress in the promotional work was placed on the city's advantages for relocation – its accessibility by air from the UK and by road and rail from other parts of the city and the Province, its advanced telecommunications facilities, low building costs, low office rentals, good labour relations, low housing costs for employees, high educational standards, abundant sporting and recreational facilities, and low crime levels. The specific additional

Creating Belfast's New Skyline

LAGANSIDE
Discover what's on the horizon,
contact the Marketing Department
Laganside Corporation Clarendon Building
15 Clarendon Road Belfast BT1 3BG
Telephone 0232 328507 Facsimile 0232 332141

**Photograph 3.3
The early
advertisement –
"Creating Belfast's
New Skyline"**

advantages of the Laganside location were the high quality infrastructure and the attractive landscaped setting close to the city centre. Initially the full page advertisement for the property journals was one titled "Creating Belfast's New Skyline" and it was a sketch of three crane tips, one with the Laganside logo appearing as a crate being lifted. This rather assertive "development" stance was softened to a more human theme in a subsequent design titled "Quay Decisions" which shows the youthful Director of Development at work in his office in an historic waterfront building with a female colleague looking over his shoulder and through the window behind them the historic quays and a hydrofoil. The message is competent staff, care for heritage, the waterfront theme, and accessibility to the "mainland". The conclusion of the accompanying script is "high standard of living in a vibrant, growing city. A city of opportunity".

Success in attracting international or UK inward office or commercial development has, however, been disappointing, mainly because of the con-

Photograph 3.4 A later advertisement – "Quay Decisions"

tinuing insecurity felt by UK investors and developers as a result of the ongoing terrorist campaign and because the deep recession of the late 1980s and early 1990s experienced elsewhere in the UK made major relocations to any northern city from the south-east unlikely, especially when London was experiencing labour surplus and plummeting rentals. Taking on board the particular difficulties of Belfast arising from the ongoing civil unrest, the Corporation's marketing strategy for inward investment is now based on the idea that "OK Belfast has its problems BUT it is a great place to do business". The marketing effort seeks to make sure that this message goes to the right people so resources are concentrated on giving tailor made one to one presentations, with contacts made to maybe 50-60 interested business people/investors per year who are identified through wider market research. For specific land use requirements such as an hotel or a cinema complex, the Corporation would go out looking specifically for suitable tenants or tenant-developers. Networking is of particular importance with emphasis placed on developing and maintaining good relations with highly placed personal contacts in Great Britain and the US. The role of the Chairman, His Grace the Duke of Abercorn, is particularly important in this respect owing to his wide network of contacts nationally and internationally.

Advertising is used mainly in the British financial and property press to reinforce the message put across in the one to one presentations and the public relations work carried out involves developing and keeping good contacts in the press to ensure that supportive editorials and good news items are regularly published, often supported by appropriate advertising. Shandwick Consultants Limited was appointed in 1992 to help maintain Laganside's profile in Great Britain and through their efforts frequent visits from mainland journalists have been arranged. "Belfast's perceived peripherality and general negative image amongst those not familiar with the city are amongst two most frequent barriers to investment. It is clear that by encouraging such people (influential journalists) to come and see for themselves and to report their impressions favourably then these barriers can be gradually broken down" (Laganside Corporation, 1992a p.16).

The general public

For the public at large Laganside's marketing involves a strong PR approach, the objective being to enthuse the public and condition them to expect good things in the Laganside area – places to walk, places to eat, sporting events and so on. The emphasis is on maintaining the "feel good" factor about the city at large and what is happening at Laganside in particular and some of the mechanisms used are sponsorship of major and minor events open to the public. Major spectacle events have included the Tall Ships Race in 1991, the Power Boat Races in 1993 and 1994, the Chinese State Circus in 1993 and a highly acclaimed performance by the Northern Ireland Opera in a disused listed building on Laganside's former gasworks site in 1994. Sporting events supported include the annual Laganside Half Marathon and the Head of the River race, a Rowing Summer School, an annual community programme of musical performances and story telling, plus Laganside bus tours (including dinner) during the summer months. Laganside has an embryonic arts strategy, somewhat restrained by recessionary pressures, which involves a range of ideas and initiatives and cooperation with the Arts Council. The strategy includes the creation of public art, the purchase of art works, sponsorship of a Folk Festival and involvement with the long established Queens Festival. The view is taken that a programme of arts events is beneficial to the Corporation's overall marketing and public relations policies. In the educational field a School Support Pack containing a high quality video, written material and a computer programme has been prepared and sent to all secondary schools in the Province, the emphasis being not only educational but also on winning the hearts and minds of tomorrow's citizens. The style of the video is upbeat and cheerful, with images of canoeing on the river, the modern industrial port activities, new building works in progress, the historical and heritage connections of the area, environmental improvements and community involvement. A riverside walkway jazz performance by school children repeated at the end of each video section provides the exciting musical backdrop.

Another mechanism used in the public relations effort is frequent "good news" stories and editorials in the local press. Throughout the six year life of the Corporation to date the local press has been highly supportive, particularly the property journals such as *Perspective, Ulster Architect* and *Specify* and the three main Belfast daily papers, with for example 48 articles on Laganside in the *Belfast Telegraph* and its associated weekly *Business Telegraph* between the end of 1992 and June 1994, sporting titles such as 'Laganside helps Shape the City of Tomorrow' (22 March 1993), 'New Era Dawning Over Belfast's River'(25 January 1994), 'Laganside Turns the Tide' (12 March 1994), and 'New Look Lagan is a Runaway Success' (24 May 1994). However some adverse publicity about the progress of schemes has crept into the press in 1993/ 1994, especially regarding the Laganbank site. Indeed delay in getting development on the ground has been a source of some embarrassment to the Corporation, although for reasons well beyond its control. This has involved problems in dealing with lands owned by several public sector bodies and in trying to attract investment during a recessionary period. The so-called "jewel in Laganside's crown" (Laganside Corporation, 1993a), the fifteen acre Laganbank site is an interesting case study of regeneration since it has lain partly vacant and derelict for many years despite its prime location to the east of the city centre. At present the site has been cleared of existing uses by the Corporation, new quay walls constructed and a road and sewer realignment scheme carried out. After a development brief was published and a number of companies submitted schemes for the site a consortium was chosen to implement the development – made up of a local contractor, O'Hare and McGovern, a local development company, Ewart plc and an American company, the Enterprise International Development Company founded by Jim Rouse who has been responsible for internationally renowned landmark projects such as New York's South Street Seaport, Boston's Faneuil Hall and Sydney's Darling Harbour. At a cost of £100 million it was to be the largest development to be undertaken in Belfast and was to feature 500,000 sq.ft. of office space, 100,000 sq.ft. of festival shopping, a 200 room international standard hotel and structured parking for 1,500 cars. A £29 million concert hall and conference centre funded by the City Council (£18 million), the EU (£4 million), Laganside Corporation and the DoE (£6.5 million) has commenced construction on the site and is regarded as an essential ingredient of the public sector subsidy of the whole scheme. Despite considerable doubts within the Council and a last ditch effort by some parties at City Hall to prevent the expenditure, work commenced in 1993 and the 2,500 seater concert hall is expected to open early in 1996 (*Belfast Telegraph*, 17 November 1993). Overall investment in the Laganbank site from the public and private sectors is expected to exceed £130 million (Laganside Corporation, 1994). The whole scheme has suffered promotional and funding setbacks, not only because of the well publicised internal wrangling of the City Council over the planned expenditure on the concert hall, regarded by some councillors as a waste of taxpayers' money and of little benefit to the less well off in the city, but also because of the breakup of the development team which won the scheme. In early 1993 the Enterprise International Development Company pulled out of the consortium in a row over consultancy fees and later in the year the American Marriot chain pulled out of negotiations related to the building of the planned four star hotel alongside the concert hall, partly it was claimed because of the worrying level of terrorist bombing activity in the city at that time. However the Corporation has signed a development contract with the Laganbank Development Company (a subsidiary of Ewart plc) and has acquired the land from the three public landowners in order to ensure the implementation of a very tight development programme in a slack property market. The most recent annual report is upbeat about progress on the site and the level of demand for the proposed offices (Laganside Corporation, 1994) and in September 1994 Hilton International entered into a joint venture with Ewart Plc for the major hotel development.

Local decision takers

The marketing aimed at local decision takers is mainly about resource allocation in a time of severe competition for scarce public resources. There are other parts of the city and other parts of the Province wanting a greater share of the cake and so Laganside has to be kept constantly in the minds of the decision takers such as the local top civil servants and through them the European Union, the main public sector landowners of the Laganside sites, politicians in charge of the main government departments in Northern Ireland, the property elite such as the top estate agents, developers and financiers, and middle class groups and societies. Not only is there frequent personal contact but also prompt supply of relevant information such as the glossy annual reports and other publicity material, as well as the development briefs for individual sites. In addition the Corporation is frequently involved in corporate hospitality events such as receptions, boat trips on the Lagan, elegant and hyped up launches of development briefs for sites, dinners, sponsorship support for activities of relevant professions, invitation only conferences and so on. In 1991, for example, two major conferences were hosted by the Corporation, one being the 300 delegate International New Towns Conference, and in the same year study tours were provided for over 1,500 people.

Local communities

Laganside's 'marketing' effort in relation to the six local communities bordering on the area is probably a reaction to the criticisms of other Urban Development Corporations such as London Docklands DC which initially more or less ignored the needs of existing low income communities in the area. Laganside Corporation, on the other hand, has realised the importance of keeping local attitudes to the proposed developments positive partly because having antagonistic neighbours would have an adverse effect on the image of the development sites. Not only are these very deprived communities but they are also divided on sectarian grounds so policies have been very much geared to keeping the local people involved and relatively content with the outcomes of consultation exercises. The Corporation has frequent meetings with local community groups and has sought to identify community needs. The two small housing sites developed, Ravenhill Reach and Laganview, have both been particularly sensitive because of their location beside existing public sector housing and every attempt has been made to work with existing tenants' groups to make sure that there is a positive attitude to the new development. In the case of Ravenhill Reach, for example, a new play area for local children is to be provided in the adjoining public sector housing and the new housing includes housing association and coownership housing as well as private housing in order to give local people the prospect of moving into the development at some stage. Likewise there has been much involvement with local community groups to ensure a feeling of ownership of the walkways so that vandalism is reduced. This has not been altogether successful on the less well used parts of the walkways where local unemployed youths have been causing extensive damage to the high quality seating and paving.

A regular work and training news sheet, *Workscene*, is circulated to all houses in the area and much environmental awareness work is carried out with local school children. In addition the Corporation has stressed that employment spin-offs from expected investment should be available to the existing communities where current male unemployment rates are 50 per

96

cent, has commissioned a skills audit and has collaborated with existing agencies in training and education programmes. Whether or not the jobs match the skills available when the time comes is another issue and any evaluation of this laudable pro community stance would need post hoc evaluation to determine the extent of real progress. As Parkinson has argued, training provision for local people does not necessarily create jobs.

> Although targeting employment through the labour market is inevitably uncertain, skills training certainly improves the job prospects of the local people. Neverthe-less, training per se does not create jobs and, at the end of the day, local employment opportunities will depend on combining an appropriately skilled population with success in stimulating private sector investment (Dawson and Parkinson, 1993).

Community consultation on the future of the derelict twenty-five acre gas-works site has been extensive, as it is sandwiched between three community groups, two perceived to be strongly nationalist and one strongly loyalist. Extensive site clearance and decontamination works by the landowners, Belfast City Council and the Department of Economic Development, began in 1992 and since then the Corporation has been involved in sustained consulta-tions with each community, the local residents tending to highlight their needs for employment, open space and community facilities. On completion of the consultant's development strategy for the area in 1994 the proposals were taken around the various communities along with an exhibition, and subse-quently the views expressed analysed. The broadbrush proposals (Belfast City Council, 1994a) include high quality open space with a waterbasin as part of a civic square, landscaped linkages with the city centre, opportunity sites for commercial, civic or community use, restored listed buildings for civic, cultural or community use, and vehicular/pedestrian circulation patterns. Stress is laid on existing visual axes, the civic potential of the site and the necessity of integrating it with the rest of the city centre and the river. In the proposed scheme a sympathy is shown to the existing star shaped road pattern in the area and possible uses mentioned are a business park, a further education college, and some sort of museum/heritage/arts use of the former gasworks buildings themselves. "Restaurants/coffee shops/craft shops linked to the interpretative backcloths of the Gasworks Industry, Lagan Navigation, or indeed a History of Victorian Belfast could thrive as part of the service sector to the new business elements within the depths of the site and draw clientele from the city centre along Ormeau Avenue to the river corridor" (Cook, 1993).

Projected images of Laganside

The images and messages implicit in the publicity sent out by Laganside – the annual reports, corporate plan, marketing strategy and other promotional material, initially designed by Future Images Limited and subsequently by the McCadden Design Group – stress vision, partnership, heritage, quality environment, culture and community. Quality environment is represented through presentations of the new riverside walkways, new weir, new cross harbour road and rail bridge plus scenic shots of the river with landscaped backdrops. Culture is illustrated by representations of the proposed concert hall and pictorial violins and brass instruments, in addition to upmarket sporting sequences such as canoeing, jogging and small boating. Heritage is expressed through frequent photographs and illustrations of traditional quay-side features, the Victorian bridges and listed buildings and their motifs. For example, the marketing brochure for the Clarendon Dock site states:

> Clarendon Dock epitomises the robust, hard working but cheerful environment that is the essence of Belfast and its people. All around there is evidence of the seagoing and shipbuilding traditions that made Belfast a great city. At one time the Dockside was the focal point of emigration as Ulster men and women left to start new lives in the New World. Today the focus is back on Clarendon Dock itself as the area enjoys a twentieth century renaissance. Clarendon Dock's original working function in the port is being replaced with a new role as a vibrant and bustling centre of business, commerce and leisure (Laganside Corporation, 1993b).

Photograph 3.5   Clarendon Dock – major infrastructural development supported by the EU

It is this selective appropriation of particular aspects of the locality's culture in furtherance of property led regeneration that causes disquiet (Neill, 1993). The present day culture of the immediate area is substantially different from the marketeer's version of reality. Indeed, whilst the population of Laganside on designation was relatively small it includes or is bounded by some of the very oldest tight knit working class neighbourhoods in inner city Belfast, for example the Markets Area, Lower Ormeau, Short Strand and Donegall Pass. The first three are widely perceived in the city to be Catholic and nationalist and the latter to be Protestant and loyalist. Territoriality in the city is so strong that the use and accessibility of sites bounding these clearly defined and segregated residential areas are very much a cause of potential conflict. Nowhere in the literature is this fact openly admitted although the Corporation's sensitive approach to the planning of the former gasworks site is clearly an acknowledgement of this situation. Realistically, from the viewpoint of the Corporation, it is not just environmental upgrading that is necessary in order to attract private sector investment but also social stability and the containment of any potential vandalism or conflict.

How then is community stressed in the marketing literature? It is stressed with many pictures of the Corporation's staff looking cheerful and enthusiastic, of happy crowd scenes, of men at work building the new structures, of schoolchildren learning about Laganside and of people enjoying leisure facilities on the river. Blue skies and a romantic evening sunset are prerequisites and naturally there is no reference to conflict, terrorism or social deprivation. The script expresses confidence and commitment: "Through real partnership we can forge ahead to build a new future for Belfast" (Laganside Corporation, 1993). "This will benefit those who will live there, those who will work there and the many thousands who will, at intervals, visit the area for business or pleasure" (Laganside Corporation, 1992b). "There is an undeniable mood of almost infectious optimism and initiative within Belfast city centre as new commercial and retail ventures take shape. Laganside is part of that success story. The foundations have already been laid but I look forward to the successful completion of the venture and to witnessing people, jobs and prosperity returning to this historic part of our capital city" (Duke of Abercorn, Laganside Corporation, u.d.).

Development as reimaging

Apart from marketing, the other element of the Corporation's work that can be evaluated with regard to its relationship with place marketing is that of planning and development. The emphasis on quality public spaces, spectacular infrastructure, flagship developments, and office, leisure, and tourism land uses is very typical of the reimaging approach taken in other post-industrial cities and analysed in Chapters 1 and 2. In order to implement the chosen strategy of supply led regeneration, major infrastructural investment is being carried out to make the area more attractive for investment by the private sector. Private sector investment thus "levered" is hoped to be at the ratio of £4 to each £1 of public sector investment when the developments are completed and there is also to be the provision of 2,500 permanent jobs apart from construction jobs (Laganside Corporation, 1992b). The main infrastructure projects, apart from site clearance and preparation work, include a £14 million weir, assisted by a £4 million grant from the European Regional Development Fund, which has been constructed across the river downstream of the former weir in order to improve the water quality and eliminate unsightly exposure of the mud banks at low tide. Although not the responsibility of the Corporation, major investment has also being undertaken recently within Laganside on the construction of cross harbour road and rail bridges linking the north of the city with the east of the city and costing £87 million. This has been partly funded by the European Union and has come in for some criticism from urban designers regarding its visual impact on the city, especially the lengths of raised roadway and rail track feeding into the bridges. With a more spectacular cross harbour suspension bridge abandoned on cost (and security?) grounds the full measure of this reimaging opportunity may have been missed. Other infrastructure works include riverside walkways which have been constructed along parts of the river with the intention of having a high quality walkway eventually extending along the one and a half mile stretch on both sides.

TABLE 3.1   European Regional Development Fund Grants

Cumulative grants from the ERDF to 1994 receivable by Laganside Corporation with respect to the following	
	£ sterling
weir	4,300,000
weir interpretative centre	229,725
walkways	4,435,751
environmental improvements	2,301,575
infrastructure	3,897,645
promotional events	245,000
TOTAL	15,409,696

Source: Annual Report 1993-1994, Laganside Corporation, Belfast.

It is the stress on quality of environment that is so illustrative of the reimaging process. The weir is not just a functional weir but provides an interesting spectacle for urban tourism with its landscaped areas at each side of the river, its walkway across the river and the unusual round visitors' centre which it is anticipated will attract around 50,000 visitors per year. Its festive blue nighttime lighting can, perhaps, be viewed as an attempt to romanticize the river. It acts as an advertisement of the river's changed role – from that of a repository of sewage to that of a pleasure area. It and the new cross harbour road and rail bridges also provide a new setting of investment and wealth for public outdoor events such as power boat racing and firework displays and purvey good visual imagery of hope and success for the world's press. Likewise the walkways are designed with high quality landscaping and materials – especially the expensive street furniture, lighting, railings and floorscape. This emphasis on quality is seen as a prerequisite in changing perceptions of the area and attracting private sector residents, service employment and urban tourists.

Furthermore, as is typical of area based reimaging strategies elsewhere, the planned land uses for Laganside are linked with service sector employment and modern upmarket lifestyles. Specifically these include shopping (festival shopping as in the Laganbank scheme not supermarket shopping), modern offices (at the McCausland, Laganbank, Abercorn and Clarendon sites),

Photograph 3.6   Clarendon Building – Laganside Office

business parks (gasworks site), tourism uses (hotel, possible youth hostel, and concert hall at Laganbank; arts/heritage facilities at the gasworks site; a marina and possible maritime museum at the Abercorn Basin site), leisure (at various sites including Maysfield where boating facilities are being developed in conjunction with the existing Leisure Centre), and private sector housing (including the proposed harbour village at the Abercorn site and the two recently developed smaller housing schemes). The heritage/tourism theme is strong in terms of land use and urban design in Laganside, in common with other waterfront developments elsewhere and indeed, generally, other post-industrial cities as argued in Chapter 1. Not only is urban tourism in such a waterfront situation heavily dependent on the generation and promotion of particular place images but also the place images supporting heritage and cultural tourism are perceived to help attract service employment and improve public self-confidence and support for the schemes (Tunbridge and Ashworth, 1992). Heritage uses planned for Laganside include the proposed museum on the gasworks site and a heritage museum for the Abercorn basin, plus street design to reflect old street patterns, maritime urban landscaping and scale as required by the plan, and even a pervading intangible maritime atmosphere conveyed through architectural motifs and nomenclature (Dargan Bridge named after a once famous Belfast civil engineer, and the Abercorn Centre named after the Chairman of the Laganside Corporation's prestigious ances-tors). Such use of heritage to sell waterfront redevelopment is regarded by some commentators as archetypically postmodern.

> The eclecticism in the use of diverse components, seemingly without logic (Relph, 1991) has in fact a new logical focus; exploitation of perceived place distinctive-ness, especially as manifested by the heritage resource. Hence the tourist-historic paradox alluded to above: the very universality of this resource exploitation gives rise to stereotypical outcomes in the broad components utilised and new functions accommodated, so that underlying the detailed sense of place now so strongly promoted there is increasingly a certain sense of 'deja vu'. Whatever the dimen-sions of the post industrial city as a whole, the tourist-historic waterfront would seem to command a prominent position in this evolving identity (Tunbridge and Ashworth, 1992).

Architecture as advertising

Not only chosen land uses or development themes but also the design of new buildings and open spaces on Laganside can be evaluated as an important element of the overall place-marketing strategy. As with architecture in other Urban Development Corporations' areas it appears that the intention is to use contextualism selectively to help local people identify with the new schemes whilst implanting postmodern elements which give the impression of an up-and-coming district. Indeed, as Crilley argues:

Buildings are viewed pre-eminently as communicative texts, which like advertisements are culturally encoded with popular meanings: and, just as all advertising follows the ancient art of rhetoric in always being an attempt to persuade potential customers that a particular commodity is worthy of purchase, so does the imagery of architecture seek to persuade the public of the virtues and propriety of the property capital commissioning it (Crilley D, 1993).

The contextualism can be seen in the choice of round copper elements for various new buildings such as the weir's interpretative centre and the Abercorn Centre, designed to replicate a theme set by the copper domes of the Victorian City Hall. This would be regarded by Crilley as an attempt by architects to give the buildings an acceptable but meretricious cultural identity and as an attempt to tap people's warm sentiments about the city and then to transfer this warmness to the Laganside development. Apart from that, new buildings so far designed in detail or built do not appear to be particularly characteristic of the city, despite being designed by a variety of Belfast based architects. The RIBA award winning Design Centre is a very modern greenish glass and steel structure. The concert hall is to be a large domed construction with Portland stone cladding, Pilkington's Planar curtain walling and brick hung at an unusual angle so that it splays outwards at the top. Uplighting is designed to make the copper domed roof appear to hover above the building. The Abercorn Centre is a beige/yellow brick postmodern building echoing the design of the weir's interpretative centre, and the redbrick Laganview apartments have unusual geometric designs with balconies and dramatic floor to ceiling triangular windows. One could argue that the architecture is placeless, that it could be in any city in the UK even in London Docklands. Indeed Neill (1993) has questioned whether some of the design concepts of Laganside are not "left-overs" from Euro-Disney. Perhaps it is also true that:

> Framed within an acceptance of the status quo, the intention is to create a mildly educational, entertaining architecture with popular commercial appeal. In fact, the architecture so derived is a powerful and tangible adjunct to place marketing. As I will show, it too bolsters attempts to overturn negative perceptions of 'marginal' redevelopment areas and erase stigmatisation of landscapes of industrial decay or those ravaged by the visual blandishments of modernism (Crilley, 1993).

On the whole appraisal of new developments from the architectural point of view has been broadly supportive, with little local adverse comment on detailed designs. There have been none of the savage attacks from the professional or general press that have greeted many of London Dockland's new buildings or, indeed, the overall postmodern assemblage of buildings. Typical might be the views expressed by the editor of the *Architect's Journal* that the design of London Docklands has "lurched drunkenly from suburban business park, to pseudo Amsterdam, to miniature Manhattan and finally to complete chaos" (Rod Hackney, quoted in Fisher and Rogers, 1992). The lack of any criticism of Laganside's architecture may in part reflect the small amount of development completed or it may reflect the strength of the urban growth coalition in the city and the power of the Corporation's promotional work, which has pulled together a form of loyalty for Laganside from the architectural and urban design professions. Nevertheless, one of the Royal Society of Ulster Architect's past presidents has said:

> The architecture at Laganside may be watered down, could become non-innovative and non-exciting. In future developments we will be more than likely to get safe architecture – more by compromise, by committee' (Thompson, 1992).

Attempts are being made, however, by the chosen consultant landscape architect, Belfast born Robert Camlin, to ensure symbolically acceptable civic and open spaces in Laganside. As designer of the major public open spaces around the new concert hall and hotel he has been carefully analysing the history, architectural forms and street/river/movement lines or axes of the city in order to use recognisable codes and pattern languages which will bring about full usage of the spaces. The question is whether the analysis will result in some selective reinterpretation of Belfast's social and economic history or an open confrontation of the issue of "Whose Culture?", a question which really needs to be posed in a culturally divided society. Will designs reminiscent of a hard working, industrious Victorian era be as acceptable to those of the nationalist community as to those of the loyalist community? Will the designer evade these issues by going for a cultural symbolism that is placeless – reproducing a form of aestheticised maritime history, with nostalgic public art compositions establishing an ambience conducive to upmarket consumption, as in Swansea's Maritime Quarter? Already reference to Clarendon Dock development as "renaissance very much in the style of St Katherine's Dock in London and Albert Dock in Liverpool" (Laganside Corporation, 1993b), the choice of names from the past for various elements of Laganside, and the logos and plaques along the new walkways could be viewed as a form of outdoor advertisement for the desired heritage/quality theme of the area in order to sell the product (to the private investor and to future occupiers) and erase the stigmatisation of a formerly derelict wasteland.

Responding to changing circumstances

The original concept plan and the Belfast Urban Area Plan 2001 have already been referred to but within that wider context the Corporation has had to adapt to changing market conditions and even changes in fashion as regards development. Certainly the Corporation is more community oriented than many other UDCs in the UK and has also made efforts to project a "green" image to reflect the new popularity of sustainability, with the publication of a colourful document called *Laganlife*. This states optimistically and with a touch of romance and nostalgia:

> From new open spaces, parks and urban squares to quiet walks along shaded boulevards, towpaths and blossoming countryside the new Belfast begins to emerge. A vibrant city finding its lifestyle, and its future, turning once again to the river ... Boats on the river, walkways, river sports, strolls along the Lagan. Badgers and foxes scampering to footfalls at night. Birdsong echoing right into the heart of the city (Laganside Corporation, u.d. p.3).

Recessionary impacts

With the UK recession having an impact on the implementation of development schemes, a new realism has also entered into the pronouncements of the Corporation's staff, tempering the visionary nature of the earlier proposals with a stress on deliverability and value. The Abercorn Centre, for example, was the first building on the three-acre McCausland site released early on by the Laganside Corporation, but progress on the overall scheme has been embarrassingly slow. The £18 million winning scheme by Aero Properties, a local development company, included 150,000 sq. ft. of ground floor retail, a multi storey car park and apartments but this later evolved into office space, then office space plus bus station. To date a 73,000 sq.ft. office building has been constructed but not the car parking or the residential element, as the offices took an uncomfortably long time to sell. The adjoining listed McCausland building has been weatherproofed by the Department of the Environment but unfortunately no full refurbishment has as yet been undertaken by the developer as originally agreed as part of the deal. The next phase of the site is the development by Northern Ireland Transport Holding Company and their subsidiary Ulsterbus of a new bus station and multi storey car park, commencing in 1994. Initially hopes for this site were high as it was regarded as an important linkage with the city centre and as the first flagship development scheme, but the practicalities of a weak property market in recessionary times have held the vision at bay.

The realities of the 1990s in the UK generally have meant that, whereas in 1989 the emphasis was on attracting substantial inward investment particularly in offices, today there are more modest plans, largely centred on the indigenous office and commercial markets and on local developers. Thus the Clarendon Dock site (thirty-five acres) owned by the Belfast Harbour Commissioners was first launched in 1990 with grandiose schemes for major office relocations and a possible European Trade Centre but the market was not there. Meanwhile the Laganside Corporation undertook the refurbishment of a fine near derelict listed dock building at Clarendon Dock as its headquarters and as a flagship development to attract interest in the site. The site's second launch in October 1993 was a much more modest affair with proposed developments including smaller scale office, residential and leisure uses in what the Corporation dubbed Belfast's new "Maritime Quarter". The press release for the site quoted the Duke of Abercorn, Chairman of the Corporation, as saying at the launch:

> I have no doubt that Clarendon Dock will shortly be regarded as the most exclusive business address in Belfast, indeed Northern Ireland; an area of tremendous maritime character and atmosphere, an historic part of Belfast, and now an undoubted magnet for those firms seeking a prestigious location with ample car parking and away from the clutter of traffic.

Clarendon Dock is currently undergoing major infrastructural works costing £4 million and funded by the EU, with significant improvements being made to the dock edge including new walls and lock gates, comprehensive new service infrastructure, the development of dock and riverside walkways, a central boulevard and a major public square. It has been a no-expense-spared approach to the design of the public spaces which include mature trees from Holland costing £6000 each and granite slabs and setts from different parts of Europe. Several important sites have been earmarked for large custom designed buildings, while smaller premises will encircle the dock itself. An architectural design panel has been appointed to oversee development at each site to ensure the protection of the overall integrity of the concept.

Residential Realities

The realities of Belfast's residential territoriality have also amended policies to some extent. Initially much of the housing provision on Laganside was intended to be relatively upmarket apartments and town houses for non-family occupants but this has been tempered with some realism about the problems of juxtaposing yuppy development cheek-by-jowl with existing low-income public housing. Thus the two recently developed sites have become mixed-tenure because of the need to fit in with the surrounding public sector estates. The one acre site at Bridge End was released with a detailed development brief for low income private housing. The commissioned architect is quoted as having said:

> We were very aware of the kinds of problem the Docklands development met in London. We didn't want to build a development full of strangers. We wanted it to be something the local community could feel part of rather than feel excluded (Acheson, 1992).

This partly completed and renamed £1.5 million Laganview scheme, comprising 32 apartments and 12 townhouses, was a joint venture between the Northern Ireland Housing Executive (the Province's unitary housing authority) as landowner and the developers, a local building company. However, phase 1 has been slow to sell partly because of its access through an existing

Photograph 3.7   Laganview Housing 1994 with river walkways in front

public sector estate. A further mainly residential ten acre site acquired by the Corporation, Ravenhill Reach, was also released by way of a development brief in 1991 and the chosen developers were a Northern Ireland construction company, Savage Brothers. The plans for the area were reached after consultation with the local population and the scheme includes 18 town houses for sale, 36 apartments for sale some under coownership (a part ownership/part rent arrangement), a 36 flat housing association scheme by Belfast Improved Homes for renting to mature single tenants, plus 5,000 sq.ft. of small unit office space adjoining a planned inlet to the river. Part of the area has been temporarily turned into a horticultural rehabilitation centre for people recovering from trauma injuries as the outcome of a review of road proposals by the DoE is carried out.

Despite this watering down of the luxury-private-sector-only concept, interestingly both housing schemes are marketed by local estate agents as providing a waterfront lifestyle, with an emphasis placed on leisure and recreational facilities, cultural attractions and proximity to the city centre with views of the upgraded river and prestige developments to be implemented on the other side of the river (Graham, 1994; Savage Brothers, 1994). The current social history of the area – the public sector housing, sectarian divisions, and high unemployment – is erased in the advertising and promotion.

Photograph 3.8   New Weir on River Lagan – a major infrastructural investment

Conclusion

English Urban Development Corporations are required by the Department of the Environment to monitor their own performance against six key quantifiable output measures, covering a wide range of their work, namely: land reclaimed, serviced and developed; infrastructure; non-housing floorspace; housing developed; private sector investment; and jobs created. No doubt there is a similar, although less formal and less public, arrangement in Northern Ireland. Nowhere in this list of quantifiable outputs is there specific mention of reimaging although this is implicit in the property led approach to regeneration espoused by Urban Development Corporations generally, and could arguably be quanitified in the amount of private sector development attracted. If one is to look at the Laganside Corporation's progress to date in altering the image of the riverfront generally, it is probably true to say that quantifiable results have been limited – very little in terms of private sector development is completed although a substantial amount is underway or planned for the near future. This may have been inevitable in Belfast since it has until recently been characterised by a stable pattern of long term development growth, despite the boom of the mid-1980s, and the requirement to escalate this growth pattern and increase additional floorspace demand from outside the Province has coincided with a recessionary period in the UK.

108

Perhaps it is also true to say that image improvements have been achieved more in relation to the home population, rather than further afield. A 1992 survey by MRC Ireland of Belfast residents' attitudes towards Laganside, for example, showed increased public awareness of the development and a generally positive attitude towards the proposed developments, including the view that it would attract tourists, improve the city's image, improve the environment and improve the living standards of those living in the area. On the other hand the attraction of inward investment has been very difficult, not only because of the recession but because of the continuing adverse press

TABLE 3.2 **Selected items of annual income and expenditure (£ sterling), Laganside Corporation, 1991–1994**

YEARS	1991	1992	1993	1994
grant-in-aid released from grant received	5,046,780	2,510,386	3,178,713	7,815,668
release from ERDF grant reserve		6,170,000	2,820,810	6,418,885
rental income		14,583	71,405	53,623
other income				1,331,000
payments to acquire major public assets	(3,546,250)	(6,022,915)	(1,951,236)	(4,380,991)
payments to acquire operating assets	(97,798)	(15,678)	(131,134)	(58,860)
operating costs	398,610	512,808	380,591	566,285
total staff costs	446,912	520,609	599,852	616,869
infrastructure and community projects	622,993	818,484	1,901,800	8,676,663

Source: Annual Reports 1991–1992, 1992–1993, 1993–1994, Laganside Corporation, Belfast

coverage of the civil conflict in the city. British Airways, for example, were said to be on the point of relocating their back office staff to Laganside in 1993 but then withdrew because of the IRA's increased bombing campaign in the city. Likewise attracting a top class international hotel chain to the Laganbank site has been very difficult, although finally accomplished in September 1994. Indeed it appears that property investors in London tend to invest outside the south-east of England only where there are guaranteed high returns and security of investment. They apparently continue to see Belfast as a risky location with the added problem of personal security for fund managers, although some recent encouraging property sales in the city centre, such as the £72.5 million sale of the CastleCourt Shopping Centre to a Middlesborough-based pension fund, reveal some success in marketing the city as an investment location. Hopes are high that the recently announced peace in Northern Ireland will be sustained and that this will have a substantial impact in terms of encouraging inward investment to the Province. A number of aid packages from the USA, the EU and the International Fund for Ireland have been promised in support of the peace process. Some commentators point optimistically to the growing confidence by the private sector in Laganside, as demonstrated by the £500,000 renovation of a riverside Victorian warehouse by a local architectural practice for office use and a boathouse (Morton, 1994).

So has the substantial expenditure on marketing and infrastructural provison designed to reimage this part of the city been worthwhile or not? That is very much a matter of opinion. There are those who feel that improving the attractiveness of a central and highly visible part of the city is indeed worthwhile, whether it results in a massive response from the private sector or not. Thus the cleaner river, the walkways, the removal of dilapidated buildings, and the building of a concert hall can only be good for the citizens of the city as a whole. As the Chief Executive has argued, Laganside is not intended to compete with other policy initiatives in the city such as Springvale and Duncairn, both very difficult inner city areas troubled with high unemployment and sectarian conflict, but to provide an additional element in the regeneration effort in a very prominent and central part of the city.

> Laganside is potentially like the aircraft carrier in the fleet. What we are trying to do is create a centre of excellence, something which can be seen from afar and represents a very easy and identifiable destination. And as that area regenerates it will spill over into the remainder of the city (Mackey, 1993).

City officials believe that Laganside Corporation's long struggle through the recessionary period has been worthwhile as the infrastructure is now largely in place and the sites available for any surge of international, national or local property development interest which might result from the end of conflict.

There are others who concentrate on the opportunity costs. The monies spent to date (Tables 3.1 and 3.2) are not insubstantial compared to the overall spending of the Department of the Environment, and there is an anticipated planned expenditure by the Corporation over the five year period 1991–1996 of £60 million. This plus the anticipated capital expenditure by the Department of the Environment, the City Council and the European Union on Laganside add up to a very considerable public sector commitment to the area. Is the goal of inward investment and image improvement worth all of this, if indeed reimaging really helps the economy to grow? Would the money be better spent on other competing schemes in the city, schemes designed to alleviate urban poverty such as The Making Belfast Work Initiative, or area based regeneration in deprived West Belfast, or even more generally on housing or education? Perhaps, as in Glasgow and Birmingham, the tide of opinion is beginning to turn away from public subsidy of such major flagship property development projects as concert halls, festival retailing and waterfront office parks. One can perhaps speculate that if peace is to be sustained in the Province a higher proportion of UK Exchequer and EU funds will need to be targeted at disadvantaged areas of the city and at social and economic development rather than at property development. Already there are signs that this is the way that civil servants responsible for urban regeneration in Belfast are beginning to think.

References

Acheson, A. (1992), quoted in 'A Housing deal to calm troubled waters', *Perspective*, vol. 1, no. 1, September/October.

Belfast City Council (1994a), *Gasworks Development Strategy*, Belfast.

Belfast City Council (1994b), *Towards a Policy and Strategies for the Arts in Belfast*, Belfast.

Berry, J.N. and McGreal, W.S. (1993), 'Public sector initiatives in the regeneration of Belfast', in *Berry, J.N. and McGreal W.S. (eds.), Urban Regeneration, Property Investment and Development*, E and FN Spon, London, pp.193–214.

Brownill, S. (1991), *Developing London's Docklands: Another Great Planning Disaster?*, Paul Chapman, London.

Building Design Partnership and Shepherd, Epstein and Hunter (1987), *Laganside*, Department of the Environment for Northern Ireland, Belfast.

Church, A. (1990), 'Waterfront Regeneration and Transport Problems in London's Docklands' in Hoyle B.S. (ed), *Port Cities in Context. The Impact of Waterfront Regeneration'*, Transport Geography Study Group, University of Southhampton.

Colenutt, B. (1991), 'The London Docklands Development Corporation. Has the community benefited?' in Keith, M. and Rogers, A. (eds), *Hollow Promises? Rhetoric and reality in the inner city*, Mansell, London.

Cook, A. (1993), *Belfast Gasworks Site Development Study*, Laganside Corporation, Belfast

Coulson, A. (1993), 'Urban Development Corporations, Local Authorities and Patronage in Urban Policy' in Imrie, R and Thomas, H (eds), *British Urban Policy and the Urban Development Corporations*, Paul Chapman, London.

Crilley, D. (1993), 'Architecture as Advertising: Constructing the Image of Redevelopment' in Kearns, G. and Philo, C. (eds), *Selling Cities . The City as Cultural Capital, Past and Present*, Pergamon Press, Oxford.

Department of the Environment for Northern Ireland, (1989), *Belfast Urban Area Plan 2001*, HMSO, Belfast.

Graham Construction (1994), *Laganview*, Dromore.

Hackney, R. (1990), *The Good, the Bad and the Ugly*, Frederick Muller, London, p.170.

Imrie R. and Thomas H. (1993), 'Urban Policy and the Urban Development Corporations' in Imrie, R. and Thomas, H. (eds), *British Urban Policy and the Urban Development Corporations*, Paul Chapman, London.

Laganside Corporation (1991), *Marketing Strategy*, Belfast

Laganside Corporation (u.d.), *Laganbank Development Brief*, Belfast.

Laganside Corporation (u.d.), *Laganlife*, Belfast

Laganside Corporation, (1992a), *Annual report 1991-1992*, Belfast

Laganside Corporation (1992b), *Corporate Plan A Vision For The Future*, Belfast.

Laganside Corporation (1993a), *Annual Report 1992-1993*, Belfast.

Laganside Corporation (1993b), *Clarendon Dock*, Belfast

Laganside Corporation (1994), *Annual Report 1993-1994*, Belfast.

Middleton, M. (1991), *Cities in Transition – The Regeneration of Britain's Inner Cities'*, Michael Joseph, London.

Mackey, G. (1993), *Development and Investment Opportunities in Laganside'*, unpublished paper given at a conference held at the University of Ulster, March 1993, Belfast.

Morrison, W. (1990), *Making Belfast Work,* Town and Country Planning Summer School Report of Proceedings, Royal Town Planning Institute, London.

Morton, R. (1994), *Edging Ahead*, Belfast Telegraph, 11 October, p. 10.

National Audit Office (1993), *The Achievements of the Second and Third generation Urban Development Corporations*, HMSO, London.

Neill, W. (1993), 'Physical Planning and Image Enhancement: Recent Developments in Belfast', *International Journal of Urban and Regional Research*, vol. 17, no.4, pp. 595–609.

Rogers, R. and Fisher, M. (1992), *A New London*, Penguin Books, London.

Sadler, D. (1993), 'Place-marketing, Competitive Places and the Construction of Hegemony in Britain in the 1980s' in Kearns, G. and Philo, C. (eds), *Selling Places. The City as Cultural Capital Past and Present*, Pergamon Press, Oxford. .

Savage Brothers (1994), *Ravenhill Reach: A waterfront development by Savage Brothers Contractors Ltd.*, Ballynahinch.

Tibbalds, F. (1992), *People Friendly Towns – Public Environment in Towns and Cities*, Longman, London.

Tunbridge, J. and Ashworth, T. (1992), 'Leisure resource development in cityport revitalisation: the tourist-historic dimension' in Hoyle, P.S. and Pinder, D.A. (eds), *European Port Cities in Transition*, Belhaven Press, London.

Whyte, J. (1990), *Interpreting Northern Ireland*, Oxford University Press, Oxford.

4 Promoting the city: image, reality and racism in Detroit

William J.V. Neill

Detroit's image has changed remarkably over the past thirteen years as billions of dollars in development have sculpted a new skyline. When the Renaissance Center was constructed, it became the symbol of the rebirth of the city of Detroit. Its completion in 1977 served as an impetus for the development that has taken place since then (Detroit Economic Growth Corporation, News Release, April 1991).

The central problem facing those who would give the city a better image is that the monster is real, and over the last 30 years it has transformed Detroit and its image. The city where people once found the American Dream in record numbers is now perceived as the city where the dream for many is to get out (Chuck Wilbur, *Detroit Metro Times*, February 1988).

Introduction

In June 1993, Coleman Young, Detroit's first black mayor, announced at the age of seventy-five that he would not be standing again for re-election. At the end of a twenty year political era, this chapter reflects on the image led economic regeneration legacy of the Young administration. Despite initial high hopes, in the aftermath of the 1967 riots, Detroit's public-private economic development partnership ended in mayoral disillusionment, with Detroit, unlike other US cities such as Baltimore and Cleveland, unable to turn an intractable outside image around.

Greater Detroit, with a black population of over 75 per cent in the core, higher than that in any comparable major American city, and with suburbs which are overwhelmingly white, is the prime examplar of metropolitan spatial apartheid in the United States (Table 4.1, Maps 4.1 and 4.2). Only

Greater Atlanta competes with Detroit for the distinction of being the most perfect 'urban doughnut': black in the deindustrialized centre, lily white on the job-rich periphery (Davis, 1993, p. 17). It was Detroit which was selected by Hollywood in the 1980s as the setting for the series of RoboCop films where law enforcement is bizarrely militarized and privatized in the face of the nightmare of urban violence running out of control. In the face of such negative image perception and at a time when image is more important than ever in the place marketing of localities (Harvey, 1989, ch. 17), this chapter focuses on the failure of economic development megaprojects, the hall-mark of development in Detroit under Coleman Young, as the spearhead of a broad reimaging strategy. Given the strength of countervailing centrifugal development forces, the city of Detroit has been more successful in imaging itself to black residents than to white outsiders.

Following preliminary remarks on city marketing and imaging generally and on the city of Detroit's historical upbeat national image until its final eclipse in 1967, the chapter periodizes the image driven urban development strategy of the Coleman Young years. This is traced through optimism in the 1970s, through struggle in the 1980s, to disillusionment in the 1990s. In a concluding section, this strategy is assessed and its serious limitations discussed in the context of current debates in Detroit and the United States on the role of racism in continuing to account for the real problems of American cities. With a new mayor and with image marketing set to assume even greater importance in Detroit, prospects for the future of the city are considered.

Historical Detroit imagery

Images of the city involve the symbolic endowment of space (Strauss, 1965, p. 3). Characteristic imagery for places as a whole and public civic imagery which is directly involved in promotion and in inducing consensus and identification draw selectively on geographical, economic, social, cultural and other aspects of the city (Strauss 1965, p. 32). Place imagery can be embedded in a variety of cultural milieus including poetic metaphor, literature, legends and even planning documents. Strauss reminds us that, in civic image terms, urban development is no stranger to the place marketing of the American city. Development and promotion have proceeded hand in hand as "the very stuffs out of which a considerable number of American towns were fashioned" (Strauss, 1965, pp. 200-208). Ashworth and Voogd (1990) explore the degree to which, in a market relations style of city management, specific city attributes, facilities and services can be "imaged" and in a demand sensitive way, marketed to specific target groups. However, they recognise the distinct business of imaging and promoting the "city as a whole" and the importance here of seeing the city generally as a place to

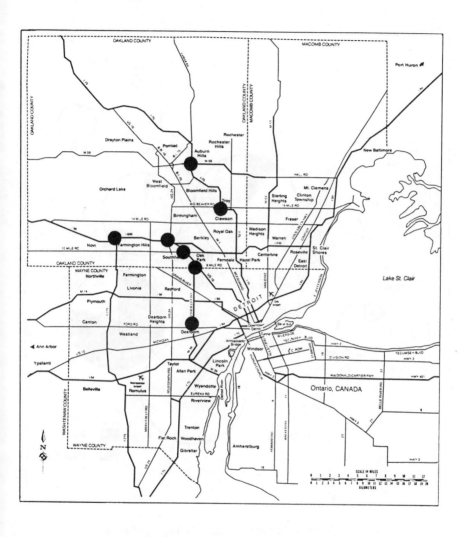

Map 4.1 Existing and emerging Edge Cities in Metropolitan Detroit (based on Garreau, 1991, p. 101)

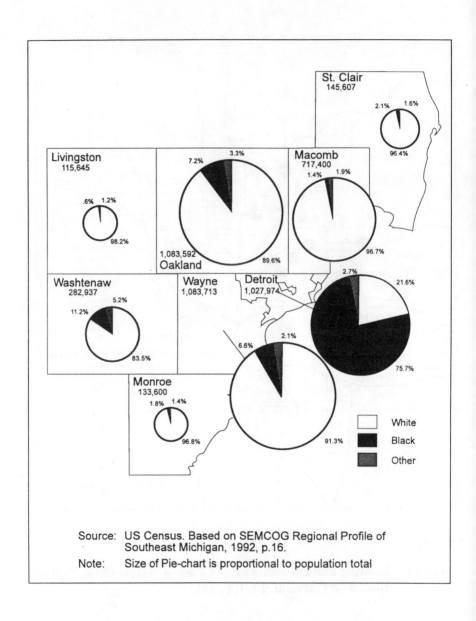

Map 4.2   Racial composition by County in S.E. Michigan (1990).

TABLE 4.1   Spatial apartheid in the Detroit metropolitan area 1990

	Population	% Black[o]	%White
City of Detroit "Doughnut core"	1,027,974	75.6	21.6
Balance of Wayne County	*1,067,059	4.7	91.2
Oakland County	1,083,592	+7.2	90.0
Macomb County	717,400	1.4	96.7
Suburban "Doughnut" Ring	2,868,051	4.8	92.0
Metropolitan Area	3,912,679	24.0	73.5

o   Percentages for blacks and whites do not sum to 100% because of the existence of small numbers of other races

*   Wayne County minus the population of Detroit and the enclave "cities" of Hamtramck and Highland Park

+   Excluding the single jurisdiction of Pontiac in Oakland County which has a large black population of over 30,000, would reduce this percentage to 4.4

Source: US Bureau of the Census

invest, work, live, recreate and visit (ibid., pp. 88-98). The "received image" to the "customer", they remind us, is the product of many factors, not least the underlying reality to which image making relates, the "promoted image" being only one factor affecting perceptions (ibid, ch. 7).

Place images which relate generally to the city as a place to invest, reside and visit, Ashworth and Voogd call the entrepreneurial, residential and tourist image respectively (Ashworth and Voogd, 1990). From the early days of the present century, Detroit's dominant image was firmly cast as entrepreneurial. The growth of the automobile industry soon began to earn Detroit the appellations of dynamic, youthful and vigorous with a reputation as a "specialized city" par excellence: the auto capital of the world, Motor City (Strauss, 1965, p. 25). *Time Magazine* in 1951, in an article celebrating the city's 250th birthday, claimed that the city best represented the spirit of modern twentieth century America, exemplified in its mass production, drive, energy, purpose and fusion of men and machines (*Time*, 1951, quoted Strauss, 1965, p. 106). Detroit claimed for itself the honour of being the "most American" city and the possessor of the most widespread and average national values (Strauss, 1965, pp.106-7).

However, in terms of the urban fabric, little of "what made Detroit Detroit" was symbolized in downtown, a problem for urban development based reimaging strategy in later years. While the Manhattan skyline symbolizes New York and the Golden Gate Bridge San Francisco, Detroit, as a blue collar factory town, has never been able to project such cosmopolitan place images.

Prelude to image collapse

Detroit's physical development agenda in the 1950s already showed acute awareness of the need to project a new image for the city in the face of accelerating suburbanization of people and employment (Tables 4.2 and 4.3). The vehicle was a public sector led growth coalition which sought a new place vision for Detroit. It prefigured the strategy and difficulties of later years under black control.

Growth coalitions can be regarded as a type of "spatial coalition", defined as "an alliance which draws support from a variety of social classes and which seeks to promote what it defines as the interests of the area in question". Such coalitions with "a stake in the area" seek the creation of a dominant, hegemonic view of place and its preferred future. (Pickvance, 1985, pp. 121-122). Growth coalitions, the most widely studied spatial coalitions in the USA, can be subdivided into the executive centred where the driving force is provided by the local state and the business centred where elements of the local business elite make the running (ibid.).

Detroit's coalition in these years was firmly executive centred. Unlike Pittsburgh where a business centred growth coalition set about the task of changing the image of the city (Strauss, 1965, p. 203), the main mover in Detroit was Mayor Albert Cobo. "Little Al – the Big Builder", despite bringing the city close to bankruptcy, was eulogized on his death in 1957 as the Mayor who had "started Detroit on its comeback" (Conot, 1974, p. 445). An urban renewal and major freeway programme combined with publicly pump primed downtown investments were the major instruments for a re-vamping of urban space which, it was predicted, would keep people in and bring them back to the city. Pride of place amongst the grand projects was a new Civic Center complex on the Detroit riverfront. This included a new 20 storey white marble City-County Building and the massive Cobo Hall and Arena, at the time the largest convention facility in the world (ibid.).

This and other futuristic physical developments attempted to give Detroit the gloss of a more cosmopolitan place image (*Detroit News* and Mayor's

Committee for Economic Growth, 1961, p. 15). A 1961 promotional publication called Detroit "America's most accessible city . . . the nation's only major area in which the freeway system begins and ends in the heart of the city" (ibid., p. 12). A Detroit guide book in 1964 presented the Civic Center Area as a "symbol of the New Detroit" (Putman, 1964, p. 11). Actual development trends, however, gave such an upbeat promoted image a ring of hollowness. The private investment response that this first of many mega projects was supposed to generate did not live up to expectations. No speculative office building was forthcoming and the new office buildings which were constructed in Detroit at this time, mainly by banks and utility companies, were in the main not the towering symbols of corporate hegemony found in other American cities. Even the new Ponchatrain Hotel, the first new downtown hotel in over thirty years, proved to be somewhat of a disappointment. On a prime site opposite the new Cobo Hall, the hotel offered only 420 rooms in one tower as opposed to over 1000 and a second tower as originally conceived (Jacoby, 1981).

More importantly, the pace of residential and economic decentralization was quite obviously by the beginning of the 1960s redefining the status of Detroit within the region (Tables 4.2 and 4.3). Between 1954 and 1961 no fewer than 29 new one-stop shopping centres opened in suburban locations (*Detroit News*, 1962, p. 28). New postwar automobile assembly plants had been constructed on land extensive sites in suburban locations such as Warren, Ypsilanti, Wayne and Wixom. In 1959, Detroit's second largest department store, Kern's, closed removing almost a whole downtown block from the tax rolls (Conot, 1974, p. 455). While large scale office decentralization only began in the 1960s, the decision by the Ford Motor Company in the mid 1960s to build its new World Headquarters in suburban Dearborn was a portent of things to come. In the fifties, drawing on permissive state legislation, 22 new suburban cities incorporated themselves on Detroit's doorstep (State of Michigan, 1983a) with the population of the City of Detroit going into sharp decline from the mid 1950s.

This was reflected in the image of the City of Detroit received by outsiders. A *Time Magazine* article carried the caption in October 1961 "Detroit in Decline". It noted the persistent unemployment in the city, the exodus of the white middle class to the suburbs and the blight that was "creeping like a fungus through many of Detroit's proud old neighborhoods" (quoted Fine, 1989, p. 17).

The general image held by blacks of their city was also unfavourable. The black population of Detroit had grown by 175,000 in the decade of the fifties to form nearly 30 per cent of the city's total (Table 4.4). In the early 1960s, in front of the symbol wall of the new City-County building a new sculpture commissioned from Marshall Fredericks was erected. This statue, which remains the official symbol of the City of Detroit, consists of a 16 foot bronze Adonis-like figure holding in his left hand a sphere as the symbol of the Deity (an object complete in itself with no beginning and no end) and in his right a Caucasian family group. It is most doubtful whether Detroit's growing black population identified with this expression of transcendent unity and order.

In the suburbs, the stark reality of black exclusion was clear, shored up by well documented racist practices. (Southeastern Michigan Council of Governments, 1976, p. 14; Widdick, 1972, pp. 141-143; Adrian et al., 1977, p. 18). Only the older political jurisdictions in the Detroit region in 1960 show minority populations of over 1.5 per cent (Table 4.4). In the city of Detroit itself, when the United States Commission on Civil Rights held hearings there in 1960, black leaders vented their concerns about discrimination in employment, education and housing and about the recruitment procedures of the Detroit Police Department (Fine, 1989, p. 6).

Ironically, it was this black dissatisfaction in the late 1950s which precipitated a temporary image revival for the City of Detroit in the 1960s. Heavy handed police tactics sanctioned by Detroit's Mayor Miriani in response to a crime wave associated in the press primarily with blacks led the black leadership to conclude that the city needed a new mayor. With 85 per cent of the black vote, Jerome Cavanagh, a young white liberal took office in January 1962 (Fine, 1989, pp. 15-16). Almost overnight, Detroit gained a new image which rested primarily on the perception that the city under its new mayor had found the road to racial peace with new policies and programmes and with liberal financial assistance from the Democratic White House in Washington (Widdick, 1972, p. 155). Until the riots in July 1967, Detroit enjoyed an image in the national press as a "model city" in terms of its ability to deal with big city problems, especially racial ones. The Motor City or "Motown" appeared as a national symbol of hope, an image which Cavanagh was willing to promote and to a degree believe. In 1965, a writer in *Fortune Magazine* personified the mayor as the "image" of the city's new consensus, "the symbol of the city's aspirations" (Fine, 1989, pp. 32-34). Just four months before the outbreak of Detroit's civil disturbances on 23 July 1967, the National Municipal League and *Look Magazine* designated Detroit as "All-American City" (ibid.). In what should probably have been a stronger lesson for attempts to improve Detroit's image in future years, the city's prestige owed much less to its ambitious building programme and much more to at least a perceived improvement in race relations.

Image collapse: 1967 Detroit riots and the aftermath

In July 1993, Robert Keller, formerly head of economic development in Baltimore and credited with that city's image turnaround, took up an appointment as President of Detroit Renaissance, the major private sector arm of Detroit's then wilting public-private sector partnership. Underlining the fact that Detroit's present image problem dates back to the 1967 riot and the well

TABLE 4.2 Population Change in S.E. Michigan 1930-1990

	Tri-County "Core" Region	Remaining SEMCOG* Counties	City of Detroit	City as % of Tri-County Region
1930	2,177,343	204,852	1,568,662	72
1940	2,377,329	236,515	1,623,452	68
1950	3,016,197	328,596	1,849,568	61
1960	3,762,360	418,994	1,670,144	44
1970	4,199,931	532,460	1,514,063	36
1980	4,043,633	638,498	1,203,339	30
1990	3,912,679	677,789	1,027,974	26

* The counties comprising the Southeast Michigan Council of Governments consist of the core counties of Wayne, Oakland and Macomb in addition to Monroe, Washtenaw, Livingston and St Clair.

Source: US Bureau of the Census, various publications

publicized social and economic ills which have befallen the city subsequently, Keller, in his first major public address, stressed that what was needed in Detroit was "a more positive self image to attract more business and jobs" and that first and foremost was the necessity to hold a "burial ceremony" for the 1967 riots (Henderson, 1993).

The memory to be buried is considerable. *Time Magazine* described the Detroit riots at the time thus:

> In the violent summer of 1967, Detroit became the scene of the bloodiest uprising in a half century and the costliest in terms of property damage in US history. At the week's end, there were 41 known dead, 347 injured, 3,800 arrested. Some 5,000 people were homeless . . . while 1,300 buildings had been reduced to mounds of ashes and bricks and 2,700 businesses sacked (*Time Magazine*, 1967, quoted Widick, 1972, p. 166).

To understand why Detroit's positive image was punctured so quickly, Widick reminds us that in the atmosphere of the Civil Rights movement, the

TABLE 4.3   City of Detroit Percentage Share of Tri-County*
Regional Employment 1948-1987 (Selected Sectors)

Year	Manufacturing %	Retail %	Services %	Wholesale %
1948	60.3	72.6	N/A	90.1
1954	53.5	63.3	N/A	76.8
1958	50.5	54.4	75.3	74.1
1962	40.6	43.4	65.8	68.6
1967	35.8	38.2	60.5	57.9
1972	33.4	28.5	46.7	44.5
1977	27.9	19.1	33.3	32.3
1982	25.7	16.3	24.4	24.8
1987	22.6	12.8	18.4	18.2

*   Wayne, Oakland and Macomb Counties, the core counties of the S.E. Michigan region.

Source: US Bureau of the Census, *Census of Manufacturers, Retail, Services and Wholesalers*, various years.

modest gains of Detroit's blacks in the 1960s were seen as tokenism rather than true social progress (Widick, 1972, p. 162). Mayor Cavanagh admitted after the riot that the Detroit effort had been "like putting a bandaid on a severe wound" (Fine, 1989, p. 37). The National Advisory Commission on Civil Disorders which reported in 1968 on events in Detroit and other American cities stated plainly:

> Race prejudice has shaped our history decisively; it now threatens to affect our future. White racism is essentially responsible for the explosive mixture which has been accumulating in our cities since the end of World War II *(National Advisory Commission,* 1968, p. 10).

In Detroit, attention was drawn in particular to the Detroit Police Department which had sparked off the riots in the city through a raid on an illegal drinking

TABLE 4.4 Minority Composition of Major Detroit Region Jurisdictions : 1960 and 1990*

	% Minority 1960	% Minority 1990		% Minority 1960	% Minority 1990
Wayne County			**Oakland County**		
Allen Park	0.5	2.1	Berkley	0.2	1.5
Dearborn	0.1	2.5	Birmingham	0.4	2.0
Dearborn Heights	N/A	2.7	Clawson	0.3	1.5
Detroit	29.2	78.4	Farmington	0.1	2.2
Ecorse	33.3	43.2	Farmington Hills	N/A	6.1
Garden City	0.2	1.4	Ferndale	0.4	4.2
Gross Point Farms	0.9	1.2	Hazel Park	0.2	3.5
Grosse Point Park	0.5	2.7	Madison Heights	0.3	4.1
Grosse Point Woods	0.1	1.7	Novi	0.3	4.0
Hamtramck	14.5	16.4	Oak Park	0.5	37.2
Haper Woods	0.1	2.2	Pontiac	17.0	48.7
Highland Park	21.4	93.6	Royal Oak	0.2	2.1
Inkster	34.7	63.9	Southfield	0.2	32.1
Lincoln Park	0.1	2.7	Troy	0.2	8.5
Livonia	0.2	2.0			
Melvindale	0.5	6.4	**Macomb County**		
River Rouge	32.4	47.2	East Detroit	0.1	1.3
Riverview	0.1	3.9	Frazer	0.0	1.7
Romulus	N/A	23.8	Mount Clemens	11.7	19.7
Southgate	0.1	3.5	Roseville	1.5	2.7
Taylor	N/A	6.8	St Clair Shores	0.3	1.3
Trenton	0.2	1.9	Sterling Heights	N/A	3.7
Wayne	0.1	9.6	Warren	0.2	2.7
Westland	N/A	5.4			
Woodhaven	N/A	4.0			
Wyandotte	0.1	1.8			

* In the 1990 Census race is broken down by the US Bureau of the Census into the following groups : white; black; American Indian, Eskimo or Aleut; Asian or Pacific Islander; other race. Minority race is defined in this table as all groups excluding whites. Major jurisdictions are defined as all Wayne, Oakland and Macomb County cities with a population greater than 10,000 in 1980.

Source: US Bureau of the Census, *Summary Population & Housing Charac- teristics for 1960 and 1990*

club. The Police Department in Detroit and other cities had come "to symbolize white power, white racism and white repression" (*National Advisory Commission*, 1968, pp. 10-11).

In the aftermath of the riots, white flight to the suburbs accelerated alongside continued economic decentralization. By 1970, the City of Detroit, now with a minority population of almost 45 per cent, due to swelled black in-migration and white out-migration, accounted for only 36 per cent of the core regional population (Table 4.2). At the same time, Detroit's relative economic position declined considerably (Table 4.3). The almost 3 million square feet of office floorspace built in Detroit during the sixties was far outstripped by the over 5 million square feet that sprang up in the suburb of Southfield (Detroit Chamber of Commerce, 1980).

When Coleman Young, on the back of racial demographic trends, was elected mayor of Detroit in 1973, Detroit was fighting the nickname "Murder City" as its homicide rate soared to 127 deaths in the first two months of 1971 alone (Blonston, 1971). Detroit's predicament seemed to be symbolized by the demoralizing move of Motown Records in the early 1970s to the West Coast.

Image reconstruction under Coleman Young: pragmatic optimism 1974-1980

In the mayoral election of 1973, with blacks yet barely a majority in the city, Coleman Young, a militant former union official, necessarily presented a campaign appealing to all groups. However, there was no doubt when Diana Ross sang at his three-day inaugural celebration that blacks now felt they were in charge (Rich, 1989, pp. 104-105). Young's twenty years' tenure and management of the city has had major implications for the image of Detroit.

A central element of reimaging Detroit under Young was a prestige development strategy harking back to the 1950s and concentrating in particular on the rebuilding of downtown. Looking back over the early, optimistic days of this strategy, Young pointed to the attempt at forging a pragmatic accommodation with the private sector. To stem the tide of disinvestment from the city in a climate of heightened inter-state and regional economic competition, downtown had been identified as "where we are able to get the maximum investment of private funds for our dollars" (Young quoted *Detroit News*, 1979). If public subsidy was necessary, then it was, as Young put it to Studs Terkel, the name of the game. While blacks had attained political power, economic power belonged elsewhere:

> I realize the profit motive is what makes things work in America. If Detroit is not to dry up, we must create a situation which allows businessmen to make a profit. That's their self-interest. Ours is jobs. The more they invest in Detroit, the more

124

their interest becomes ours. That is the way the game is played in America today. I don't think there's gonna be a revolution tomorrow. As a young man I thought it. I think the revolution's for someone else (Young, quoted Studs Terkel, *Detroit Free Press*, 1980).

The inspiration for Young's prestige development agenda was the new flagship Detroit Renaissance Center which opened on the riverfront in 1977 and which for a short time promised a reversal of economic fortune for the city under a new growth coalition with the private sector as leader or at least full partner. The instrumental force had been the major economic power elite Detroit Renaissance Inc., formed in 1970 as "an organization of top leaders of the top corporations in the Detroit area pledged to commit their personal talents and some of their corporate clout to effect a physical and economic revitilization of the city of Detroit" (Graves, 1975, p. 186). With a pivotal role played by Henry Ford II, public relations and "corporate responsibility" blended with concern for the continued viability of the central business district and its fixed investments and with a certain basic concern for social stability lest the corporate sector should be seen to be writing off the city entirely. At this time it was also possible to believe that Castells' general argument also applied to Detroit, namely that the city centre was "a keypoint of the self-definition of an economic and cultural elite. The luxury buildings that rise so full of pride in the place of the demolished slums would have no explanation without this analysis" (Castells, 1977, p. 299).

The Detroit Renaissance Center, a towering prestige hotel, office and retail complex dominates the Detroit skyline (Photograph 4.1). It has become, as it was intended, a new symbol for the city featuring in much promotional literature and testifying to the corporate power in Detroit which on this occasion flexed its muscles for the city through the catalytic role of Henry Ford II. The President of Detroit Renaissance Inc. indicated that, when he took his job in 1971, a consensus had been reached by the organization to sponsor such a major reimaging project:

> By the time I arrived it had been decided that the top priority of Detroit Renaissance would be a project of such scale that it would change the image of downtown Detroit as a place that had had a net outflow of investment for 25 years. Beyond that the project had to be so impressive to the eye that everyone would say 'Hey, something important is happening in downtown Detroit'. Because it was to begin the renaissance of the city, it had to take place on the riverfront where Detroit started in the first place. And finally, it had to be of such magnitude that it would cause other new investments downtown. We didn't think new office buildings would have great impact if they were just scattered around downtown along with a new hotel. We needed to have a physical mass (McGill et al., 1978).

At the dedication ceremony for the "Ren Cen" on 14 April 1977, Henry Ford II spoke of the development as a "catalyst for the renewed growth of Detroit".

Photograph 4.1
Detroit's
Renaissance Center:
symbol of city
rebirth in the 1970s.

The *Detroit Free Press* reporting on the event carried a front page picture of a smiling Coleman Young and Henry Ford shaking hands with the Renaissance Center as a backdrop. The accompanying story referred to the achievement and hope symbolized by the Renaissance Center and the public-private sector partnership symbolized in the handshake (*Detroit Free Press*, 1977). In the history of urban flagship developments seldom can a project have promised so much and delivered so little. Yet despite having been described as "inept" and "wasteful" (Molotch, 1988, p. 34) the main problem with the Renaissance Center has been the direction it set for the city's development agenda during the rest of Young's tenure.

The following year a public-private partnership was institutionalized in an overhaul of the city's development apparatus and a strategy of what proved to be folly embarked upon with the city expensively pursuing reluctant private capital and generally trying to build its way out of regional problems of racism, inequality and uncontrolled suburban sprawl. A newly formed private

126

non-profit Detroit Economic Growth Corporation (DEGC) assumed a lead hands-on economic development role for the city involving promotion, deal making and implementation. The board of directors, appointed by the mayor, was drawn from the highest corporate ranks in the private sector and Detroit Renaissance Inc. in particular. With funding from city and private sources, the staff of the Growth Corporation have since its inception also serviced subsidiary development agencies of the city (an Economic Development Corporation and Downtown Development Authority) responsible for specific forms of financial assistance available to new development projects. The other major player in Detroit's economic development strategy has been the city's Community and Economic Development Department (CEDD) under the direct control of the mayor and responsible for legal, regulatory and background financial aspects of development. The DEGC and CEDD working in concert under the watchful eye of Coleman Young sidelined the Detroit Planning Department on development issues and from an early stage this City strategy thus faced charges of project opportunism and lack of an adequate co-ordinated land use plan (Ravitz, 1988). Perhaps owing to the mesmerizing presence of the Renaissance Center and its corporate promise which turned out to be hollow, criticisms that trying to replicate this success might involve excessive opportunity costs for Detroit's neighbourhoods, that a human capital strategy might better address the needs of Detroit residents and that changing Detroit's outside image might involve more prosaic matters such as improving city services and trying to improve difficult race relations, seem to have been crowded out of policy debate in the office of the mayor.

City economic development strategy documents from the mid to late 1970s present a "wish list" of big ticket development projects involving tax breaks and liberal amounts of public assistance from city, state and especially federal sources to encourage further private sector investment all within the spirit of the stated corporate intention of rolling Detroit's renaissance forward. (City of Detroit, 1978a; City of Detroit, 1978b). A Moving Detroit Forward Plan of 1977, drawing on the favoured relationship enjoyed by Young with the Carter White House, proposed no less than $2.5 billion in federal development funds for Detroit over a five year period (City of Detroit, 1977). Within the grand building strategy, various projects, which were to meet varying fates in the 1980s, were still at the concept stage. These included a proposal for a one billion dollar plus subway along Detroit's main commercial corridor, Woodward Avenue, linking the central business district to the suburbs, and a quarter of a billion dollar elevated People Mover designed to tie together various activity centres within the Central Business District (CBD) itself. A $220 million downtown shopping centre (Cadillac Square Mall) was envisaged anchored by three new department stores. A major new hotel, office and upper income apartment complex costing $70 million was forseen for a prime site opposite the Renaissance Center and linked to it by a futuristic skywalk (Millinder Center). The idea of a high rise

127

and high income 2000 unit apartment complex on the Detroit River to the west of the Renaissance Center was being strongly mooted by Max Fisher and Al Taubman, two major multimillionaire local property developers prominent in the Detroit growth coalition of the time, the latter ironically having made his fortune in building suburban shopping malls (Darden et al., 1987, p. 55).

Major projects for which ground breaking actually took place in the 1970s in the wake of the Renaissance Center included a new $31 million public plaza (Hart Plaza) which opened in 1979 on the riverfront between the Renaissance Center and the Detroit Civic Center. The same year saw ground breaking for a second phase of the Renaissance Center itself involving the Rockefeller Realty Corporation and Ford Motor Land Development Corporation in the addition of two new 21 storey octagonal office towers at a cost of $70 million. However, the jewel in the crown of Young's development efforts during these years was undoubtedly the completion in 1979 at a cost of $46.6 million in city financing of a new 21,000 seat sports arena also on the riverfront. The Joe Louis Arena has prevented the loss of the Detroit Red Wings Ice Hockey Team to the suburbs, a real possibility after the departure of the Detroit Lions football team to the Pontiac Silverdome closer to its suburban patrons (English, 1980). Combined with other investments, including $250,000 spent on environmental improvement in the ethnic Greektown restaurant and nightlife area, Detroit looked forward to a downtown which had "the potential to become an around-the-clock activity center: a place to live, work and be entertained" (City of Detroit, 1977, p. 24).

Detroit Renaissance Inc. and the Greater Detroit Chamber of Commerce took on the job of marketing the "Renaissance City". A national image campaign including a supplement in *Fortune Magazine* overrode the Central Business District Association's initially more modest, locally based image campaign, centered on the slogan, "The Image of Our Town starts with ME" (Central Business District Association, 1992, p.12). To showcase the "new Detroit" Detroit Renaissance Inc. brought the Formula One motor racing Grand Prix to Detroit which from 1982 to 1988 was a premier flagship event to reimage the city and to inspire confidence (Zurawik, 1982). To international television viewers, it was the towering corporate structure of the Renaissance Center, around which the course was designed, which formed the dominant symbol of the Motor City.

Actual regional development trends at the end of the 1970s put such boosterism in perspective. Continued white flight reduced the population of Detroit by over 300,000 between 1970 and 1980 (Table 4.2), increasing the minority population to two thirds. As one reviewer noted in 1979:

Reading the press releases about Detroit's renaissance, it's hard to believe we're in a fight for survival. But we are, and the odds on Detroit's winning are not necessarily improving (Cheyfitz, 1979, p. 57).

128

The reviewer noted that despite tenuous economic revival downtown, most of Detroit's 139 square miles had not been touched by the developers' renaissance and that with a shrinking property tax base, the city was being deprived of the ability to provide essential services. The city's share of core regional employment fell substantially across the board in the 1970s (Table 4.3) and the near bankruptcy in 1979 of the Chrysler Corporation, with fifteen plants in the City of Detroit, was enough to dent even official optimism (Woutat, 1980).

In the 1970s, over 100 Economic Development Corporations, with powers to offer low interest financing to new business investments, had been established in Detroit's suburbs (State of Michigan, 1983). In the heightening Detroit versus suburbs economic competition, the city in the 1970s spawned 6 million square feet of new office space but suburban downtowns in Southfield and Troy together built 10 million square feet (Detroit Chamber of Commerce, 1980). In 1970, running parallel with plans for the Renaissance Center, Henry Ford II had begun development of a massive 2,300 acre site surrounding Ford's World Headquarters in suburban Dearborn. The intent was to create over a number of years a new Dearborn town centre and surrounding residential community (Wilson, 1993). Against such developments, Detroit's growth coalition in the 1970s has been described as simply providing the "rhetorical cover" that enabled many businesses to get out of town (Chafets, 1990, p. 22).

Nevertheless, by 1980 the image of Detroit held by black residents and by outsiders had changed. Although the Renaissance Center was criticized for being symbolically aloof from the rest of the city clustered behind a massive fortress-like berm which runs along its front (Bulkeley, 1977), this physical ambivalence was undoubtedly overshadowed by the image of Young brokering Detroit's development agenda at the "big table" with the white corporate elite. This image of the mayor dealing eyeball to eyeball with the white economic establishment on his own terms was deliberately cultivated by Young and was an important element in giving blacks, through himself, a sense of ownership of the city. It must, however, be set alongside other measures designed to make black Detroiters feel that at last they had a stake in the city's future. Of black appointments to city office none was more important than the appointment of a black Chief of Police. The central issue of Young's first mayoral election campaign had been the erosion of black confidence in the city's predominantly white police department (Bledsoe, 1990, pp. 14-15). By 1980, due to an aggressive affirmative action policy, 35 per cent of the police department was black, with a high proportion of these officers ranking above patrolman (*Time*, 1980, p. 26). In the same year, 94 per cent of Detroit blacks held a favourable impression of the mayor and his pursuance of such policies (Kiska, 1980, p. 36).

In 1980 there were also signs that Detroit was shaking off the tag of "Murder City" and was tentatively beginning to turn its image to outsiders around. The crime rate had receded to become more in line with that of the average large American city (*Congressional Quarterly*, 1980, p. 1927) and national media coverage focused on the potential for recovery symbolized by Detroit's Renaissance Center and the city's determinedly upbeat mayor, even if inevitably harbouring some doubts as to ultimate success when measured against the scale of the city's problems (Guzzardi, 1980; *Time*, 1980). At this time, it was still possible, in the face of scepticism, to argue that flagship megastructures and developments such as Chicago's Water Tower Place, Atlanta's Peachtree Center, Baltimore's Charles Center and Inner Harbour and Detroit's Renaissance Center signified the comeback of cities in general in competition with their suburbs (Von Eckardt, 1979). Riding on such fragile optimism, Young, in 1980, had enticed the Republican party to hold its national convention in Detroit's new Joe Louis Arena. It put the city on the convention map and was a sign of a short lived national image turn-a-round (*Congressional Quarterly*, 1980).

Renaissance postponed : Detroit's public-private partnership under strain, 1981-1987

While there is inevitably a degree of arbitrariness in periodizing the flow of events, nevertheless, 1987 marks the next significant watershed in understanding the evolution of Detroit's image led development agenda. Twenty years after the Detroit riots, the year saw the death of Henry Ford II, hitherto the most important private sector face in Detroit's loose coalition of growth interests. More importantly, November 1987 saw publication of a private sector Strategic Plan for Detroit which, with its luke-warm and even sour reception in the mayor's office, represented the last gasp of Detroit's public-private sector partnership under Young.

The context for Detroit's development agenda in the 1980s had changed significantly. While the city was already endeavouring to stave off fiscal crisis with an accumulated budget deficit in 1981 of $132 million (City of Detroit, 1981), the Reagan and Bush years were to see a drastic decline in federal revenue support from 26 per cent of Detroit's budget in 1980 to only 8 per cent in 1991. State budgetary support, within the spirit of Reagan's New Federalism, showed a small proportionate increase from 18 per cent to 22 per cent over the same period, but revenues to fund city operations had to be increasingly derived from local sources (Citizens Research Council, 1991, p. 2).

As a response to national economic decline, the reinvigoration of the private sector within a resurgence of enthusiasm for the cultural tradition of "privatism" was to involve an emphasis on individual solutions and a retrenchment of the public sector (Barnekov et al., 1989). At a time when competitive cut-throat civic entrepreneurialism was to move up a gear, it was a mixed blessing to be imaged as the "Motor City". With the American auto

130

industry at the heart of debates over lack of competitiveness (Bluestone and Harrison, 1982) and with the scheduling for closure by the Chrysler Corporation of seven of its fifteen production facilities within the city of Detroit between 1980 and 1983 (City of Detroit, 1983, p. 9), this long standing appellation was likely to conjure up rust-belt images of deindustrialization.

While the eyes of the regional corporate establishment were increasingly focusing on market survival, the development agenda of the Young administration continued to concentrate on big ticket, image conscious projects, with the city increasingly swimming against the tide to keep a development momentum going. An early indignity was the sale in 1982 by Ford Motor Company and other local equity partners of Phase I of the Renaissance Center itself after heavy accumulating losses. Detroit's symbol of rebirth ignominiously passed at a knock down price to an investor group headed by a developer from Chicago (Fireman et al., 1982). Of more than symbolic importance was the closure in 1982, after 100 years in the city, of Hudsons, Detroit's last major department store (Stanton, 1982). The decision was a death blow to city plans to revive retailing downtown by incorporating Hudsons as one anchor store into a major new shopping precinct (the Cadillac Center project).

The failure to secure a subway or at least a light rail system for the city on its main commercial corridor, also a key component of Young's Moving Detroit Forward Strategy of the 1970s, ranks as a considerable disappointment during this period (Neill, 1988). While major federal funding for construction was actually on offer, dating back to a commitment made by the Ford administration, this came to nothing because of federal insistence that regional consensus be reached on a dedicated local revenue source to subsidize fares. Already in 1981 Young had referred to suburban opposition to such underwriting of a subway as "racism and bigotry by suburban politicians seeking favour with their constitutents" (McClure, 1981). In the opinion of a senior transportation planner in Detroit, to suburbanites a subway conjures up images of graffitti and marauding violent blacks being given easier access to whites beyond the city limits (Interview, 1991). While the imagery of a surface light rail system was likely to meet with less suburban opposition, Detroit's mayor tended to the view that anything other than a subway would be an insult to the city (Neill, 1988). Here one researcher has pointed out how "fantastic imagery" is now the most important factor in the making of urban rail investments in US cities : "rail is not something emerging from a process of analytic reason but from drives such as penis envy and the lust for power" (Richmond, 1989). It is likely that, in the failed reimaging bid of Young for a Detroit subway, the price paid in the resulting regional transportation stalemate has been an under-investment in much needed bus transportation (Smart, 1989).

A number of other megaprojects were, however, either substantially underway or completed during this period. By far and away the largest were the opening in 1985 of a new General Motors assembly plant on the site of a bulldozed neighbourhood within the city of Detroit and the coming into service in 1987 of the Detroit downtown People Mover. The former project, in the words of Young's official biographer, was "aimed at the retention of jobs and the city's image as the center of the American automobile industry" (Rich, 1989, p. 170). The latter, by putting an automated, elevated monorail ring around the CBD "would change the skyline and advance a new futuristic image of the city" (Rich, 1989, p. 192). Both projects were pursued aggressively by Detroit's mayor with a heavy commitment of the city's overstretched treasury and protest concerning the heavy opportunity costs involved.

The General Motors project involved the demolition of an entire neighbourhood. Following an offer by the corporation to the city in 1980 to spend part of its $40 billion world wide investment programme on a new assembly plant in Detroit if 500 acres of land could be found, Poletown on the city's eastside and overlapping with the enclave municipality of Hamtramck was designated for demolition. In a Herculean effort, bordering on desperation but aimed at stemming the tide of disinvestment from the city, the General Motors project represented the Young administration's most important attempt up to that time at redevelopment outside the CBD. The end of 1981 was to register the demolition of sixteen churches, twenty five bars and stores, thirty three warehousing and industrial sites, two public schools, one hospital, one post office, six petrol stations and one thousand five hundred homes in the city's ethnic Poletown neighbourhood (Blonston, 1981). Hailed by General Motor's chairman as signifying the "industrial rebirth" of Detroit (*Citizen*, 1980) the Poletown project, creating 3,000 auto industry jobs, involved heavy federal, state and local subsidies to the value of $200 million excluding a twelve year property tax abatement from an ailing city to the world's largest industrial corporation.

In the downtown People Mover, Detroit has likewise paid a heavy financial price for a project with a major image component (Photograph 4.2). Lobbied for heavily by Young but starting out in 1982 as a project of the regional transportation authority (SEMTA) with primary funding from the federal government, the People Mover was taken over amidst considerable acrimony by the city in 1985 when its future was in grave doubt because of cost over-runs which Detroit's suburbs were not prepared to meet. The People Mover construction itself, with many cranes in evidence, was seen by Young as adding to Detroit's "building reputation" and thus inspiring investor confidence. And the project, by tying together spatially fragmented land uses downtown, would bolster Detroit's aspirations as a service centre with convention business as an anchor (Rich, 1989, pp. 192-193). However, the potential of Detroit's futuristic People Mover has remained unrealized despite the fact that Miami is the only other major US city to have one in its CBD. From the beginning, ridership figures were disappointingly low and

Photograph 4.2   The Detroit Downtown People Mover

expected pedestrian activity around its stations has not materialized. The system, while fully automated, costs more money to operate than it takes in as farebox revenue (Smart, 1989).

Of lesser scale than Poletown or the People Mover but, nevertheless, ranking as first tier prestige commercial and residential developments, a handful of projects in particular stand out which were either completed or substantially underway between 1981 and 1987. All were the recipients of twelve year property tax abatements and in most cases other substantial public subsidies. The successful letting of a new 350 unit upmarket apartment building (Trolley Plaza) completed in 1981 proved that downtown living was marketable in an industrial city with no such tradition. This paved the way for what remains Detroit's residential flagship development, two multi-storey residential apartment towers which opened on the Detroit riverfront west of the Renaissance Center in 1985. Riverfront West and its marina together with the Renaissance Center dominate the Detroit waterfront as seen from Canada. Riverfront West is Detroit's major attempt so far at establishing an image of downtown residential cosmopolitanism, taken for granted by its Midwest rival Chicago. A twelve year tax abatement, saving the developers $700,000 annually, reinforces the fact that reimaging the city in Detroit's case has not come cheap (Detroit Downtown Development Authority, 1983).

A second commercial prestige project also opened in 1985. The Millinder Center, consisting of a 32 storey 340 unit apartment tower, adjoining 20 storey first class hotel and additional office and retail space, is connected to both the nearby Renaissance Center and the City-County Building by glass enclosed skywalks. With a People Mover station passing through the atrium space, the development is an impressive image show piece. Again the price tag has been considerable. On a $71 million project, direct private developer equity has been only $7 million. A $33 million long term loan from the State of Michigan Pension Fund, a $13 million federal Urban Development Action Grant, and $25 million in various types of loan subsidy and grant from the city of Detroit have been the price of spawning this additional critical mass of development which attempts to link the bunkered Renaissance Center safely to the rest of the Central Business District (ibid.). On a somewhat more modest scale, 1985 also saw the opening with public subsidy of Trappers Alley in the city's downtown Greektown district consisting of 180,000 square feet of new restaurant space and speciality retailing. In 1987, the Vice President of the DEGC pointed to the Trolly Plaza, Riverfront Apartments and Millinder Center as having built up a core of activity and confidence which was set to snowball. The optimistic prediction was that in three or four years time market forces would work on their own and that the "blanket of comfort" involved by way of public subsidy in such future projects would no longer be necessary (Dobson, quoted Barron, 1987). Other major developments underway at the time were still, however, to varying degrees dependent on the public purse. While major new buildings such as Riverfront Apartments and the Joe Louis Arena had filled out Detroit's riverfront west of the CBD, Stroh River Place and Harbortown in particular represented the extension of the "downtown renaissance" to Detroit's east riverfront. After the ending in 1985 of a 135 year brewing tradition, when Stroh's announced it would no longer produce in Detroit (the unthinkable equivalent of Guinness moving out of Dublin), the city was forced to settle for the Stroh Corporation becoming a property developer on 30 acres of run down land $1^1/_2$ miles or so east of the Renaissance Center. Stroh's corporate headquarters were temporarily relocated to River Place in a substantial mixed use development consisting primarily of offices and upmarket riverside apartments and penthouses (City of Detroit, 1985). Harbortown, an adjacent development, complements River Place in revitalizing and reimaging this stretch of Detroit's industrially denuded riverfront to project a more attractive image of an exciting city lifestyle with consumption and recreational behaviour to match. Also begun in the mid 1980s, a 48 acre site by 1987 had begun to sprout more upmarket penthouses, apartments and townhouses with tennis courts and swimming pools, all based around a marina and lagoons with moorings for about 150 boats (City of Detroit, 1985; Barron, 1987). The project was, however, dependent on $6.5 million of federal Urban Development Action Grant funds and various other forms of state and city financial assistance (City of Detroit, 1985).

Despite such on the ground achievements and associated promotional hype, it was clear by 1987, on the twentieth anniversary of the riots, that the aspirations of the Moving Detroit Forward programme, put together in Mayor Young's first term of office, were not being matched by reality. The property and flagship led Renaissance agenda attempting with the grand gesture to turn the image of the city around, thus to inspire investor confidence, stem the tide of disinvestment, invite suburbanites to rediscover the true potential of the city, and create positive spin-off or trickle down effects to Detroit's poor neighbourhoods, was palpably not coming to pass. An array of hard fought for, one-off prestige projects could not hide the reality of the devastating impact of the wider dynamics of regional economic change and racial polarization on the city. Detroit's image led developments seemed increasingly divorced from the problems and concerns of the city's neighbourhoods. Correspondingly, the marketing image campaign of the city adopted in 1984 settled on the rather modest if risqué slogan "Do it in Detroit" to encourage some suburbanites to shop and dine in downtown.

The nature of racial and economic polarization between city and suburbs, which led increasingly during these years to outspoken frustration and anger on the part of Coleman Young, will be examined later. However, in terms of raw numbers, in the 1980s Detroit lost over 175,000 people (Table 4.2; Map 4.3). The suburb of Southfied had become the new downtown of white Detroit and, moreover, was acting as a magnet for members of the black middle class anxious to leave the problems of the central city (Chafets, 1990, p. 139; Table 4.4). Despite the number of manufacturing jobs never recovering after the recession of the early eighties and the competitive shake out in the auto industry in particular, by 1987 total jobs in the Detroit region had increased to beyond pre-1980 levels (Figs. 4.1 and 4.2). This job growth involving a large expansion of service employment was, however, focused in Detroit's suburbs with the relative economic position of the city again declining significantly between 1982 and 1987 (Table 4.3). In 1987 the unemployment rate in the city of Detroit stood at over 20 per cent while the rate for the region as a whole had dropped to around 6 per cent (City of Detroit, 1992). More telling, given the low labour force participation rate in Detroit as people became discouraged, is the Census Bureau estimate that in 1985 only half of black men aged 25 to 64 in the Detroit area were employed (Farley, 1987). While in 1979 22 per cent of all City of Detroit residents lived in households with income below the poverty line, by 1984 this had increased to 43 per cent (Neithercut, 1987, p. 8).

A task force report on unemployment in Detroit reporting in 1987 singled out "one overriding and alarming fact of life in Detroit : the chronic and severe unemployment among minorities between the ages of sixteen and thirty" (Detroit Strategic Planning Project, 1987, p. 59). The closure of Hudsons and the departure of Stroh's had been body blows to the city's economic development plans. The Poletown project involved the rationaliza-

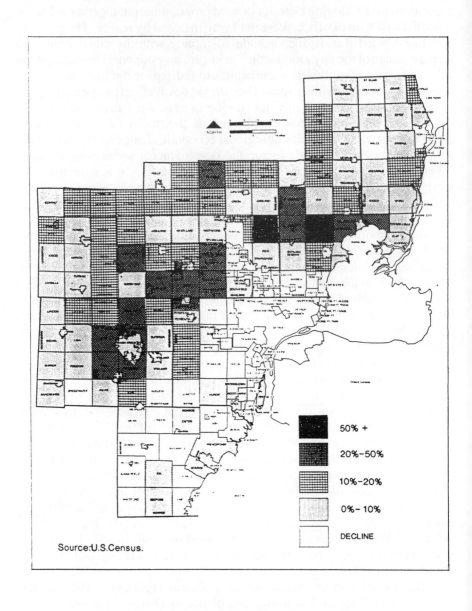

Source:U.S.Census.

Map 4.3   Population change in S.E. Michigan 1980–1990

tion of General Motors jobs within Detroit rather than the provision of net additional jobs. Even the president of Detroit Renaissance Inc. in relation to the departure of Stroh's noted that "the symbolism of another major facility becoming obsolete in the inner city has its negative image connotations. It makes revitalization of the city tougher" (quoted Gavrilovich and Blossom, 1985).

Perhaps out of embarrassment at such disinvestment of Detroit Renaissance Inc. members from the city of Detroit, the organization in 1985 initiated a Detroit Strategic Planning Project (DSPP). The idea was to breathe new life into a public-private partnership that had begun to turn sour by spending $1 million in private sector raised resources to investigate and prepare action plans for the major problems which were ailing the city (Neill, 1991). In a major exercise in private sector led planning, five task forces encompassing crime, education, image, jobs and race relations reported in 1987 (DSPP, 1987). The luke warm reaction of Detroit's mayor to what appeared a mixed bag of band-aid solutions signalled the end of Detroit's public-private sector partnership under Young (Neill, 1991).

From the mid 1980s, the image of Detroit, which was increasingly presented by Young and which struck a chord with a majority of the city's residents, was of a black city surrounded by hostile white suburbs. That this was a successful way of consolidating political power is suggested by a poll in 1985 which showed that the mayor enjoyed 82 per cent support amongst Detroit blacks (Rich, 1989, p. 116). In a notorious interview with the Canadian Broadcasting Corporation in 1986, Young declared that he was not in favour of unilateral disarming of the people of Detroit while the city faced hostile suburbs armed to the teeth (Chafets, 1990, p. 155; Mackie, 1987). By 1987 a new sculpture had appeared downtown in a more prominent position than the bronze Adonis which symbolized the aspirations of a previous Detroit. Now a huge clenched black fist, another tribute to the Detroit boxer Joe Louis, swings in the middle of Jefferson Avenue, the city's thoroughfare along the riverfront (Photograph 4.3). What undoubtedly signifies determination with a measure of defiance in Detroit undoubtedly also signifies menace beyond Eight Mile Road, Detroit's northern boundary line.

To outsiders generally, the image of Detroit had deteriorated precipitously since the false dawn of the visit of the Republican Party Convention in 1980. In 1983, with care packages arriving in Detroit from Germany, it was reported that Detroit was seen as "the leading symbol of social and economic failure in America" (*Detroit Free Press*, 1983). In 1987, the *New York Times* observed how various downtown developments in Detroit were "promising, but painfully slow and isolated. The run-down artery (of Woodward Avenue) once symbolized the city's blue-collar glory . . . Now drug dealers use the corner telephone booth as an office" (quoted DSPP, 1987, p. 94). With 686 homicides in Detroit in 1987 (almost 63 per 100,000 residents) the city was again the Murder Capital of the USA (Chafets, 1990, p. 30). Reporting on this

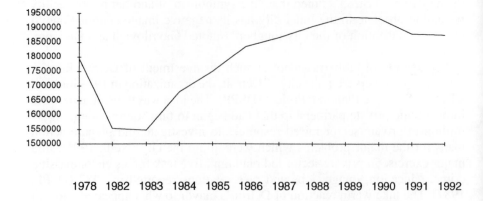

Figure 4.1   Total Employment in Detroit MSA* 1978–92

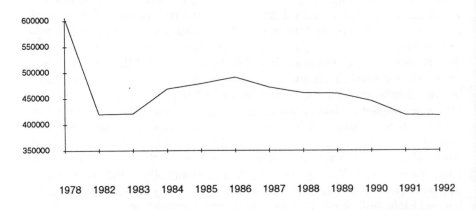

Figure 4.2   Manufacturing Employment in Detroit MSA* 1978–92

* There is a break in the continuity of the data from the end of 1983 due to the US Census Bureau redefinition of the Detroit Metropolitan Statistical Area. The effect is to slightly increase the values for 1984 onwards.

Source: Compiled from data supplied by Michigan Employment Security Commission, Bureau of Research and Statistics.

**Photograph 4.3
The Fist of Joe
Louis: a new symbol
for Detroit since the
mid 1980s.**

in the British *Guardian* newspaper, one journalist captioned her story by describing Detroit as "the city of the six-year-old with a machine gun". More children under the age of sixteen were shooting and killing each other in Detroit than in any other city in the United States (Mackie, 1987). When the twentieth anniversary of the riots brought what Young called a media "feeding frenzy" to the city, the report of the DSPP not surprisingly argued that "at this juncture in Detroit's history, it is especially and strategically important that Detroit have a clearly defined and managed image to present to the world" (DSPP, 1987, p. 96). However, six years later, at the end of Young's tenure as mayor in December 1993, this was precisely what the city did not have.

City under siege : Detroit 1988-1993

The final years of the Young administration saw an embattled, almost bunker mentality, which defined relations between the black city of Detroit, the

139

"hostile white suburbs" and the white corporate establishment. With the rhetoric of renaissance more difficult to sustain, the planning director of America's sixth largest city was to present it as comparable with a Third World city struggling for survival in a post colonial situation (Chafets, 1990, pp. 177-178).

Even the Los Angeles riots in 1992 did not make "the thousand pound gorilla of the urban crisis" central to presidential electoral debate (Davis, 1993, p. 5). At the level of State Government in Michigan, for Detroit it was to be a case of moving to even lower importance in gubernatorial priorities. A Democratic governor, who had for eight years placed urban issues "on the backburner" while endeavouring to improve the competitiveness of the state's automotive economy in general, was replaced in 1991 by a right wing, budget cutting Republican (Neill, 1991). Detroit was to hit the financial skids in 1989 with consecutive annual multimillion-dollar budget shortfalls throughout the rest of Mayor Young's tenure (*Detroit News*, 1993a). Detroit Renaissance Inc., with its members living and investing in the suburbs, had been reduced to the status of "a joke" in the opinion of the president of the Detroit Central Business District Association (Edgecomb, 1993). However, the thought of accusations of hypocrisy and bad faith did not restrain the Chairman of Detroit Renaissance Inc. from stating publicly in June 1993 that the mayor was the problem in Detroit's deteriorated public-private sector partnership and should go (Glancy, 1993).

The image-conscious blue ribbon megaproject continued to be the hallmark of Young's development strategy up to the end (Figure 4.3). While in the beginning such a policy could be generously given the benefit of the doubt, latterly it appeared as quixotic. Two new skyscrapers substantially funded by public subsidy arose downtown. The 29 storey and 500,000 square feet Madden office building, adjacent to the Cobo Conference Center, opened with the aid of $9.5 million in various forms of public financing in 1990 (DEGC, 1992). The even larger 44 storey and one million square feet One Detroit Center opened with the aid of $38.5 million in various forms of public subsidy in 1992 (ibid.). Located next to the City-County Building at the foot of Woodward Avenue, the Gothic design office structure introduces monumental postmodernism to Detroit's central business district. A major $225 million city financed expansion to the Cobo Conference and Exhibition Center had been completed in 1988 enabling Detroit to boast the fifth largest convention facility in the United States and the largest contiguous exhibition area of any centre in the country (DEGC, 1991). By 1992 a $25 million expansion to Detroit City Airport with a planned $16 million runway extension to come was another much touted cornerstone of Young's ongoing redevelopment plan the city. Conceived to compete for commuter traffic with Detroit Metropolitan Airport in the suburbs, the east side city project came in for criticism as being built more on grandiose wishful thinking and image considerations than any sensible cost-benefit analysis (Hamada et al., 1993).

140

However, without doubt the most "successful" grand project realized during the final years of the Young administration was a repetition of the Poletown experience, this time to secure a new Chrysler assembly plant within the city's borders. In January 1992 Chrysler launched production of a new Jeep Grand Cherokee at its Jefferson North Assembly Plant on Detroit's east side. To retain 2,500-3,000 Chrysler jobs relocated from an out-moded facility meant more radical urban surgery at considerable financial cost. The acquisition and clearance by the city of a 380 acre site for Chrysler involved the demolition of 630 homes and 76 commercial premises and the relocation of 3,500 people (City of Detroit, 1990). Including site clean up and infrastructure costs, the total public sector bill was $264 million (ibid.). The Chrysler Corporation characterization of the project not unnaturally chose to emphasize an all too rare reinvestment in the city rather than the background picture of general disinvestment:

> This new assembly plant not only symbolizes a renewed commitment to the City of Detroit, to Chrysler's experienced workforce, and to the environment, it also represents Chrysler's recognition of the importance of coalescing public and private resources to redevelop urban America (Chrysler Corporation, 1992).

Other major developments realized in the closing years of Young's mayoral tenure included the building of the first new residential subdivision in the city in decades and a revival of the downtown theatre district on run down Woodward Avenue, the city's main commercial corridor adversely commented on by the *New York Times* in 1987. The former, Victoria Park subdivision begun in 1992 near the new Chrysler plant, was only possible because the city had readied the land for construction complete with new infrastructure and then given it away for development (*Detroit News*, 1993b). The revival of Detroit's theatre district in the northern fringe of downtown with some financial help from the city was actually triggered by the catalytic role of a local pizza baron Mike Illich, Chief Executive Officer of Little Caesar's Pizza, who opened the renovated 5,000 seat Fox theatre in 1989. Financial institutions in Detroit had notably refused to invest in the project of a revitalized theatre district (Williams, 1987). The Fox, the largest remaining movie palace in the United States, is now complemented by the renovated State and Gem theatres and various upmarket restaurants and there was speculation in 1993 that, with a possible Detroit casino and new sports stadium as part of the future plans of Mike Illich for development around the theatre district, the city could sprout a new entertainment and sporting hub (Lam, 1993; Gallagher, 1993a). Indeed in 1993, one could be forgiven for thinking that Detroit's place vision owed more to the local "Big Cheese" than to the local "Big Three" automakers. In 1994 plans for the realization of "Foxtown" proceed with the carefully crafted help of image makers from Walt Disney (Goodin, 1994).

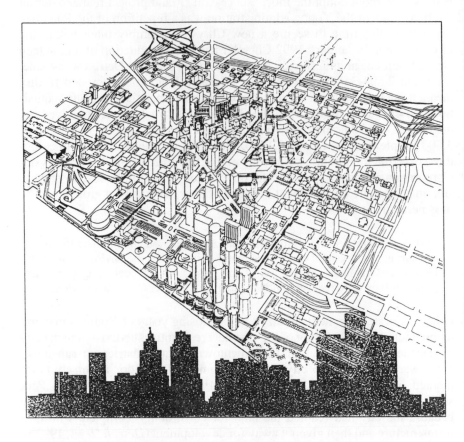

Figure 4.3   Detroit Economic Growth Corporation: Long-range development concept for downtown Detroit (circa 1987)

Despite such talk in 1993 of a renewed renaissance in Detroit based on entertainment, the arts and sport, actual wider development trends warranted a much less sanguine appraisal. Downtown, the DEGC was forced to write off a $7.5 million loan to the Madden Building shortly after it opened in order to ensure the struggling development's continued viability. One of Detroit's older skyscrapers, the Ford Building, was sold for a bargain basement price in 1991. And the One Detroit Center, the newest skyscraper with its one million square feet of new Class A office space, had triggered off another round of "musical buildings". As a review of the Detroit office market pointed out in 1992:

Most of the tenants filling the new buildings come from other downtown offices, leaving landlords the job of wooing new lessees from other buildings in a merry-go-round of deals that might include no rent for several months or free upgrading of space (Detroit Chamber of Commerce, 1992).

In 1993, a task force put together by the Central Business District Association (CBDA) reported on the major problem of vacant and deteriorated commercial buildings downtown (CBDA, 1993). The weakness of the office market in the CBD was remarked upon in that "only a few tenants with major space requirements have moved into the District within the past 15 years" (ibid., p. 6). One of these was the relocation of the Little Caesar's Pizza headquarters from suburban Farmington Hills to the refurbished Fox theatre and its crowning ten storey office building. Detroit's plight was unwittingly summed up by the director of the city's Community and Economic Development Department when celebrating the move as "the first time a major company has moved into the city in more than thirty years" (Moten, quoted in City of Detroit, 1988, p. 77).

While the construction of new office developments with substantial public assistance in the form of grants, loans and tax incentives was regarded in the CBDA report as necessary to keep existing tenants in downtown, it was leaving millions of square feet of office space, particularly in the deteriorating buildings of the north and west ends of the CBD, either vacant or less than 50 per cent occupied. Nearly 20 per cent of the 500 buildings in the CBD in 1992 were totally vacant (CBDA, 1993, pp. 1-2). Other downbeat notes to Detroit's development agenda in the closing phase of the Young administration must also include the fact that no major hotel building took off downtown based upon optimism over the enhanced convention potential of the expanded Cobo Hall. And in May 1993 the decision of Southwest Airlines, the major carrier at Detroit's City Airport accounting for 90 per cent of passengers, to relocate to Detroit Metro called into question one of the mayor's pet grand projects (Bratt et al., 1993). In the same month, to the consternation of the mayor and neighbourhood leaders in Detroit, the city's Ombudsman presented a proposal to the city council suggesting that residential abandonment and population thinning was so bad that the city should close some neighbourhoods down (Map 4.4). With populations relocated to viable areas and the cost of basic city servicing reduced, blighted areas would be landscaped and parts of the Motor City returned to pasture (Usborne, 1993).

In suburban Oakland County on the other hand, pasture land was being devoured for development. From 1979 to 1992, Oakland County lost only 5 per cent of its jobs in manufacturing and gained 63 per cent in non-manufacturing jobs making it the "economic front runner" in Michigan (Grimes and Fulton, 1993, p. 8). This success, in contrast to the city of Detroit's continued overall economic decline, was in part due to state industrial policy promoting the northwest Oakland County suburbs as the anchor of "Automation Alley" hosting the largest concentration of machine vision and robotics firms in the United States (Hill, 1990, p. 52). In 1992, when the Chrysler Corporation announced that it would be moving its corporate headquarters from Highland Park, an enclave "city" surrounded by the city of Detroit, it was not to Detroit's CBD, but to its Auburn Hills technical centre in north Oakland County. A major report published in 1991 by the Southeastern Michigan Council of Governments predicted that if such sprawl continued, by the year 2010, 40 per cent more land would be needed in the region for development despite population growth of only 5 per cent (Southeastern Michigan Council of Governments, 1991, p. xii).

There can be little doubt that at the end of the Coleman Young administration in 1993 Detroit was firmly reimaged in the eyes of the majority of its residents as a black city. One of its African American Congressmen described it as "the black capital of the United States" (Crockett, quoted Chafets, 1990, p. 121), while the director of the city's welfare department put it in interview thus:

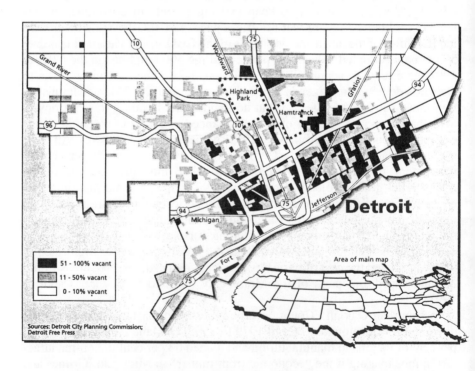

Map 4.4   Residential abandonment in the City of Detroit
©**The Economist, May 1993**

Detroit is an environment where you can forget about being black. I don't think about being black, because everybody is. This is a very different place from the South Bronx, LA or Jackson, Mississippi. Here, our government is black (Cassandra Smith-Gray, quoted Chafets, 1990, pp. 178-179).

Or in the words of one outside observer:

Young may not have provided [black Detroiters] with the safest streets or most efficient services; nor has he been able to raise their standard of living. But he has given his constituents something even more valuable : a feeling of empowerment and personal worth. Detroit is one of the few places in the country where blacks can live in a sympathetic, black-oriented milieu (Chafets, 1990, p. 178).

While prestige development projects, sometimes bearing the name of prominent black Detroiters (Joe Louis Arena, Millinder Center), gave some physical expression to empowerment, of greater importance in black identification with the city was political control itself. Already by 1980, under black administration, African American incumbency at city managerial and professional levels had increased to 32-42 per cent owing to political appointments and affirmative action (Eisinger, quoted Fainstein and Fainstein, 1993). By 1990, the Detroit police department had the most integrated force of any major city in the US with more than half of its senior officers being black (Chafets, 1990, p. 39). In 1993, in fact, a court ruling declared that affirmative action to promote blacks to sergeant within the police department was no longer necessary (*Detroit Free Press*, 1993). Survey results in 1990 indicated, however, that while there were no longer black/white differences in evaluations of the quality of police protection in Detroit, overall the quality itself was deemed to be low (Bledsoe, 1990, p. 15). In the wake of the Rodney King trial which pointed the finger at racist brutality within the Los Angeles Police Department and sparked the LA riots in April 1992, Detroit remained calm despite outbreaks of violence in other cities (Read et al., 1991). During a serious local incident in November 1992, when a black male Detroiter died after suffering blows from white police officers, Young issued a statement saying that he had not worked for years to change a once violently racist police department only to see his efforts sabotaged by such an act (*Economist*, 1992). Owing to such comments, which tried to make the point that the general image of the Detroit Police Department was not a violent racist one, Detroit again remained calm. Two Detroit police officers were subsequently convicted of second degree murder.

Sensitivity to Detroit being perceived by its inhabitants as a black city was revealed in the dissatisfaction with a poster produced by Detroit Renaissance Inc. to market the 1993 Detroit Grand Prix which since 1989 had been downgraded to Indy cars owing to the Motor City's inability to meet the financial and other demands of Formula One organizers (Detroit Renaissance Inc., 1993). The poster juxtaposes Georges Seurat's pointillist painting of

French leisure, "Sunday Afternoon on the Island of La Grande Jatte", with Indy cars and Detroit's skyline (Photograph 4.4). The people in the poster are all white which drew black claims that it misrepresented the city's image. The Executive Director of the Race Relations Council of Metropolitan Detroit commented:

> It happens all the time. It's a slap in the face. It builds walls. It's sending a message that you're not important even when it's done without ill-intent (Parish, quoted Atkins, 1993).

One prominent black business leader also commented:

> Subliminally it's saying to white folks, 'We aren't looking for a bunch of black folks to be here, either, so come on down. You're safe' (Coleman, quoted Atkins, 1992).

The schizophrenia involved in marketing Detroit brought out by the rather trivial poster issue was remarked on by one Detroit media consultant:

> These people never admit that it's a black city. They always look for some symbolism. The Ren Cen is not Detroit (Mongo, quoted Bratt, 1993).

However, the haemorrhaging of the black middle class to the suburbs is indicative of a less than universal African American willingness to identify positively with "the black city of Detroit". In the words of one black critic of Coleman Young in 1988:

> The participants in the 'black flight' will not hesitate to tell you that they are leaving because the elected black political leadership has failed to provide protection for them and their families . . . At some point black politicians must be held accountable (Dilliard, 1988, p. 566).

While a closer examination of arguments relating to the relative importance of white racism and black responsibility in accounting for the problems of Detroit is dealt with in the concluding section, Bledsoe has noted how in Detroit a downward spiral results from the departure of such quality conscious residents, which in turn produces a further deterioration in the quality of municipal services (Bledsoe, quoted MacGregor, 1993, p. 11).

The persistently negative image of Detroit at the end of Young's tenure, despite a twenty year image led development strategy, was perceived by business interests as a serious handicap for the Detroit region generally. The Greater Detroit Chamber of Commerce reported in 1993 that "the local and national reporting of criminal activity, the most visible image deterrent, appears to have kept significant improvement out of reach" (Greater Detroit

ITT AUTOMOTIVE DETROIT GRAND PRIX XII

JUNE 11, 12, 13, 1993

Photograph 4.4   Controversial poster for the 1993 Detroit Grand Prix: a place image without African Americans based on a painting by George Seurat ©Detroit Grand Prix and Detroit Renaissance Inc. Reproduced with permission.

147

Chamber of Commerce, 1993). The *Detroit News* with a primarily suburban readership was more scathing:

> The city [Detroit], the very purpose of which is to deliver basic services to its citizens, charges high prices for inefficient and unreliable services. Crime is out of control and the police department is at its lowest manning strength in decades . . . The result is an abandoned major city, whose nasty national reputation hurts the area as a whole (*Detroit News*, 1993c).

In 1993, with "the national image of Detroit as a dangerous wasteland", regional recruiters were finding it difficult to entice potential employees in other states to give the Detroit region a chance (Roush, 1993). Suspicion lingered locally that Comerica, formerly Detroit Bank & Trust, had changed its name in order to overcome negative image connotations. Hollywood had inflicted the negative "Robocop" image on Detroit in films depicting random urban mayhem, but the local Detroit tradition of 'Devil's Night' was a self-inflicted image disaster. A book of the same name focused unflattering national media attention on Detroit in 1990, as outsiders, to the consternation of the mayor, were told how Detroiters once a year burnt down their city for entertainment. The author, in a book not unsympathetic to the city's problems, described the origin of 'Devil's Night' thus:

> . . . in 1983, for reasons no one understands, America's sixth largest city suddenly erupted into flames. Houses, abandoned buildings, even unused factories burned to the ground in an orgy of arson that lasted for seventy-two hours. When it was over the papers reported more than eight hundred fires. Smoke hung over the city for days.

> What at first appeared to be a bizarre outburst turned into an annual tradition. By 1986, Devils Night had become a prelude to Halloween in Detroit in the way that Mardi Gras precedes Lent in New Orleans, or the Rose Bowl parade ushers in the New Year in Pasadena (Chafets, 1990, pp. 3-4).

After losing his temper and uttering expletives on a national television programme where 'Devil's Night' was discussed, in November 1990, Young led a delegation to television executives in New York demanding more positive image coverage for his city (*Detroit Free Press*, 1993). In the wake of such turmoil, the March 1991 issue of *Detroit Monthly* suggested only half-facetiously that Detroit reimage itself by playing up its bland aspects and relabelling itself as "America's Dullest City":

> As we approach the city's three hundredth anniversary, it's clear that metro Detroit's salvation can only come about once we recognize, accept and promulgate our dullness. After all, that other stuff isn't working (Barron, 1991).

148

"That other stuff" had included a marketing effort launched in 1988 with a $1 million budget to blur the distinction between city and suburbs by promoting the concept of "Greater Detroit" as a "world technology centre". This was a public sector initiative by a loose confederation of interests calling itself the Greater Detroit Economic Development Group and was composed of executive leadership in Wayne, Oakland and Macomb counties and the City of Detroit joined by the State of Michigan Departments of Commerce and Transportation. The informal arrangement was popularly known as "Six Pack" (Manning-Thomas and Lontz, 1991). The effort to present a common face to the nation and the world produced a series of glitzy promotional films with Motown sound tracks (Chafets, 1990, p. 173) but by 1993 the name "Greater Detroit" had not taken root. In the opinion of some commentators:

> Five years later the name is used by just about the same number of people as it was then, the relatively small group of planners and optimists who thought it up (Gallagher and Bell, 1993).

Oakland County in particular by 1993, under a new hard line County Executive, had decided to cut itself loose from the "Six Pack" notion of Greater Detroit and was endeavouring to distance itself in image promotion from the City of Detroit. Projecting itself as the region's "world technology centre" to counter the rust belt image of deindustrialization, strong unionization and high taxes, the county in an economic development promotional video struggled to overcome its own anonymity while at the same time barely mentioning the city of Detroit or showing black faces (Oakland County, 1992). Also in 1993, Oakland County in a significant symbolic gesture withdrew its financial support from the Metropolitan Detroit Convention and Visitors Bureau.

Racism and the limits of the possible: development policy under Coleman Young reconsidered

In the November 1993 election two black candidates vied to succeed Young as mayor of Detroit. The winner, Dennis Archer, with the black vote split but with support from the remaining whites in the city, polled 57 per cent on a platform of partnership with the white suburbs and business community in order to solve the city's problems. Reflecting more the stance of the outgoing Young, Archer's opponent, Sharon McPhail, implied that her adversary was an "Oreo" candidate and "tool of suburban interests" (Walker; 1993; *Economist*, 1993). With Detroit's new mayor endeavouring to construct a new vision for the city and yet another election being seen as symbolic (*Crain's Detroit Business*, 1993) this section reflects on the interplay of race and class factors which define the limits of optimism in Detroit. Young's image led development agenda is critically considered against what could realistically have been regarded as feasible. A concluding section of the chapter comments on the prospects for an improvement of Detroit's image in the future.

One unconvincing conceptual platform from which to judge Detroit's predicament is a conservative one based on neoclassical economic ideas of optimizing producer and consumer behaviour. This viewpoint, which enjoys considerable currency in Detroit's suburbs, puts emphasis on the role of individuals and individual political jurisdictions in being responsible for their own welfare and future. Tying into the strong home rule tradition in Michigan local government, the argument is that the city of Detroit must make itself competitive and attractive to business and residents by dealing more effectively with its crime problem, seriously endeavouring to reduce crippling city taxes, delivering more satisfactorily and efficiently a host of city services and generally entering into more effective intraregional competition. Black conservatives such as Thomas Sowell, Clarence Thomas and Shelby Steele can be cited as sharing this perspective which argues that blacks have played the victim too long and must be judged by the same standards as other Americans (Hacker, 1992, p. 52).

This conservative view has been articulated strongly by the influential newspaper the *Detroit News* which has a primarily suburban readership. The following comments from an editorial in 1993 as part of a series of articles on "redefining the city" echo strongly the argument put forward by the economist Charles Tiebout in the 1950s concerning the allocative efficiency of metropolitan fragmentation, that is the proposition that the consumer, in shopping among different communities which offered varying packages of local public services and in selecting as a residence the community which offered the tax-expenditure programme best suited to his tastes, was ensuring a tendency towards optimality in local government services (Tiebout, 1956).

> It's our view that "urban sprawl" while real enough, is a much-misunderstood phenomenon. Though often assumed to be a bad thing, it can also be seen as the result of individuals exercising their preferences about where and how to live and work. It is not so much the cause of the decline of the older inner cities as the effect of bad policies that reinforce the preference for a decentralized mode of living. The city is being redefined. We would argue that the goal of public policy should be to give people as much individual freedom as possible to make their own decisions about where to live. If that means urban "sprawl" so be it . . . in a tax-conscious, crime ridden age, urban sprawl also represents citizens shopping for the best buy for their tax dollar (*Detroit News*, 1993d).

Perhaps, not surprisingly, the *Detroit News* launched its "Redefining the City" series of articles with a contribution from Joel Garreau who celebrated the fact that Americans as a whole were redefining the city on the edge of metropolitan cores (Garreau, 1991). Detroit, Garreau argued, is "the birthplace of Edge City" dating back to the decision by General Motors after

150

World War I to build its headquarters not in downtown Detroit but in a then peripheral location accessible to downtown by car (Garreau, 1993). The implication is that instead of bemoaning the decline of "old Detroit", Detroiters should not feel guilty in inventing a new spatial future by riding the crest of a renewed wave of city building (Map 4.1).

The conservative stress on individual and municipal agency, by not adequately addressing the wider social realities of economic power, economic change and racism, fails to provide a realistic standard against which to judge the economic development record of Coleman Young. In broad terms, the early promise of Detroit's public-private partnership, with the allure in calmer economic times of some influence over power in corporate boardrooms, was short lived. Economic restructuring, which has shaken the Detroit region since the late 1970s, has intensified competitive pressure in the regional labour market as a whole transcending balkanized political jurisdictions, however much local economic proactivity is hyped.

Racism continues to be a major social force with a stark spatial expression structuring job, housing and educational opportunities. Here Fainstein has recently referred to the considerable scholarship of the last five years or so which emphasises the continuing significance of race in explaining the situation of African-Americans across the entire black class structure and suggests that a research focus on the pathology of an urban black underclass serves to divert attention from wider social processes (Fainstein, N., 1993). In one important contribution emphasing the continuing significance of racism in America, Andrew Hacker puts it thus:

America has always been the most competitive of societies. It poises its citizens against one another, with the warning that they must make it on their own. Hence the stress on moving past others, driven by the fear of falling behind. No other nation so rates its residents as winners and losers.

If white America orchestrates this arena, it cannot guarantee full security to every member of its own race. Still, while some of its members may fail, there is a limit to how far they can fall. For white America has agreed to provide a consolation prize : no matter to what depths one descends, no white person can ever become black (Hacker, 1993, pp. 29-30).

This view that blacks continue to be racially oppressed and are, therefore, victims was expressed strongly by Coleman Young at a conference on race relations in Detroit in 1987:

. . . let me hasten to tell you what my definition of racism is. As a victim, I think I ought to have a degree of expertise on the matter. It's just like the patient on the operating table. The doctor has to ask you does it hurt because he can't tell. The patient can. And so the person who is the victim can tell you about racism . . . .

151

Now I view racism not as a two-way street. I think racism is a system of oppression. I don't think black folks are oppressive to anybody, so I don't consider that blacks are capable of racism. Blacks are perfectly capable of bigotry and do harbour bigotry. But we don't impose racism or racist policy or racist oppression on anyone (Young, 1987).

Cornell West in his recent book *Race Matters* in sympathetic vein argues that the existence of existential angst and the shattering of civil society in significant pockets of black America cannot be divorced from the workings of US capitalist society and especially "the lived experience of ontological wounds and emotional scars inflicted by white supremacist beliefs and images permeating US society and culture". These "beliefs and images", argues West, "attack black intelligence, black ability, black beauty, and black character in subtle and not-so-subtle ways." (West, 1993, pp. 17-18).

Such a critique of conservative analysis provides a better vantage point from which to consider a number of criticisms made at the end of Young's tenure of dogged pursuit of an image led development agenda. The "new consensus" emerging, as Detroit's corporate sector hyperbolically effuses over the new possibilities opening up to the city under the direction of its new mayor, includes the judgements that past development policy was top heavy with flagship projects, was too opportunistic and was inadequately linked to an effective and coordinated campaign to market the city and that the "race card" of projecting the image of the city as victim was overplayed. These criticisms are considered in turn.

In pursuing prestige projects, the opportunity cost in terms of resources foregone for neighbourhood investment and small business development has been considerable. The Detroit Economic Growth Corporation, for example, by 1993 had written off $25 million in bad loans with another $14 million in delinquent loans pending (Cannon, 1993). More positively, with the pump priming of grants, infrastructural investments and property tax concessions, at the end of the Young era, Detroit did have a new skyline and was the only city in the country to have two modern auto plants within its borders. However, measured against the general economic and social plight of the city, such accomplishments pale and fall short of the early promise in the 1970s of kick-starting a more general economic renaissance. By this standard image led development in Detroit, by hoping to change perceptions of urban space as a locale for investment, has been a failure.

Criticism of mayoral policy, must, however, be tempered by the knowledge that the development agenda followed by Young with an emphasis on downtown was not unlike that followed by a host of other American cities. Quite simply, available economic development strategies were limited with business seeing no profit in investing in poor neighbourhoods (Fainstein and Fainstein, 1993, p. 13). Indeed, the Poletown and Jefferson Avenue projects can be read, within the Young strategy, as boldly trying to break free from the corporate service centre expansion development agendas governing elsewhere. Despite the initial building of the Renaissance Center, the City of Detroit has had a most difficult job enticing a recalcitrant private sector into backing such a strategy. At a time when the limitations of "big bang" property led regeneration, even with more full blooded private sector backing, are being recognized (Turok, 1992; Imrie and Thomas, 1993) this must stand as a major reason why disillusionment with the private sector was so strong in Young's last years. There is a harsh irony here in the fact that the corporate sector in the end blamed the mayor for frosty public-private relations. Even in better circumstances, as Imrie and Thomas have recently argued, while property led regeneration is a necessary part of urban revival "it is neither a sufficient nor an adequate response to the multiple tasks involved in the revitalization of cities" (Imrie and Thomas, 1993, p. 88). Corporate disinvestment continues from Detroit, a city which is compelled to warehouse a vastly disproportionate number of the region's economically disadvantaged and which is increasingly treated as a pariah by suburban jurisdictions unwilling to share appropriate fiscal responsibility.

The claim that development policy under Young was too opportunistic and that the plan for the city was in the mayor's head has been given credence by the intention of the present mayor, Dennis Archer, to formulate a more binding "master plan" against which to evaluate projects. Examples of opportunism under Young which are cited include the less than central attention given to design and the rather ad hoc approach taken to the overall development of Detroit's riverfront. In 1991, a proposal of Young's to offer Comerica Bank a prime site on the riverfront to entice the bank to remain in the city would have involved the demolition of the present Ford Auditorium. The fact that the auditorium is padlocked owing to lack of municipal funds did not stop this particular extreme example of opportunism being blocked by voter referendum.

In Young's defence, it is hardly surprising that, in a context of galloping disinvestment and adequate opportunity for "corporate blackmail", opportunism became an active policy response. And on the design issue it is arguable that, with the "bunkered" Renaissance Center, in the early seventies Detroit was in the vanguard of the security led design which was frighteningly described by Davies in relation to Los Angeles (Davies, 1990, ch. 4) and which constrains possibilities for the production of more permeable, less privatized public spaces.

There is a degree of credibility to the charge that Detroit under Young paid insufficient attention to actively using the media to market a more positive side to the city, including its development achievements. Other cities such as Cleveland and Pittsburg, which have improved their image, have targetted the national media with positive stories. Even after the publication of the Detroit Renaissance Inc. Strategic Plan in 1987, which identified image as a crucial issue needing remedial action, no agency took on this basic public relations function. Perhaps Detroit Renaissance Inc. was afraid of the charge of hypocrisy. In defence of the Young administration it must be remembered that the Detroit area, because of the auto industry, is permanent host to reporters from the national media in the way that many other cities are not. To "feed the national media" in such circumstances is vastly more difficult. Thus while Cleveland's image turnaround since municipal bankruptcy in 1978 has been characterized as "a triumph of public relations" (Krumholz, quoted Gallagher, 1993b) Detroit continues to present the American urban nightmare without any counterbalancing media soft focus.

In terms of overplaying the race card, it is certainly true that a basic contradiction if not schizophrenia emerged between reimaging Detroit to outsiders, with racial victim imagery increasingly intruding, and the reimaging of the city to resident African-Americans. The latter process, while more successful in terms of establishing black identification with city government through reforms in the Detroit police department for example, was not wholly successful either. The claim from some blacks that perhaps victim status was being overplayed, especially in the latter part of Coleman Young's tenure, is undoubtedly reflected in the election of Dennis Archer, a former Michigan supreme court justice, as Young's successor on a platform of bridge building with Detroit's suburbs as opposed to a greater emphasis on the victim theme by his opponent. The following contrasting assessments illustrate how, while the achievement of Young in reimaging the city for blacks has been considerable, it could not adequately address the identity crisis in black America (West, 1993).

[By 1989 Coleman Young] had built a black city-state in the heart of the American middle-west, given his people a government that spoke their language, streets and parks named for their heroes, city jobs and contracts and more political control than blacks have ever had, anywhere, in North America. He had, more than any other politician in the country, created a city in his own image (Chafets, 1990, p. 226).

If the office of the mayor of Detroit were held by a white mayor under the circumstances of today, there would be wall-to-wall blacks marching around the City-County Building with clenched and upraised fists demanding the mayor's head (Dillard, 1988).

The case that white racism should not excuse blacks from holding their politicians accountable to high standards of performance and that greater agency involving a more positive sense of empowerment is necessary to overcome a nihilistic threat based on self hate within sections of the black population has recently been forcefully argued by Cornell West. Rejecting both the market solutions of new black conservatives by insisting that race still matters greatly and the black liberal position with its continued stress on victim status, West argues in general terms that a "love ethic" is necessary to overcome the black "disease of the soul" in "a last attempt at generating a sense of agency among a downtrodden people" (West, 1993, p. 19).

Judged by this yardstick which acknowledges victimhood but also hope, claims that Young overplayed the race issue, perhaps with an eye to re-election, engender a more sympathetic hearing when coming from Detroit blacks rather than white suburbanites and business interests. The popular verdict of the latter that Young was " more angry than constructive" (Greig, 1994) downplays the reason for anger in a region where a casual glance at spatial geography makes it clear that race does indeed continue to matter.

What future for the pariah city?

Over fifteen years ago one urban sociologist identified pariah status as one possible future for aging central cities such as Detroit. Black political control of the pariah city would be a "hollow prize" involving political control over an economically sterile environment. Doubt was expressed as to whether "the metropolitan apple can long flourish while its core rots" (Hill, 1978, p. 230).

Detroit at present seems set to prove that this in fact can happen. Suburbs, Edge Cities, state and federal government, which either face or espouse a conservative critique of traditional liberal solutions, find neither resources nor will to define policies to reverse present trends. On these present trends, the *Detroit News* has predicted that Detroit is in danger of becoming "America's first real ex-city" (Greig, 1994). The trend projections of the regional planning agency to the year 2010 less melodramatically put the city of Detroit on a continued downward spiral of economic decline, continued racial segregation and social distress (Southeastern Michigan Council of Governments, 1991).

Countering Joel Garreau, David Rusk, a former mayor of Albuquerque, has recently restated the unpopular argument that metropolitan wide govern-mental structures and regional income redistribution must be part of the solution to the problems of cities like Detroit (Rusk, 1993a). In a speech to a Detroit audience of decision makers in mid 1993, Rusk made the case that regional government and responsibility sharing was necessary in Detroit to avoid "a metro area organized as a garrison state to try to contain a year-round Devil's Night" (Rusk, 1993b). The case for some form of regional govern-ance and responsibility sharing, including perhaps some form of sharing of the regional property tax base, has been made many times before in metro-politan Detroit, not least in a major study of uneven development in SE Michigan published in 1987 (Darden et al., 1987). However, given the strong Jeffersonian tradition of home rule local governance in Michigan, employed at present to legitimize suburban class and racial privilege, racial polarization and continued sprawl driven in part by fear form the more likely scenario.

Despite the success of the present Mayor Archer in persuading President Clinton to hold his Big Seven "Jobs Summit" in Detroit in March 1994, there

155

is no evidence that the tackling of such urban issues features strongly on the Clinton White House agenda . While it is likely that eighteen square miles of "America's most severely distressed big city ghetto" (*New York Times*, quoted *Crain's Detroit Business*, 1994) will be designated as one of President Clinton's six federally assisted urban "empowerment zones", with a two year infusion of tax breaks and other incentives to businesses which employ zone residents, this can be but modest help in a struggle to turn the city around.

As Mayor Archer, with a more managerial style, turns his attention to the city's $80 million budget deficit and chronically deteriorated city services such as rubbish collection, street lighting and police protection, he is simultaneously in 1994 talking Detroit up as an "entrepreneur's dream" and possible future "urban jewel" (*Economist*, 1994).

Ultimately it proved impossible for Coleman Young to balance a representation of place with which black Detroiters could identify with the needs of upbeat city marketing to outsiders and potential investors. While the possibility of the emergence of a reinvigorated more broadly based growth coalition with a place vision offering some hope to Detroit cannot be ruled out, a more realistic question is probably the degree to which Mayor Archer can continue to talk the language of moderation and coalition building against the continuing realities of racism, decentralization and disinvestment.

References

Adrian, Charles et al. (1977), *Governing Urban America*, 5th Ed, McGraw Hill, New York.

Ashworth, G.J. and Voogd, H. (1990), *Selling the City: Marketing Approaches in Public Sector Urban Planning*, Belhaven Press, London.

Atkins, Elizabeth (1993), 'Grand Prix Poster revs up race, marketing issues', *Detroit News*, 7 June.

Barnekov, T., Boyle, R. and Rich, D. (1989), *Privatism & Urban Policy in Britain and the United States*, Oxford University Press.

Barron, John (1987), 'Designing Detroit', *Detroit Monthly*, May, pp. 88-95.

Barron, John (1991), 'We're America's Dullest City; talk it up!', *Detroit Monthly*, March, pp. 56-63.

Bledsoe, Timothy (1990), *From One World, Three: Political Change in Metropolitan Detroit*, Center for Urban Studies, Wayne State University, Detroit.

Blonston, Gary (1971), 'Why Detroit's Homicide Rate is Skyrocketing', *Detroit Free Press*, 7 March.

Blonston, Gary (1981), 'Poletown: the profits, the loss', *Detroit Free Press*, 22 November.

Bluestone B. and Harrison B. (1982), *The Deindustrialization of America*, Basic Books, New York.

Bratt, Heidi (1993), 'Prix poster leaves black Detroiters out of picture', *Detroit News*, 3 June.

Bratt H.M. et al. (1993), 'Southwest's exit deals blow to City Airport expansion plan', *Detroit News*, 20 May.

Bulkeley, William (1977), 'Developers call Detroit Complex the Renaissance, but there is skepticism that it signals a rebirth', *Wall Street Journal*, 15 April.

Cannon, Angie (1993), 'Twenty five million dollars in bad loans lost by city agency since '78', *Detroit News and Free Press*, 27 June.

Castells, Manuel (1977), *The Urban Question: A Marxist Approach*, Massachusetts Institute of Technology Press.

Central Business District Association (1992), *Annual Development Report: Commemorative Edition*.

Central Business District Association (1993), *Revitalizing Detroit's Central Business District: A report and 5 year strategic plan to eliminate vacant and deteriorated commercial building conditions*, January.

Chafets, Ze'ev (1990), *Devil's Night and other true tales of Detroit*, Random House, New York.

Cheyfitz, Kirk (1979), 'The Incredible Shrinking City', *Detroit Monthly*, vol. 2, no. 7, pp. 57-60.

Chrysler Corporation (1992), 'Jefferson-Connor Industrial Revitalization Project: A Cooperative Effort between Chrysler Corporation and the City of Detroit', memo to Clement Dinsmore, Counsel, US Senate Committee on Banking, Housing and Urban Affairs, 21 July.

Citizen (1980), 'New Plant will usher area rebirth Murphy tells Rotary', *The Citizen* (a newspaper serving Hamtramck, north Detroit, Warren and Highland Park), 6 November.

Citizens Research Council of Michigan Detroit, (1991), *Fiscal Trends of the City of Detroit*, Detroit.

City of Detroit (1977), *Moving Detroit Forward: A Plan for Urban Economic Revitalization*.

City of Detroit (1978a), *Annual Report (1976-1977) to Economic Development Administration*.

City of Detroit (1978 b), *Overall Economic Development Program*.

City of Detroit (1981), *Report of the Budget Planning and Stabilization Committee*, April.

City of Detroit (1983), *Introduction and Synopsis to Detroit Master Plan*.

City of Detroit (1985), *The Detroit Riverfront Comes Alive*, Executive office of the Mayor.

City of Detroit (1988), *Detroit '88*.

City of Detroit (1990), *Jefferson/Connor Industrial Revitalization Project*, Status Report, 23 July.

City of Detroit (1992), *1990 Census and other socio-economic data*, Planning Department.

Congressional Quarterly (1980), 'Detroit Hosts First National Party Convention', 12 July, pp. 1926-1927.

Conot, Robert (1974), *American Odyssey*, William Morrow & Co, New York.

Crain's Detroit Business (1993), 'Looking for Detroit's Vision: New mayor is a symbolic first step', 29 November.

Crain's Detroit Business (1994), 'Zone just one step in revival effort', 21 March.

Darden Joe T. et al. (1987), *Detroit: Race and Uneven Development*, Temple University Press, Philadelphia.

Davis, Mike (1990), *City of Quartz: Excavating the Future in Los Angeles*, Verso, London.

Davis, Mike (1993), 'Who Killed LA? A Political Autopsy', *New Left Review*, no. 197, pp. 3-28.

Detroit Downtown Development Authority (1983), *Annual Report 1982-83*.

Detroit Economic Growth Corporation (1991), *News Release*, April.

Detroit Economic Growth Corporation (1992), *A Report on Development Activity*.

Detroit Free Press (1977), 'Detroit Hails City Renaissance', 16 April.

Detroit Free Press (1980), 'How Mayor Young got heavyweight status', 6 October.

Detroit Free Press (1983), 'Care Packages for Detroit', 27 February.

Detroit Free Press (1993), 'Highlights of Twenty Years', 23 June.

Detroit News (1962), 'Sixth Quinquennial Survey of the Detroit Market'.

Detroit News (1979), 'Tax Breaks for business?' 7 October.

Detroit News (1993a), 'Detroit's Budget Fantasy', 15 April.

Detroit News (1993b), 'Is Older Cheaper? Maybe', 1 June.

Detroit News (1993c), 'Suburbanization & Competition', 4 June.

Detroit News (1993d), 'The Great Sprawl Debate', 30 May.

Detroit News and Mayors Committee for Economic Growth (1961), *The Real Detroit*.

Detroit Renaissance Inc. (1993), 'The Detroit Grand Prix: A Race History'.

Detroit Strategic Planning Project (1987), *Final Report, Detroit Renaissance Inc.*

Dillard, Ernest (1988), 'Detroit Perspectives' in Henrickson, Wilma Wood (ed.), *Detroit Perspectives*, Wayne State University Press 1991, Detroit, pp. 565-567.

Economist (1992), 'Overkill', 21 November, pp. 72-73.

Economist (1993), 'Detroit's mayor – A job fit for heroes', 28 August, pp. 45-46.

Economist (1994), 'Detroit: a man, a plan', 12 March.

Edgecomb, Diane (1993), Interview with the author, June.

English, Carey (1980), 'An arena grows in Detroit, and trouble blooms all over', *Detroit Free Press*, 29 June.

Fainstein, Norman (1993), 'Race, class and Segregation: Discourses about African Americans', *International Journal of Urban and Regional Research*, vol. 17, no. 3, pp. 384-403.

Fainstein, Susan and Fainstein, Norman (1993), 'Urban Regimes and Racial Conflict: Economic and Political Consequences of Black Incorporation in the US', paper presented at the Fulbright Colloquium, 'Managing Divided Cities', sponsored by the Centre for the Study of Conflict and the Department of Philosophy and Politics, University of Ulster, Jordanstown, 6-8 September.

Farley, Reynolds H. (1987), 'An historical perspective on current differences', paper presented at a Conference on Race Relations sponsored by the Detroit Strategic Planning Project, Detroit, 25 July.

Fine, Sidney (1989), '*Violence in the Model City: The Cavanagh Administration: Race Relations and the Detroit Riot of 1967*', The University of Michigan Press, Ann Arbor.

Fireman, Ken et al. (1982), 'Original Partners sell the Ren Cen at a loss', *Detroit Free Press*, 29 April.

Gallagher, John (1993a), 'Illich says he'd pay for stadium itself', *Detroit Free Press*, 16 June.

Gallagher, John (1993b), 'Cleveland Creeps Along', *Detroit Free Press*, 28 June.

Gallagher, John and Bell, Dawson (1993), 'Regionalism faces a legacy of failure', *Detroit Free Press*, 3 June.

Garreau, Joel (1991), 'Edge City: Life on the New Frontier', *Anchor Books*, New York.

Garreau, Joel (1993), 'Detroit: The birthplace of Edge City', *Detroit News*, 30 May.

Gavrilovich, P. and Blossom, T. (1985), 'Stroh Won't Brew Here Anymore', *Detroit Free Press*, 9 February.

Georgakas, Dan and Surkin, Marvin (1975), *Detroit: I do mind dying*, St Martin's Press, New York.

Glancy, Alfred (1993), comments at Greater Detroit Chamber of Commerce, Mackinac Conference, 3 June.

Goodin, M. (1994), 'Stadium can't ensure survival but Illich consults Disney to make Foxtown Friendly', *Crain's Detroit Business*, 28 March.

Graves, Helen, M. (1975), *New Detroit Committee/New Detroit Inc: A case study of an Urban Coalition*, Unpublished PhD thesis, Wayne State University, Detroit.

Greater Detroit Chamber of Commerce (1980), *The Detroiter Office Guide*.

Greater Detroit Chamber of Commerce (1992), *Metro Detroit Office Guide*.

Greater Detroit Chamber of Commerce (1993), *A Report on the Strategic Plan for the Economic Development of Southeast Michigan*.

Greig, Geordie (1994), 'From Motown to no town', *Sunday Times*, 20 March.

Grimes, Donald and Fulton, George (1993), *The Economic Outlook for Oakland County in 1993-94*, report prepared for Economic Development Division, County of Oakland, Michigan.

Guzzardi Jr, Walter (1980), 'A determined Detroit Struggles to Find a new Economic Life', *Fortune*, 21 April, pp. 74-85.

Hacker, Andrew (1992), *Two Nations: Black and White, Separate, Hostile and Unequal*, Ballantine Books, New York.

Harvey, David (1989), *The Condition of Postmodernity*, Basil Blackwell, London.

Hamada, Tarek et al. (1993), 'City blamed for airline's departure', *Detroit News*, 21 May.

Henderson, Angelo B. (1993), 'New Renaissance chief presses vision for future', *Detroit News*, 30 June.

Hill, Richard Child (1978), 'Fiscal Collapse and Political Struggle in Decaying Central Cities in the United States' in Tabb W and Sawers L (eds), *Marxism and the Metropolis: New Perspectives in Urban Political Economy*, Oxford University Press, pp. 213-240.

Hill, Richard Child (1990), 'Federalism and Urban Policy: The Intergovernmental Dialectic', Ch 3 in Swartz T. and Peck J. (eds), *The Changing Face of Fiscal Federalism*, M. E. Sharpe Inc., New York.

Imrie, R. and Thomas, H. (1993), 'The limits of property-led regeneration', *Environment and Planning C : Government and Policy*, vol. 11, pp. 87-102.

Interview (1991), Interview by the author of a senior Detroit transportation planner, June.

Jacoby, Al (1981), Author's interview with the Co-ordinator of the Mayor's Committee on Commercial and Industrial Development under Mayor Miriani in Detroit.

Lam, Tina (1993), 'Casino plan floats near Fox Theater', *Detroit Free Press*, 29 May.

Kiska, Tim (1980), 'Whites trusted less; violence is rejected' in McGehee, S. and Watson, S. (eds), *Blacks in Detroit*, a reprint of articles from the Detroit Free Press, Detroit.

MacGregor, Susanne (1993), 'Reconstructing the divided city: problems of pluralism and governance', paper presented at Fulbright Colloquium, 'Managing Divided Cities', sponsored by the Centre for the Study of Conflict and the Department of Philosophy and Politics, University of Ulster, Jordanstown, 6-8 September.

Mackie, Lindsay (1987), 'Baby, it's murder in Detroit', *Guardian*, 21 July.

McClure, Sandy (1981), 'Subway 'No' Vote Blamed on Racism', *Detroit Free Press*, 14 January.

McGill, Andrew and Young, Barbara (1978), 'One Man Shakes a City', *Detroit News*, 8 October.

Molotch, Harvey (1988), 'Strategies and Constraints of Growth Elites', ch. 2 in Cummings, Scott, (ed.), *Business Elites and Urban Development*, State University of New York Press, Albany.

Neill, William J.V. (1988), 'Transportation Planning in Detroit: Conflict and the Evolution of Practice', *Planning Practice and Research*, Winter, pp. 13-18.

Neill, William J.V. (1991), 'Motown Blues: No answer in privatized planning', *Town and Country Planning*, vol. 60, no. 3, pp. 86-87.

Neill, William J.V. (1991), 'Industrial Policy in Detroit: The Search for a new regional development model in the home of Fordism', *Local Economy*, vol. 6, no. 3, pp. 250-270.

National Advisory Commission on Civil Disorders (1968), Bantham Books, New York.

Neithercut, Mark E. (1987), *Detroit Twenty Years After: A statistical profile of the Detroit Area Since 1967*, Centre for Urban Studies, Wayne State University, Detroit.

Oakland County (1992), Promotional video.

Pickvance, C.G.(1991), 'Spatial Policy as Territorial Politics: the side of spatial coalitions in the articulation of 'spatial' interests in the demand for spatial policy' in Rees, G. et al., (eds) *Political Action and Social Identity*, Macmillan, London, pp. 117-142.

Putman, Beatrice Morgan (1964), *An illustrated Guide to Dynamic Detroit*, Industrial Publishing Corporation, Detroit.

Ravitz, Mel (1988), 'Perils of Planning as an Executive Function', *American Planning Association Journal*, Spring 1988, pp. 164-165.

Reed, Christopher et al. (1992), 'Riots fire US race divide', *Guardian*, 1 May.

Rich, Wilbur C. (1989), *Coleman Young and Detroit Politics: From Social Activist to Power Broker*, Wayne State University Press, Detroit.

Richmond, Jonathan E.D. (1989), 'Theories of Symbolism, Metaphor and Myth; and the development of Western Rail Passenger Systems, or Penis Envy in Los Angeles', paper presented at annual conference of Association of Collegiate School of Planning, October .

Roush, Matt (1993), 'City Image: If you rebuild it will they come?', *Crain's Detroit Business*, 22 November.

Rusk, David (1993a), *Cities without Suburbs*, Woodrow Wilson Center Press, Washington D.C.

Rusk, David (1993b), Remarks to the Greater Detroit Chamber of Commerce, Mackinac Conference, Michigan, 3 June.

Southeastern Michigan Council of Governments (1976), *Land Use Trends in SE Michigan*, Detroit.

Southeastern Michigan Council of Governments (1991), *The Business as Usual Trend Future: The Data Base*, Detroit, January.

Stanton, Barbara (1982), 'Hudson's Giving up on Downtown Store', *Detroit Free Press*, 15 April.

State of Michigan (1983a), data supplied to the author by the State Boundary Commission.

State of Michigan (1983b), data supplied to the author by the then Office of Community Development.

Strauss, Anselm L.(1961), *Images of the American City*, The Free Press of Glencoe, New York.

Suburban Mobility Authority for Regional Transportation (SMART) (1989), *A summary history of regional public transportation governance in SE Michigan*, Detroit, May.

Tiebout, Charles M. (1956), 'A Pure Theory of Local Expenditures', *Journal of Political Economy*, October.

Time Magazine (1980), 'Resentment is building in the nation's black urban ghettos', 16 June.

Thomas, June Manning and Lontz, William (1991), *Intergovernmental Cooperation for Economic Development: Greater Detroit's Six Pack*, Michigan Partnership for Economic Development Assistance and Michigan State University, E. Lansing.

Turok, I. (1992), 'Property-led urban regeneration: panacea or placebo?' *Environment and Planning* A, vol. 24, pp. 361-379.

Usborne, David (1993), 'Motor City Fights against fulfilling a death wish', *Independent*, 31 May.

Von Eckardt, Wolf (1979), 'New Mood Downtown', *Transaction, Social Science and Modern Society*, vol. 16, no. 6, pp. 4-7.

Walker, Martin (1993), 'The mayor's race to the finish', *Guardian*, 30 October.

West, Cornell (1993), *Race Matters*, Beacon Press, Boston.

Widick, B.J. (1972), *City of Race and Class Violence*, Quadrangle Books, Chicago.

Wilbur, Chuck (1988), 'Detroit's Strategic Plan: Image', *Metro Times*, 3 February, p. 12.

Williams, Ron (1987), 'Detroit Loves a Good Demolition' in Henrickson, Wilma Wood (ed.) *Detroit Perspectives*, Wayne State University Press, 1991, Detroit, pp. 555-559.

Wilson, Melinda (1993), 'Fairlane: The Final Pieces', *Detroit News*, 30 June.

Woutat, Donald (1980), 'When Chrysler Hurts, Detroit Hurts', *Detroit Free Press*, 13 May.

Young, Coleman (1987), 'Personal Observations on Race Relations in Detroit', speech given at a Conference on Race Relations sponsored by the Detroit Strategic Planning Project, 25 July.

Zurawik, David (1982), 'What price Prix?', *Detroit Free Press*, 1 June.

5 Tackling Detroit's rust belt image: Industrial policy experimentation in the home of Fordism

William J.V. Neill

An alternative image of economic development . . . would shift from the mascu-line metaphor of cuthroat competition for mobile capital to a more feminine image of nurturing the strengths of the local context. The alternative image of economic development based on embeddedness shifts attention from cutting the costs of capital to upgrading the skills of labor and nurturing the context of self-generating economic development (Logan and Swanstrom, *Beyond the City Limits*, 1990, p. 21.).

Introduction

The American Midwest has recently been reviled as "the rust belt" with Detroit as its heart. This chapter reports on the efforts of State government in Michigan in the 1980s and continuing through industrial extension services of the Michigan Industrial Technology Institute in the 1990s to move beyond promotionalism to tackle rust belt imagery at source. This has involved developing interventionist supply side economic policies for the mature industrial district centred on S.E. Michigan. This is a region which is almost synonymous with a whole production and consumption system, Fordism, now deemed by many theorists to be in decline (e.g. Albrechts and Swyngedouw, 1989; Harvey, 1989; Murray 1989). Federalism in the United States permits regional economic experiment and debate going beyond the US notion of free market privatism which has inspired many policy ideas in Britain since the 1980s (Barnekov et al. 1989). The chapter reports on a neo-Progressive policy practice experiment in Michigan which was inspired by developing theories of "flexible specialization" and post-Fordist debates on the future of mass manufacturing. Emerging directly from an early realization by key policy actors that prestige reimaging projects in Detroit were of themselves no answer to threatened deindustrialization (Luria and Russell, 1981) the Michigan experience raises important questions concerning the role of small business, regional agglomeration economies and the degree to which corporate power can be "tamed" and brought under the influence of local economic strategies.

Detroit and the Japanese Competitive Threat

The Detroit region with a population of around 4,500,000, about half the Michigan total, has always been the backbone of the state's industrial economy. "Motown" itself, with a population of around 1,000,000, is predominantly African-American and is surrounded by a suburban collar of mostly white suburban jurisdictions. Amid fractious division one of the few issues on which city and suburbs have been agreed is the Japanese threat to the regional economy as a whole.

Japanese auto makers by 1990 claimed about a third of the world market of 46 million vehicles (*Business Week*, 1990). On the domestic turf of the "Big Three" (General Motors, Ford and Chrysler), Japanese US sales of cars, from both imports and transplants, have raised questions about the future of Detroit as an industrial district centred on the auto. While the threat of a few years ago that Japan might wrest global economic leadership from the US has passed, Japanese prowess in industries such as steel, electronics and cars continues to be the principal cause of Japan's $50 billion trade surplus with America (Farrell, 1994). From a market share of 20 per cent in 1980 Japan's capture of US passenger car sales reached almost 30 per cent in 1992. (Table 5.1) While this has subsequently fallen back somewhat aided by an appreciating yen which makes Japanese cars on average about $2,300 more expensive than American equivalents (Dickson, 1993), a research report commissioned by the Michigan Commerce Department and published in 1993 was nonetheless nervously entitled *Michigan: Still the Automotive State?* (McAlinden and Andrea, 1993). Michigan is faced with the reality that, of the 11 transplant assembly plants opened by the Japanese in semi-rural towns of the lower Mid-west, Upper South and Canada in the 1980s and 1990s, only one, Mazda, is in Michigan (*Business Week*, 1989; *Business Week*, 1994a; Kennedy and Florida, 1992). Taking advantage of locations elsewhere with less union influence, Japanese carmakers have combined high automation with worker adaptability and close working relationships with suppliers who often provide components in modules to be assembled by robots. Japanese firms have led the way on quality, have reduced the product development cycle to three to four years, and have plants which can be more flexibly reprogrammed and which can run profitably at lower levels of output. In the space of 10 years Michigan has seen Tennessee, with major Nissan investments, emerge from modest beginnings to become a significant automotive state accounting for almost 9 per cent of US production in 1993 (Dickson, 1994). While the position of Detroit's Big Three has improved since Chrysler's second flirtation with bankruptcy in 1991 and the staggering $4.5 billion losses by GM in the same year, Japanese cars are headed for record sales of over 3.5 million vehicles in the US in 1994 (*Business Week*, 1994d). In March 1994 Toyota opened its second US auto plant, not in Michigan, but in Georgetown, Kentucky (*Business Week*, 1994a).

TABLE 5.1   Japan's share of US passenger car sales

	per cent
1980	20.0
1990	27.0
1991	29.2
1992	29.7
1993	27.1
1994	28.4

Source: Done, 1991 and *Business Week*, 1994d. Data for
1990-94 refer to first 4 months of each year.

The flexible specialisation thesis: a signpost but no policy blue-print

Michigan's industrial policy experiment to counter threatened regional economic decline was informed by both on-going developments in the automotive industry and the Japanese experience in particular and by the extensive and continuing debate over the future of mass manufacturing. The latter is the focus of the present section. Already in 1984 "flexibility" was picked up as a key concern. The major industrial policy document of the new Democratic Governor who assumed office in 1983 was entitled *The Path to Prosperity* (State of Michigan, 1984). Prepared by a governor's task force charting out a long term economic strategy for the state this rejected the notion that Michigan should drift towards a service economy of the future. It raised the spectre of Michigan becoming "an industrial museum, the Liverpool of the late 20th century" (p. 70) and argued that despite the growing importance of services,

164

manufacturing continued to be the engine that drove the Michigan economy and determined the state's prosperity. To a considerable degree Michigan's industrial problems, the report advanced, "are the problems of the Detroit metropolitan area" (p. 108). The economic choices for Michigan were put in stark terms. The State could:

1. Get poor – reduce wages to Sunbelt and Third World levels.

2. Get out – abandon durable goods manufacturing for information services and other high tech activities.

3. Get smart – which meant "shifting from making familiar products with routine standardized processes, that can be replicated easily in low wage states and nations, to making new products and existing products with more complex, flexible processes that are protected from such competition by their dependence on human skills. Only in this way can Michigan's economy get competitive without 'getting poor'" (State of Michigan, 1984, p. 52).

The "get smart" strategy was the one endorsed. The State would target its effort to "economic base" export or import substituting industries, which drove the economy and would let the "local market economy", which feeds off the economic base, take care of itself. A State policy review of the *Path to Prosperity* in 1989 continued to endorse the strategy of competing, not with muscle power, but brain power and highlighted the upgrading of the skills of Michigan's existing work force along with investment in education as "the top priority of Michigan's economic development strategy for the 1990s" (State of Michigan, 1989, p. 57). An application of the thinking of the American industrial policy analyst and present Labour Secretary under President Clinton, Robert Reich, who drew attention in 1983 to the implications of flexible manufacturing systems, is clearly evident and received citation in the original Michigan strategy report. Reich argued then that while high volume, standardized production facilities could be established anywhere, production processes that depended on skilled labour must stay where the skilled labour was. Industrialized countries should not abandon older industries like automobiles but rather should restructure them towards higher value-added and technologically more sophisticated businesses. In the car industry this meant precision-engineered automobiles and auto components. The lowest skilled standardized segments of production could be allowed to migrate to developing countries (Reich,1983).

Echoing this theme in 1984, Piore and Sabel published their book, *The Second Industrial Divide*, which made an impact in the United States by arguing that America's difficulties resulted from the limits of mass production and presenting "flexible specialization" as an alternative model offering the possibility of reversing economic decline. Mass production was characterised by the use of special purpose machines and semi-skilled workers to

165

produce standardized goods. Flexible specialization on the other hand, taking advantage of programmable technologies, was based on skilled workers producing customized goods in smaller production runs for niche markets. Heightened competition in global markets, volatility and uncertainty, and increased differentiation in consumer tastes gave a competitive advantage to networks of flexible small firms benefiting from economies of agglomeration in industrial districts. In the face of volume market penetration by large Japanese auto producers, Michigan was never likely to adopt a simple reading of early flexible specialization arguments, by seeing the nurturing of small firms, which can challenge large corporations in producing for niche markets, as the answer to foreign competition. Rather Michigan State policy in the 1980s and continued through the Michigan Industrial Technology Institute in the 1990s developed in engagement with flexible specialization ideas but was also influenced by critique questioning the possibility of an independent dynamic role for small firms in industries still dominated by multi-national corporations. Before considering such arguments it can be said, however, that at its most basic level neo-Progressive industrial policy towards Detroit has been based on a realization that "while the physical barriers to capital mobility have increasingly been overcome by technology, many sectors of capital remain dependent on what could be called a social ecology of skilled labor that ties them to specific geographical contexts" (Logan and Swanstrom, 1990, p. 20).

Recent debate surrounding the flexible specialization thesis, while acknowledging the role of new programmable technologies and the possibilities for small and medium sized firms under new conditions, has centred more on the role of large corporations and industrial organization. Concerning the latter, research confirms the existence of "vertical disintegration" as a widespread phenomenon (Harrison, 1994) whereby important aspects of production are externalised and carried on by smaller independent suppliers forming contractual arrangements with a larger company. The result is a superior, more flexible way of responding to market uncertainty and differentiation through the creation of a more effective learning system which also minimizes transaction costs amongst all parties. Partly as a result of this it has thus been argued that small firm dominance is a myth and that:

> a substantial part of the restructuration that has taken place (in this era), including the expansion of the small business sector, has evolved under the control of larger firms, thus raising doubts about claims for the viability of independent, innovative and dynamic small enterprises, whose rise is due to their superiority over large corporations (Sengenberger and Pyke, 1992, quoted Harrison, 1994, pp. 15-16).

More recently Sabel has endeavoured to incorporate such observations into flexible specialization theory. Claiming that the relationship between the economy and its territory is changing, Sabel points to a possible renaissance of regional economies based not only on cooperative networking between proximate small firms using new technology to produce for niche markets but also on the flexibility deriving from "an emergent and spreading corporate form which blurs familiar distinctions between large and small firms" (Sabel, 1989, p. 7). Large firms, Sabel claims, are imitating and allying with small firm industrial districts through the process of vertical disintegration. In the last fifteen years, Sabel states, "many of the largest multinationals have shifted strategy. Often without explicitly repudiating the mass-production model, they have begun to organize production on the lines of flexible specialization. They have been moved to do this by their previous failures, by the exemplary successes of the new industrial districts and by their fear of Japanese competitors – who are themselves perfecting systems of flexible production" (Sabel, 1989, p. 31). This point is also made by Hirst and Zeitlin who identify the Third Italy (Emilia Romagna in northern Italy) and Japan as "the most successful regional and national economies that have followed flexible specialization strategies" (Hirst and Zeitlin, 1991, p. 11).

A number of problems, however, can be identified with such adaptations to the original core of flexible specialization ideas. Firstly, given the importance of large firms to economic restructuring it is questionable whether a continued primary focus on the secondary industrial sector as an independent beacon of progress and innovation can be justified (Curry, 1993; Harrison, 1994). Secondly, there is the danger of falling victim to what Amin and Robbins refer to as "vulgar theory" which seeks "to condense all new industrial spaces into one spatial form (the 'industrial district') as well as one structural process (for example, vertical disintegration)" (Amin and Robbins, 1990, p. 21). With a totalizing vision there is a danger of falsely discerning the birth of a new sociotechnological paradigm and endowing it with universally possible progressive characteristics (Curry, 1993, p. 102). As Curry has recently argued, the loose association of firms in the countryside of northern Italy bears no resemblance to the organization of the auto industry, for example, thus calling for comparative study of the real conditions of production in a rich variety of industrial districts (Curry, 1993; Perulli, 1993, p. 108). Thirdly, the argument has been strongly made that Japanese industrial organization should be studied in its own right and that something is lost if we conflate, for example, the Third Italy with Toyota City. It is incorrect to ascribe to the regionally agglomerated subcontracting networks of Japan the title of flexible specialization since while the Japanese economy may have flexible aspects the dynamic direction of the industrial economy does not reside with the small firms sector (Curry, 1993). In that Japan has over the last decade or so exported its automobile production methods to the heart of traditional Fordism the following section reviews further theory which has attempted to understand such post-Fordist techniques and which in turn has influenced neo-Progressive industrial policy in Michigan.

From flexible specialization to lean Fordism: understanding the Japanese automobile industry

It is hardly surprising that Japanese automobile production techniques have been of interest to economic planners in Michigan. The Massachusetts Institute of Technology study of the future of the automobile industry (Womack et al., 1990) has been of particular interest and would seem to lend support to Sabel's characterisation of future trends, at least in this sector, but with the terms flexible production and lean production preferred to that of flexible specialization. In relation to product range and output volume, the study points out that in 1990 Toyota, the prime harbinger, was offering customers around the world as many products as GM even though it was half GM's size. Production runs per model for the volume Japanese auto companies currently average around 125,000 per year, roughly half that for Western high volume companies who change models less frequently in any case. In general, all the major automobile markets are now characterized by an increase in the number of models and a decline in volume per model (Clarke and Fujimoto, 1991, p. 36). Recent research confirms that the average sales of the five best selling passenger cars in the US have declined to 300,000 units, representing a halving of volume since 1970 (McAlinden and Smith, 1992, p. 16). However, niche marketing and highly attuned market responsiveness are not solely or even mainly a product of flexible programmable technology. With parts designed for ease of assembly, niche products do not always involve components customised from scratch. This squares with recent research commissioned by the Michigan Commerce Department itself which concluded that:

> At the level of final consumers, variety is apparently increasing, especially among foreign-based producers. But this increased variety is also apparently quite superficial, even cosmetic. Certainly, it is not inconsistent with less variety and longer production runs for many or most of the parts that go into cars, although it is also true that at least some suppliers are reorientating their capacity toward smaller, shorter-series plants (Luria, 1990).

It is the vertical disintegration aspects of flexible production that the MIT auto study most firmly endorses. Japanese success rests primarily on superior industrial organization. Independent or semi-independent suppliers are bound together in a non-bureaucratic market responsive hierarchy committed to quality, efficiency and superior product development performance, which is ensured by cooperation and sharing of information within the network. While the traditional US supplier system has been characterised by many suppliers dealing with auto companies on the basis of short term contracts in an adversarial relationship where one supplier is played off against another, the Japanese structure emphasizes long-term relationships where first tier suppliers provide subassembled units from parts produced by lower tier suppliers

168

(Clark and Fujimoto, 1991, p. 138). The teamwork labour process in assembly plants breaks with Taylorism in encouraging on the job learning with no rigid separation between design/conception and execution (Kaplinsky, 1988). Spatial agglomeration is central to the lean production system which the MIT study describes:

> Once a lean producer starts down the path to assembly in a major regional market, the logic of the system tends powerfully to bring the complete complement of production activities, including product development, along as well. And sooner rather than later, as is happening in North America (Womack et al., 1990, p. 255).

The MIT study fits Sabel's more recent conception of subsidiaries of multinationals along with small firms nurturing the growth of industrial districts:

> The activities of the giant corporations would more closely resemble and actually blend into the activity of the industrial districts. An engine plant which participates in the design of the engine and depends on highly specialised local suppliers to produce it is both part of the multinational car firm *and* an independent industrial district (Sabel, 1989, p. 40, emphasis original).

Some theorists, however, while recognizing agglomeration tendencies within the auto industry put more stress on multinational control than on the potential local autonomy of industrial districts. Schoenberger argues that in the face of market differentiation and instability "spatial linkages will be strengthened as intensified flexibility and adaptability require much tighter coordination of all phases of the manufacturing process from design and engineering through final assembly" (Schoenberger, 1987). However, she points to the corporation's ability to construct agglomeration economies away from traditional industrial centres. Hill, while recognizing the tiered nature of Japanese automobile industrial organization and how auto manufacturers "have managed to extend the specialization and timing integral to modern factory production to a much wider regional space" (Hill, 1989, p. 463), nevertheless stresses the importance of the transnational production systems in which major corporations are embedded in explaining developments within the industry. Amin and Robbins, reviewing the literature on industrial districts, stress the "vast alternative body of work which views contemporary transformations as a threat to localities as they become fragmented, integrated into, and subjugated by international forces beyond their control and victims of more intensified inter-regional competition" (Amin and Robbins, 1990, p. 29).

There is debate then over the degree to which regional economies can be masters of their own destiny and indeed whether capitalism, as the MIT study predicts, is bringing forth a new productive machine of organizational and technological relationships which will "change the world". A dissenting voice on the MIT study is provided by Wood who argues that Japanization of the auto industry can be interpreted in more Fordist mass production terms

(Wood, 1988). The study has likewise been criticized for presenting a "sanitized" description of lean production and for exaggerating its emancipatory potential in particular. "Kaizen", the Japanese process of continuous improvement, Babson argues, is stressful with workers often only reacting to management initiatives. Lean production he argues is in fact "mean production" since it "has the potential to be as or more oppressive than mass production, but still generate *obedience* with a system of performance/merit pay that punishes 'slackers'" (Babson, 1993, p. 20, emphasis original). Given the emancipatory dimension stressed by flexible specialization literature which influenced the neo-Progressive policy in Michigan to be described shortly, such scepticism is salutary. It contrasts, for example, with the perspective of Hirst and Zeitlin who, characterizing Japan as flexibly specialized, argue that:

> In each of its institutional forms, flexible specialization depends for its long term success on an irreducible minimum of trust and cooperation among economic actors, both between managers and workers within the firm and between firms and their external subcontractors ... such cooperation depends in turn on the establishment of rules limiting certain forms of competition such as sweated wages and conditions, as well as a collective institution for the supply of non-market inputs such as technological information or trained labour (Hirst and Zeitlin, 1991, p. 7).

However, there is agreement that at least in the auto industry, the region is a significant geographical entity in the reconstitution of organized capitalism. The remainder of this chapter considers Michigan's industrial policy in Detroit in this context.

Car wars: Detroit's Big Three fight back

The backcloth to Michigan policy is the "Japanizing" of regional economies in the US by the auto companies themselves. The location of the Japanese transplants provided ample evidence to Michigan economic planners of how even a sector specific industrial agglomeration such as Detroit can be bypassed in favour of greenfield locations:

> Within an advanced capitalist country such as the USA, the range of skills needed to support a more integrated production complex are, if not ubiquitous, at least widely available. .... What might be perceived as the natural advantage of an existing industrial agglomeration can still be severely diminished in the face of the corporation's power to create an industrial landscape of its own choosing (Schoenberger, 1987, p. 211).

This, of course, is precisely what the Japanese transplants have done in the United States. Transplant assembly plants now possess the capacity to assem-

170

ble over 2.5 million vehicles annually in the US with a new supporting supplier infrastructure of 259 parts manufacturing facilities with Japanese investment interest which have opened since 1981. Based on JIT production techniques such suppliers are located within 5 hours driving time or 200 miles of their major transplant assembly customer (McAlinden and Smith, 1992, p. 37, pp. 42-44). Lean as Japanese transplant production may be, scale economies for important components remain important and dedicated as opposed to flexible supplier facilities are part of the extended industrial production system. Vehicle engines and transmissions, for example, can still only be produced efficiently in volumes between 600,000 and 700,000 and is only feasible at all, even for the Japanese, at 300,000 units or higher (McAlinden and Smith, 1992, pp. 45-49). This contributes to the $30 billion in annual auto parts imports to the US (McAlinden & Smith, 1992, p. 14). And Japanese stamping facilities, located within or adjacent to their assembly operations, are thought to be effective precisely because they specialize in the production of parts for very few vehicle platforms or models assembled in the host facility and sometimes for only one (McAlinden and Smith, 1992, p. 38).

The employment impact on the Detroit region of the domestic auto companies' struggle to become leaner has been substantial. In Michigan, by 1987 the State's manufacturing industries had matched their 1979 output levels with roughly 200,000 fewer workers (State of Michigan, 1989). The Big Three auto makers reduced their US employment by 164,000 during 1979-89 partly through increased outsourcing, a job loss figure which increased to almost one quarter million during the 1990-91 recession. Between 1979 and 1991 GM, Ford and Chrysler closed no less than 80 facilities and reconverted or built 38 plants (McAlinden and Smith, 1992, p. 22). Locationally this has involved a recentralization of production in the Mid-West and Mid-South but often avoiding higher cost and more labour militant urban and industrially mature areas. Catering to fragmentation in consumer demand for a wider variety of models involving more vehicle platforms, more model variations and more flexibility in plants, recentralization has enabled transport economies as assembly plants service national as opposed to regional markets. Assembly plants that once produced identical models for a local area now distribute their products throughout the country (Rubenstein, 1992, p. 291). The Mid-South and Mid-West area between the I-75 and I-65 interstate highway corridors and bounded in the south by I-20 has now been dubbed the U.S. "automotive box" (McAlinden and Smith, 1992, p. 22).

Simultaneously, as Rubenstein argues, the labour climate in US auto plants has been influenced by the adoption of post-Fordist work rules inspired by Japanese management practices. Acceptance of more flexible and potentially stressful Japanese-inspired work rules has sometimes been made a condition, although not a guarantee, of keeping a plant open (Rubenstein, 1992, p. 270). Holmes and Rusonik (1991) attribute the withdrawal by the Canadian autoworkers from the United Auto Workers union in 1985 to the Canadians wanting to restore the traditional Fordist industrial relations system regarding wage rules and the maintenance of uniformity between companies and plants with respect to wages and work rules. The Canadians were also unenthusiastic about direct participation in management decision-making. In contrast, the UAW had accepted the wide application of "quality circles" and "team-working" and had agreed to lower wage rates for newly hired workers and broader job descriptions for all employees.

At individual company level it is Chrysler and Ford that have been leading the Big Three in the comeback trail against the Japanese, clawing back market share since 1992. Chrysler after studying and implementing production techniques used at Honda has fought its way back from alarming losses in 1991 and has successfully launched in 1994 a new inexpensive small car, the Neon, competing on price and quality with the best output of the Japanese lean production system. In April 1994 Chrysler was able to announce a best ever quarterly net profit of $938 million and had reduced its product development cycle to three years (Woodruff and Miller, 1993; *Economist*, 1994b). Ford has also been successful in restructuring. In 1992 the Ford Taurus symbolically replaced the Honda Accord as the No.1 selling car in the US (Woodruff, 1993). In the US, Ford, with a product development cycle reduced to four years, is now a low cost producer with its Atlanta factory rated as the most efficient car plant in North America (*Economist*, 1993). This successful restructuring has sometimes involved renegotiation of rigid job-control contracts. The contract at the Wayne, Detroit, plant in 1990 was renegotiated towards a team concept as a condition of allocating the new Ford Escort to the facility. Plant retooling emulated as closely as possible the organization of a comparable Mazda facility in Japan (Rubenstein, 1992, p. 273). Emphasis is also placed in the MIT study on teamwork amongst Ford workers "ignoring the technical details of the contract on a massive scale in order to cooperate and get the job done" (Womack et al., 1990, p. 283). With the launch by Ford in 1993 of its new "World car", the Mondeo, paralleling Japanese models such as the Honda Accord and Toyota Corolla and the reorganization of its product development in 1994 on a global basis, there is little doubt that auto companies continue to seek opportunities to produce in volume in search of economies of scale which continue to matter (*Business Week*, 1994b).

The picture painted of General Motors in the MIT study is of the world's largest industrial concern struggling, with too many managers, workers and plants, to adapt to Japanese productive techniques. The company has tried unsuccessfully to automate itself out of trouble and has had as much as 70 per cent of the value of its output accounted for by in-house production. In the mid 1980s GM launched the idea of its Saturn plant, a project to build cars in an entirely new way in pursuit of Japanese type efficiency. There would be "no layoffs at the plant, hierarchical distinctions would be minimized, time clocks would be done away with, work rules would be minimized, 20 per cent of all pay would come in the form of performance bonuses, and participatory decision-making would be the rule" (Osborne, 1988, p. 168). Because the Saturn project was considered so central to GM's future, a study prepared for the Michigan Senate saw the decision by GM to locate the $4,000 million project in Tennessee as ominous for Michigan's future (Hudson Institute, 1985, pp. 3-9). In 1994, however, while Saturn cars have been well received by the American public the project still remains barely profitable due to lacklustre productivity (*Economist*, 1994c). The company in 1994, while now profitable in its North American operations, still operates with the least efficient plants in North America, while trying to adapt from being a bureaucratically heavy full-function manufacturer of cars to being more like Toyota, a designer-assembler. In 1994, GM still manufactured over 65 per cent of the parts used in its cars as opposed to 50 per cent for Ford, 30 per cent for Chrysler and even less for Japanese manufacturers (*Economist*, 1994a). Given that the American industry has a long way to go to remake itself in the image of Japanese lean production, it is significant that the success of the New United Motor Manufacturing Inc. (NUMMI) plant in Fremont, California, a joint venture between GM and Toyota, with all senior managers supplied by the latter, has placed Fremont amongst the most efficient US car factories (*Economist* 1992). The most potent competition in the future according to the Chairman of Ford, will still come from Japan (Kerwin, 1994). Although under competitive price pressure Japanese manufacturers have recently been reducing the number of models, sharing more components in different cars and stretching product cycles (*Business Week*, 1994c), flexibility in meeting demand remains further advanced than with Big Three producers. Many more Japanese assembly plants allow the production of several very different models on the same line. Hence while model changeover time can take weeks and even months in Big Three facilities this can be a matter of days in Japanese plants (*Business Week*, 1994e, *Business Week*, 1992). As recently observed in the *New York Times*:

> At the General Motors Corporation, for example, a key Canadian plant that manufactures the Lumina mid-size car was shut in November to prepare for the 1994 version. The factory stayed closed for three months, and is still not expected to reach its full assembly line speed until August. By contrast, Honda's assembly plant in Marysville, Ohio, was able to switch from the 1993 Accord to the 1994 model in one weekend, and was up to full speed in a matter of weeks (Bennet, 1994).

Detroit: Michigan policy for a mature industrial district

In describing the reasons for the crisis of the Mid-West auto industry Clarke (1986) referred to "ossified class relations" and claimed that only a restructured class bargain would save the Detroit region as an auto producer. While

State of Michigan officials have worked with a corporatist model in mind (Hill, 1989) this has been within the constraints of Michigan's reputation for having a poor business climate with pressure, therefore, to keep down business costs (mainly tax and social wage expenditures) and to step somewhat gingerly when public intervention in the economy is discussed. Framed within a neo-Progressive outlook which seeks to accomplish social objectives through economic development strategies rather than through Great Society type programmes of the 1960s (Osborne, 1988), certain novel aspects of Michigan's industrial policy stand out.

The role of research and theory

The AIM Project (Auto in Michigan Project) was established early in the first administration of Democrat Governor, James Blanchard, who assumed office in 1983. This pulled in researchers from the university sector and the Department of Commerce itself "to understand the concrete implications for Michigan of a changing automotive economy" (AIM, 1986). Later the Michigan Commerce Department through its PRIME programme (Programme of Research in Modernization Economies) continued to monitor the flexibility debate. By the end of the decade State policy-making was informed by a proliferating post-Fordist literature. What is clear is that Michigan was not finding in the flexible specialization debate a rationale for easing out of mass manufacturing or for seeing small and medium sized firms as an independent engine for growth in the Detroit economy. No simple prescription of niche marketing through small batch production or simple high tech band wagon was seen as saviour of the Detroit region's manufacturing base. Research by the Michigan Commerce Department concluded that there was "little support for the view that smaller units of production – individually or in groups – can or are likely to replace a large share of the output of larger, more mass-production units". Referring to the recent work of Sabel that treated small-firm networks primarily as a preferred form of organization of large firms' supplier bases, the research argued that "public programmes should assist small firms to arrange with large-firm customers the kind of orders that play to the productivity strengths of programmable technologies used to produce intermediate goods, so as to harness flexibility to cheaper mass-consumption goods" (Luria, 1990). Research commissioned by the Michigan Commerce Department from the Michigan Industrial Technology Institute on industrial modernization in the state found both mass and batch producers alike automating their process equipment and challenged the view that the critical contribution of automated technology was to improve the efficiency of small-lot production (MITI, 1990, p. 58). Technology itself, as opposed to better industrial organization in general, was identified as "delivering at best marginal flexibility and quality improvements to the vast majority of adopters" (MITI, 1990a, p. 100). The research also concluded that "proximity matters".

Most of the informal cooperative activities uncovered in the study interviews involved firms located in close proximity either within a single county or adjacent counties (MITI, 1990, p. 123).

The Michigan Modernization Service

The Michigan Modernization Service and the State-established Michigan Industrial Technology Institute have been the flagship vehicles mediating between post-Fordist theory and industrial policy practice. MMS was concerned in the main with research and development especially of programmable manufacturing technology and its diffusion to small and medium sized Michigan firms (MMS, 1987a). The intention, to quote from a MMS work plan, was to create a "culture of continuous industrial modernization" and a "customized environment" for that purpose. The MMS defined a role for the State in fostering cooperative networking and sharing of information between smaller firms, particularly those involved in putting together modules of components for the automobile manufacturers (MMS, 1987b). Local area modernization plans based on local economic analysis began preparation in 1988. These focused, in particular, on local linkage analysis. The following description of LAMP (Local Area Modernization Plan) indicates the key role which small and medium-sized inter-firm linkages were seen as playing in Michigan's strategy:

> Viewing the manufacturing base in aggregate and in its components will enable the (Michigan Modernization) team to glean common characteristics among groups of firms which can be addressed via common solutions . . . (Modernization plans) will enable the identification of opportunities for firms to increase sales through consortial arrangements. This could take the form of the increased linkage of local firms by increasing the amount of intra-community sourcing of material, tooling and parts. It may be possible for area firms to enter new product markets through jointly producing a set of components that form a large module, or through linking processes with products (e.g. one firm doing precision machining of another firm's castings). The impact of this effort could prove particularly significant among firms which supply products and services to the automotive industry, where the automakers are moving toward modular sourcing of components from a smaller number of suppliers. This shift in auto industry sourcing patterns threatens the viability of smaller suppliers, unless they are able to market themselves to the higher-tier suppliers (MMS, 1987b).

Employing eight full-time staff and 23 private contractors MMS had an annual State budget of approximately $3,500,000 before its abolition in 1991. On a relatively modest budget Michigan's relationship with flexible specialization and post-Fordist theory went beyond mere flirtation in a few State reports. In the 1990 financial year, $317,000 in MMS funding was committed alongside $422,000 in local match to support 17 Manufacturing Alliance

175

projects (Fig. 5.1) between local groups of firms, trade associations and trade unions (MMS, 1991). The strategy had switched from technology as the main solution to competitiveness to incorporate the wider aspects of industrial organization also:

> MMS initially focused almost all of its efforts on helping its customers under-stand, acquire, and implement programmable automation technologies. What we learned over time is that throwing technology at a firm can cause as many problems as it solves. Global competitiveness requires a transformation in many aspects of the business, from shop floor organisation and quality control, to human resource management and organizational development, and strategic business planning and marketing. Technology is a tool to help achieve lower costs, higher quality, and faster delivery, but it only works if the basic production system is already well-tuned (MMS, 1991).

The work continues: the Michigan Industrial Technology Institute

In 1991 an incoming Republican Governor, John Engler, harkening to the simpler, less government economic nostrums of the Reagan era abolished the MMS. However, the extension service work has continued and in fact has expanded five fold with the establishment of a new Midwest Manufacturing Technology Centre at the Michigan Industrial Technology Institute. The latter, founded in 1981 in Ann Arbor with door step faculty expertise from the University of Michigan, had already been carving out a distinctive place for itself in industrial application research into automated manufacturing and robotics (Bartsch, 1985, pp. 28-31). With major carry over funds voted during the last days of the Democratic Blanchard administration matching a five year $13,000,000 federal grant from the National Institute of Standards and Technology, the continuance of neo-Progressive industrial policy for Detroit is likely to be assured in the medium term with the Clinton adminis-tration now endorsing an expanded programme of 170 manufacturing exten-sion services around the country (Luria et al., 1993). In addition, a collaborative research and development project between Detroit's Big Three and Washing-ton, to develop an ecologically friendly vehicle for the 21st century, is the most striking initiative so far in the Clinton administration's new industrial policy (Rudolph, 1993).

In discussing the operating philosophy of MITI, individual members of staff would be the first to admit that theoretical issues are still being wrestled with. Nevertheless, a case is made for placing priority on allocating manufac-turing extension resources to small and medium sized enterprizes in "core industrial agglomerations" in which "the tendency for industrial capacity and expertise to be densely concentrated has spawned rich local networks of large traded-goods producers and their SME suppliers (Luria et al., 1993). To the extent that large corporations can be embedded in such industrial districts where an institutional and supportive climate encourages firms to take the

MICHIGAN MODERNIZATION SERVICE
(REPORT TO MICHIGAN LEGISLATURE, 1991)
MISSION

The mission of the Michigan Modernization Service (MMS) is to help strengthen the competitive position and growth potential of Michigan's small and medium-sized manufacturers. Patterned after the Agricultural Extension Service, MMS provides direct services to smaller manufacturers to help them achieve and maintain global competitiveness.

Products and Services

1) Service to individual Firms

MMS serves as a catalyst to help firms implement world class manufacturing practices in their operations in order to improve quality and productivity, reduce costs, and expand markets. To accomplish this, MMS field teams provide an assessment of a firm's current performance against best manufacturing practice, and recommend specific steps for the customer to take to achieve continuous improvement toward world class manufacturing standards.

A typical field team consists of three individuals - one with a manufacturing or industrial engineering background, one with expertise in industrial training and human resource management, and one with expertise in industrial market analysis. These individuals are generally private contractors with many years of experience in manufacturing.

The MMS assessment focuses on issues related to: a) shop floor productivity and quality, including the introduction of new technology; b) human resource management and technical training; and c) analysis of market risks and diversification opportunities.

The typical MMS engagement involves five days of time from each of the members of the field team. No fee is charged for this service. MMS has provided this service to over 600 firms since its inception in 1985.

2) Manufacturing Alliances

Many of the competitiveness issues faced by small and medium-sized manufacturers cannot be addressed by any single firm and are best addressed through collaborative actions by groups of firms. Experience in other economies (Japan, West Germany, northern Italy, etc.) has demonstrated that small firms can improve global competitiveness if they combine resources to achieve cost efficiencies and economies of scale.

MMS serves as a catalyst to encourage the development of these new forms of competition in the Michigan manufacturing base. To accomplish this, MMS provides grants to trade associations, trade unions and groups of firms to solve problems or capitalize on opportunities that could not be capitalised on by individual firms.

Examples include opportunities to improve customer-supplier relationships, building industry links to the state R & D infrastructure, group firm marketing efforts and sector-specific training strategies.

In addition, MMS has initiated a process of assisting industrial trade associations to engage in strategic planning to identify the key issues facing their industry, and organise their association resources to address those issues.

Figure 5.1   Michigan and its response to the need for a State post Fordist industrial policy

MISSION

The mission of the Midwest Manufacturing Technology Center is to improve the productivity, quality, and manufacturing capability of foundation firms important to the Michigan and Midwest economy, and to enhance the knowledge, resources, and cooperative action of organizations that support modernization of the U.S. industrial base.

MMTC's activities are primarily focused in six areas:

Technology Assistance. Sector-specific programs to assist firms in evaluating, specifying, selecting, implementing, and optimizing appropriate tools, technologies and methods.

Technology Transfer. Interaction between the research community and commercial vendors to make new process technologies more readily available to foundation firms.

Continuous Improvement. Focused user groups to bring firms together to solve common problems, implement long-term changes, and promote commitment to quality.

Benchmarking Service. Manufacturers receive objective, detailed measures on how they compare to other, similar firms across the country.

Resource Network. Alliances with complementary capabilities and a common commitment to service Michigan manufacturing to give firms access to a broad range of expertise.

Councils. Six strong advisory councils which act as the "voice of the customer" and direct MMTC's services toward critical industry needs.

Source: MMTC, Annual Report, April 1992

Figure 5.2   Midwest Manufacturing Technology Center

"high road" to competitiveness through investment in plant and people as opposed to the "low road" of cutting wages, the hypermobility of capital can be dampened. This concept of agglomeration extends beyond that in traditional neoclassical economics recently described by Harrison where local economies are conceptualized as collections of atomistic competitors:

> By contract, modern industrial district theory emphasizes the interdependence of firms, flexible firm boundaries, cooperative competition and the importance of trust in reproducing sustained collaboration among economic actors within the districts (Harrison, 1992, p. 471).

As described in a paper produced by MITI staff:

> (Core agglomeration) firms don't just happen to be near each other and share a regional labor market; they do business with each other in a way that connects them as if, in some ways, they were complementary plants of a single enterprise. These agglomerations are an especially rich source of what some economists term increasing returns. When a manufacturer in one of these agglomerations improves its cost and quality performance, it also creates a competitive advantage for its in-cluster customers and suppliers. When government helps such a firm, it supports an entire regional web of interconnected companies. Indeed, the case for focusing on agglomerated places rests in no small measure on the inter-firm learning – formal and informal – that occurs there. Remediating technical laggards and improving both average and best manufacturing practice in such places is likely to have positive ripple effects (Luria et al., 1993).

With a less experimental and more client driven approach to the fostering of inter-firm cooperative linkages, the role of the Midwest Manufacturing Technology Center presently emphasises a renewed focus on technological diffusion with networking somewhat downplayed compared with the work of the Michigan Modernization Service. This has undoubtedly been influenced by the pressure on the Michigan Industrial Technology Institute, the host body, to be self-sustaining by the mid 1990s (MITI, 1992). The mission and major areas of MMTC activity are summarized in Fig. 5.2.

Lessons from the Detroit industrial policy experience

A number of lessons can be learnt from the Michigan supply side regional industrial policy experience. Firstly, we should be wary of hyperbole when considering the possibilities for progressive regional reregulation referred to in some flexible specialization literature. It would be naive to think that the peripatetic tendencies of corporate capital had been brought under control in Detroit. Large firms, not smaller ones, have been driving corporate restructuring in the US auto industry and despite a modest $1 million investment by

General Motors in the Michigan Industrial Technology Institute (Bartsch, 1985, p.31) the Big Three have not been greatly interested in regional corporatism. Rather geographical factors and the continued advantages of existing agglomeration economies in the wider Detroit region have bolstered industrial policy experimentation in Michigan. In 1992 S.E. Michigan was still the location of fifteen motor vehicle final assembly plants and one in every five motor vehicles produced in the US was assembled in Greater Detroit, a ratio which had actually increased from one in six in 1980. Additionally, the Detroit region has been gaining importance as a world automotive technical and administrative centre. Since 1990, Toyota, Nissan, Isuzu and Fiat have moved into the region and opened new technical centres (Semcog, 1992, pp. 34-36). Attempts at regional partnership with smaller and medium sized capital in economic restructuring also punctured hyperbole and brought Michigan neo-Progressives up against the limits of what can be secured for workers. While encouraging firms to take the "high road" to global competitiveness by investing in technology and people, the argument that Lean Production as distinguished from traditional Fordism, actually empowers management more than workers is well known to MITI staff.

Secondly, it is clear that practice and market complexity continue to run ahead of any full theoretical understanding which can wholly guide supply side policy intervention. As Castillo has recently remarked "we are witnessing a period of deep reflection and great effort by social scientists . . . who are seeking to take on board and interpret phenomena which probably affect capitalist societies more radically than has occurred for some time" (Castillo, 1994, p. 4). Confronted with the concrete reality of complex economic change Michigan supply side intervention has heeded the advice of Sayer (1989) and moved away since the 1980s from endorsing any simple bi-polar model of economic change. Thinking in terms of opposites (e.g. Fordism versus flexible specialization) "carries with it a series of dichotomous assumptions which limit our ability to understand the changes taking place. It obliges us to think in terms of ruptures (before and after) rather than in terms of complex processes" (Castillo, 1994, p. 11).

Thirdly, Detroit industrial policy practice, implemented at a time when potentially contingent geographical factors favoured recentralization of the automobile industry in the Mid-West and within the context of a particular industrial district where social conflict existed alongside important embedded relationships, can give only limited insight into the ability of regional political action to replicate industrial districts elsewhere. Nevertheless, despite its uniqueness, Michigan experience is an example of one existing industrial district rejecting the role of passive spectator in the face of the investment decisions of major corporate capital. Supply side intervention has been supported by the knowledge that "regions matter because agglomerations matter" (MITI, 1989, p. 7). Reasserting a production rather than consumption view of "the city", deindustrialization rust belt imagery in Detroit has been addressed at source complementing the all too frequent surface reimaging of city marketeers. Unfortunately the particular problems of the city of Detroit have not been central in this endeavour. As one commentator noted, Michigan's Democratic Governor, James Blanchard, who initiated State level neo-Progressive supply side industrial policies in the 1980s, made no significant efforts to bring the poor into the development process (Osborne, 1988, p. 172). The *Path to Prosperity* document which launched Michigan's experiment ten years ago simply stated that:

> In the absence of any proven means for funnelling regional job development away from suburbs and into inner cities, policies to reduce urban unemployment will have to focus on giving central city residents better access to jobs outside the city (State of Michigan, 1984, p. 111).

Or as one MITI staff member put it provocatively in interview in 1993: "I haven't thought about central cities in ten years."

References

AIM (1986), Auto in Michigan, Newsletter, vol.1, no 3, June, Michigan Industrial Technology Institute, Ann Arbor.

Albrechts, Louis and Swyngedouv, U.W., (1989), 'The Challenges for Regional Policy under a Flexible Regime of Accumulation', in Albrechts, L., Moulaert, F., Roberts, P., and Swyngedouw, U.W. (eds), *Regional Policy at the Crossroads: European Perspectives*. Jessica Kingsley Publishers in association with Regional Studies Association, London.

Amin, A., and Robins, K. (1990), 'The re-emergence of regional economies? The mythical geography of flexible accumulation'. *Environment and Planning D, Society and Space,* vol. 8, pp. 7-34.

Babson, Steven (1993), 'Lean or Mean: The MIT Model and Lean Production at Mazda', *Labor Studies Journal*, vol. 18, no. 2, pp. 3-24.

Barnekov, T., Boyle, R. and Rich, D. (1989), *Privatism and Urban Policy in Britain and the United States,* Oxford University Press, Oxford.

Bartsch, Charles (1985), *Reaching for Recovery: New Economic Initiatives in Michigan*, Northeast-MidWest Institute, Center for Regional Policy, Washington, DC.

Bennet, James (1994), 'Japanese made gains in June vehicle sales', *New York Times,* 7 July.

Business Week (1989), 'Shaking up Detroit', 14 August, pp. 30-36.

Business Week (1990), 'Car Wars – Special Report', 9 April, pp. 36-47.

Business Week (1992), 'Detroit's Big Chance', 29 June.

Business Week (1994a), 'Toyota, it's back on track', 4 April.

Business Week (1994b), 'Borderless Management', 23 May.

Business Week (1994c), 'New from Nissan: Reverse Sticker Shock', 23 May.

Business Week (1994d), 'Detroit, Check your Rearview Mirror', 6 June.

Business Week (1994e), 'Motown's struggle to shift on the fly', 11 July.

Castillo, Juan José (1994), 'Post-Fordism: what are you talking about? More on the reorganization of production and the organization of work', Paper presented at the 13th World Congress of Sociology, Bielefeld, Germany, July 18th-23rd.

Clark, Kim B.and Fujimoto Takahiro (1991), *Product Development Performance: Strategy Organisation & Management in the World Auto Industry*, Harvard Business School Press, Boston, Mass.

Clark, G.L. (1986), 'The crisis of the midwest auto industry', in Scott, A.J. and Storper, M. (eds), *Production, Work, Territory: The geographical anatomy of industrial capitalism*, Unwin Hyman, London.

Curry, James (1993), 'The Flexibility Fetish', *Capital & Class*, vol. 50, Summer, pp. 99-126.

Dickson, Martin (1993), 'Hard pedalling on the comeback trail', *Financial Times*, 2 June.

Dickson, Martin (1994), 'Third Place in US new car production', *Financial Times*, 25 May.

Done, K. (1991): 'Big Three batten down the hatches', *Financial Times*, 5 February.

Economist (1992), 'New factories for old', 3 October.

Economist (1993), 'Ford: Mondaine or mundane?', 8 January.

Economist (1994a), 'Taking GM apart', 7 January.

Economist (1994b), 'America's car industry: following Chrysler', 23 April.

Economist (1994c), 'General Motors: a younger wave', 2 July.

Farrell, Christopher (1994), 'Is the Japanese Dynamo Losing Juice?', *Business Week*, 27 June.

Harrison, Bennett (1992), 'Industrial Districts: Old Wine in New Bottles?', *Regional Studies*, vol. 26, no. 5, pp. 469-483.

Harrison, Bennett (1994), 'The Myth of Small Firms as the Predominant Job Generators', *Economic Development Quarterly*, vol. 8, no. 1, pp. 3-18.

Harvey, David (1989), *The Condition of Postmodernity*, Basic Books, Oxford.

Hill, R. C. (1989), 'Comparing transnational production systems: the automobile industry in the USA and Japan', *International Journal of Urban and Regional Research*, vol. 13, no. 3, pp. 462-479.

Hirst, P. and Zeitlin, J. (1991), 'Flexible specialization versus post-Fordism: theory, evidence and policy implications', *Economy and Society*, vol.20, no.1, pp. 1-56.

Holmes, J. and Rusonik, A. (1991), 'The break-up of an international labour union: uneven development in the Northern American auto industry and the schism in the UAW', *Environment and Planning A*, vol. 23, no. 1, pp. 9-35.

Hudson Institute (1985), *'Michigan Beyond 2000: A study prepared for the Michigan Senate*, Indianapolis, Indiana.

Kaplinsky, R. (1988), 'Restructuring the capitalist labour process: some lessons from the car industry', *Cambridge Journal of Economics*, vol. 12, pp. 451-470.

Kenney, Martin and Florida, Richard (1992), 'The Japanese Transplants: Production, Organization and Regional Development', *Journal of the American Planning Association*, vol. 58, no. 1, Winter, pp. 21-38.

Kerwin, Kathleen (1994), 'Value will keep Detroit moving', *Business Week*, 10 January.

Logan, John R. and Swanstrom, Todd (1990), 'Urban Restructuring: A Critical Review', chapter 1 in Logan, John R. and Swanstrom, Todd (eds), *Beyond the City Limits*, Temple University Press, Philadelphia, pp. 3-24.

Luria, Dan (1990), 'Automation, Markets and Scale: Can Flexible Niching Modernize American Manufacturing?' *International Review of Applied Economics.*

Luria, Daniel et al.(1993), 'Fixing the Manufacturing Base: The Allocation of Manufacturing Extension', *Journal of Policy Analysis and Management,* vol. 12, no. 4.

Luria, Dan and Russell, Jack (1981), *Rational Reindustrialization: An Economic Development Agenda for Detroit*, Widgetripper Press, Detroit.

McAlinden, Sean P. and Smith, Brett C. (1992), *The Changing Structure of the US Automotive Parts Industry*, Office for the Study of Automotive Transportation, University of Michigan, Transportation Research Institute.

McAlinden, Sean P. and Andrea, David J. (1993), *Michigan: Still the Automotive State?*, The Office for the Study of Automotive Transportation, University of Michigan, Transportation Research Institute.

Michigan Modernization Service (1987a), *Business Plan,* 13 April.

Michigan Modernization Service (1987b), *Local Area Modernization Plan Project,* Work Plan, 17 April.

Michigan Modernization Service (1989), *Local Area Modernization Plan (LAMP) Project,* internal memorandum, 3 January.

Michigan Modernization Service (1991), *Report to the Legislature,* 28 February.

MITI (1989), 'Fixing what's broke where it counts: agglomeration in the core industrial economy', *Technecon*, vol. 1, no. 2.

MITI (1990), *The Michigan Foundation: A Study of the Modernization Process in Michigan's Small and Medium Sized Manufacturers*, A report prepared for the Michigan Modernization Service.

MITI (1992), *Industrial Technology Institute Times*, vol. 3, no. 1.

MMTC (1992), Midwest Manufacturing Technology Center, Annual Report for 1991.

Murray, Robin (1989), 'Fordism and Post Fordism', in Hall, Stuart and Jacques, Martin (eds.) *New Times,* Lawrence and Wishart, London.

Osborne, David (1988), *Laboratories of Democracy: A new Breed of Governor Creates Models for National Growth,* Havard Business School Press, Boston, Mass.

Perulli, Paolo (1993) 'Towards a Regionalization of Industrial Relations', *International Journal of Urban and Regional Research*, vol. 17, no. 1, pp. 98-113.

Piore, M. and Sable,C. (1984), *The Second Industrial Divide,* Basic Books, New York.

Reich, Robert (1983), *The Next American Frontier*, Times Books, London.

Rubenstein, James M.(1992), *The Changing US Auto Industry: A Geographical Analysis*, Routledge, London.

Rudolph, Barbara (1993), 'Star Wars for Cars', *Time*, 11 October.

Sabel, C.F. (1989), 'Flexible Specialization and the Re-emergence of Regional Economies', in Hirst, P. and Zeitlin, J. (eds), *Reversing Industrial Decline? Industrial Structure and Policy in Britain and Her Competitors,* Berg, Oxford.

Sayer, A. (1989), 'Post Fordism in Question', *International Journal of Urban and Regional Research,* vol.13, no.4, pp. 666-692.

Schoenberger, E. (1987), 'Technological and Organisational Change in Automobile Production: Spatial Implications', *Regional Studies,* vol.21, no.3, pp. 199-214.

SEMCOG (1992), *Regional Profile of Southeast Michigan*, Southeastern Michigan Council of Governments, Detroit.

State of Michigan (1984), *The Path to Prosperity: Findings and Recommendations of the Task Force for a long term Economic Strategy for Michigan.*

State of Michigan (1989), *Beyond the Rust Belt: The Path to Prosperity Revisited.*

Womack, J. P., Jones, D. and Roos, D. (1990), *The Machine that Changed the World,* Macmillan, New York.

Wood, S. (1988), 'Between Fordism and Flexibility? The US Car Industry', in Hyman, R. and Streeck, W. (eds), *New Technology and Industrial Relations,* Blackwell, Oxford.

Woodruff, David (1993), 'Why Detroit doesn't need the protection it wants', *Business Week*, 8 February.

Woodruff, David and Miller, Karen Lowry (1993), 'Chrysler's Neon', *Business Week*, 3 May.

6 Beyond the hype: targeting social deprivation in Belfast's public housing estates

Brendan Murtagh

Introduction

In the event that peace does establish itself in Belfast and Northern Ireland the city's other image problem is likely to move to political centre stage. Social deprivation and income inequality induced by unemployment or low paying employment threaten the stability of any future political settlement. This chapter reviews deprivation in Belfast and recent government initiatives designed to alleviate it. While a major public sector housing programme over the last twenty years has provided the city with some of the best social housing in the United Kingdom, indices of social distress stubbornly persist. In a situation of limited resources this chapter suggests the need for a more targeted application of those available. The chapter stresses the significance of consumption sector cleavages in understanding the poor, who they are and where they live in Belfast. Drawing on the work of Peter Saunders (1986, 1989 and 1990), it concludes that the restratification of British society has implications for understanding local society, the relationship between space and society and the role of land use planning. Saunders argues that restratification is based on the control and ownership of individual consumption including health, education, transport and housing. This is not to deny that social class and, crucially, religion are two important sectors of cleavage in the stratification of local society. Rather, it challenges assumptions underpinning the logic of spatial programmes whose point of departure correlates poverty with a particular religious grouping. Developing this contention, the chapter uses a range of empirical data to explore the reality of the distribution of deprivation in the city. In particular, it highlights the relationship between social malaise and public sector housing estates. It suggests that this provides a point of departure to move the policy debate beyond the hype and closer to the reality.

The face of deprivation: Belfast's other problem

Studies in urban deprivation have had a relatively long history in Belfast. In 1853, Rev. W.M. O'Hanlon's Walks Among the Poor of Belfast revealed, "Indescribable scenes of poverty, filth and wretchedness..." in an area to the north of the city centre (Quoted in Bardon, 1982, p. 103). More rigorous and advanced analyses in the mid 1970s have followed. Boal et al. (1974) applied Principal Component Analysis to seven and then ten (Boal et al., 1978) indicators of social malaise and identified concentrations of deprived wards in the inner city and in West Belfast. Similarly, in 1976 a government led project team identified the same two zones using sixteen social, economic and demographic indicators:

> One is characterised by unemployment, low incomes and overcrowded housing resulting from large family size. This has a West Belfast distribution. The other is an inner city syndrome distinguished by substandard housing, poor physical environment, low incomes, lack of skills and a concentration of persons suffering from different forms of physical handicap whether associated with age or health (Project Team, Belfast Areas of Need, 1976, p. 61).

The persistence of poverty and relative deprivation resulted in a re-analysis of social and economic conditions in the city using 1981 Census data (Policy Planning Research Unit (PPRU), 1987). That study showed that little had changed since the Belfast Areas of Need (BAN) Report in 1976 and that "for the most part, the same wards are still relatively deprived. A group of wards in the city extending West and South West have significantly higher levels of multiple need than other wards in the BUA" (PPRU, 1987, p. 27).

Knox (1978) recognised the problems caused by using available indices of need to construct statistical analyses of social malaise. He criticised the use of census related data in some multivariate analysis of deprivation because the indicators selected often overlapped in terms of the dimensions of disadvantage they attempt to explain. He argued that:

> Non-census data are particularly important in providing a more explicitly social dimension to area profiles and territorial social indicators and in compensating for the bias of census based Small Area Statistics (SAS) towards housing, demographic and employment indicators. Non-census data thus form the major and very often the only source of information about fundamental domains of life such as health, leisure, social stability, security and environmental quality (Knox, 1978, p. 78).

For this reason, indicators were selected by the author from the Northern Ireland Housing Executive's 1985 Belfast Household Survey to provide a more sensitive account of the reality of spatial poverty in the city. Surveys are carried out by the Housing Executive in mid Census years to update the

186

social, economic and demographic profile of the city. A total of 22,000 households were surveyed in 1985 (NIHE, 1985). The under-use of housing based empirical data sets for trend analysis has been pointed out elsewhere (Murtagh, 1992a). In short, all valid and reliable data connected with space and society have a role to play in understanding deprivation and should be developed in a way that increases that understanding.

Fifteen variables were selected by the author for detailed analysis at ward level (Murtagh, 1993). These included: total unemployment; multiple household unemployment; female unemployment; supplementary benefit; housing benefit; family income supplement; dependency ratio; public rented housing; head of household income below £60 per week; overcrowding; Net Annual Valuation of dwelling below £60 per annum; dwelling unfitness and lack of basic dwelling amenities. The main data sources used were the Greater Belfast Household Survey 1985 of approximately 22,000 households in the city (NIHE, 1985) and the Northern Ireland House Condition Survey of the previous year (NIHE, 1984), both carried out by the Northern Ireland Housing Executive. A ward based data set was constructed from both surveys and subjected to a series of statistical analyses.

The first stage correlation analysis was carried out on the combined data set and the results are shown in Table 6.1. Patterns of association are immediately apparent. For example, multiple household unemployment has a high correlation co-efficient with both female unemployment (.68) and total unemployment (.88). Other relationships can be established between state benefits such as housing benefit and supplementary benefit (.82). Indicators of poor housing conditions are also strongly correlated. For example, the correlation score between dwelling unfitness and amenity deprivation is .91. However, public rented dwellings correlated strongly with a number of indicators including, for example, total unemployment (.77), supplementary benefit (.83), housing benefit (.74), low car ownership (.80) and low income (.68). In order to unravel the relationship between these factors and to consider their spatial distribution in Belfast, it was necessary to employ more advanced factor analysis techniques. This was carried out in the second stage.

Principal Component Analysis (PCA) is a statistical technique used to identify a relatively small number of factors that can be used to represent relationships among sets of many interrelated variables. The basic assumption of PCA is that underlying dimensions, or factors, can be used to explain complex phenomena. The data set, when subjected to this type of analysis, showed that the first four factors account for 73.8 per cent of the total variance. The contribution of each variable to the four factors is shown in Table 6.2. The indicators with highest loadings, or percentages, contribute most to the factor and give its overall character.

The efficacy of factor analysis in this project has been in the reduction of a large number of variables to a smaller number of factors for each case. In this respect a factor score was computed for each case (or ward). The first factor

Table 6.1 Correlation Analysis of Deprivation Indicators

Variable	HOH Unemployed	Female Unemployed	No Car	HOH Unskilled	Supplement Benefit	Housing Benefit	Family Credit	Dependency Ratio	Public Rented Housing	Household Unemployed	Low Income	Over-crowding	NAV	Unfitness	Missing Amenity
HOH Unemployed	1.00	.68	.34	.32	.46	.26	.30	.23	.38	.57	.26	.34	.16	.01	.03
Female Unemployed	.68	1.00	.69	.43	.66	.43	.07	.26	.63	.88	.63	.47	.38	.32	.30
No Car	.34	.69	1.00	.54	.81	.59	.19	.32	.80	.83	.80	.45	.51	.47	.53
HOH Unskilled	.32	.43	.54	1.00	.61	.56	.27	.32	.55	.49	.51	.31	.37	.31	.33
Supplementary Benefit	.46	.66	.81	.61	1.00	.82	.26	.43	.83	.78	.68	.47	.32	.25	.32
Housing Benefit	.26	.43	.59	.56	.82	1.00	.21	.35	.74	.54	.65	.36	.22	.13	.32
Family Credit	.30	.07	.19	.27	.26	.21	1.00	.25	.15	.18	.10	.07	.20	.14	.13
Dependency Ratio	.23	.26	.32	.32	.43	.35	.25	1.00	.21	.33	.40	.01	.18	.01	.02
Public Rented Housing	.38	.63	.80	.55	.83	.74	.15	.21	1.00	.77	.69	.38	.22	.28	.35
Household Unemployment	.57	.88	.83	.49	.78	.54	.18	.33	.77	1.00	.64	.47	.30	.26	.28
Low Income	.26	.63	.80	.51	.68	.65	.10	.40	.69	.64	1.00	.26	.52	.46	.57
Overcrowding	.34	.47	.45	.31	.47	.36	.07	.01	.38	.47	.26	1.00	.23	.02	.03
NAV	.16	.38	.51	.37	.32	.22	.20	.18	.22	.30	.52	.23	1.00	.74	.74
Unfitness	.01	.32	.47	.31	.25	.13	.14	.01	.28	.26	.46	.02	.74	1.00	.91
Missing Amenity	.02	.30	.53	.33	.32	.32	.13	.02	.35	.28	.57	.03	.74	.91	1.00

Table 6.2 Factor Analysis of Deprivation Indicators

Variable	Factor 1	Factor 2	Factor 3	Factor 4
HOH Unemployed	.08	-.02	.80	.39
Female Unemployment	.42	.25	.78	.04
No Car	.71	.42	.41	.03
HOH Unskilled	.59	.24	.20	.29
Supplementary Benefit	.82	.13	.40	.17
Housing Benefit	.87	.01	.13	.13
Family Credit	.03	.13	.11	.83
Dependency Ratio	.49	-.07	-.07	.61
Public Rented Housing	.80	.15	.38	-.04
Household Unemployment	.60	.18	.67	.08
Low Income	.74	.44	.18	.05
Overcrowding	.26	-.02	.68	-.15
NAV	.14	.83	.16	.17
Unfitness	.12	.94	.03	.01
Missing Amenity	.22	.94	-.02	-.02
Total variance accounted for by factor	47.2%	14.9%	8.3%	3.4%

extracted can be labelled state dependency. The profile of the factor is low ownership of dwellings and cars leading to dependency on public sector housing and transport. Furthermore, dependency on the state for cash resources is reflected in a high co-efficient for supplementary benefit and low head of household income. This is the most significant factor as it accounted for 47.2 per cent of the total variance in the data. Spatially, this factor is concentrated in a ring of wards in the inner city and parts of West Belfast. However, there is a significant extension of this type of deprivation into East Belfast. In addition, it is prevalent in outer areas to the North and West of the city. The second factor, which accounts for 14.9 per cent of the variation in the data, reflects poor housing conditions shown by high co-efficients for low Net Annual Valuations, dwelling unfitness and lack of basic amenities. This has a mainly inner city distribution, with a short southward extension to the area around Queen's University where there is a high proportion of poor quality private rented dwellings. Unemployment was the third factor extracted and accounted for 8.3 per cent of total variance. Spatially it is concentrated in three main areas which are West Belfast, a narrow spine of wards extending into the north of the city and inner East Belfast. Finally, the dependency deprivation factor reflects a drain on available household income. This is shown by high factor loadings for dependency ratio and family income supplement. This factor accounts for only 3.4 per cent of the variance and while less spatially specific it was dominant in wards in the inner city and outer parts of North Belfast.

In summary, this analysis has identified five main areas of malaise. The inner city and West Belfast concentrations of deprivation highlighted by studies in the seventies and eighties are again identified in this study. However, there are also a strong northward spine and shorter but significant concentrations in wards in the inner east of the city and in outer Belfast. Spatially, this correlates closely with the distribution of public sector housing estates and deprivation in the outer city is almost exclusively linked to large single estates such as Rathcoole in the north and Twinbrook in the west.

However, as both Knox (1987) and Boal (1978) have pointed out, the use of the ward as a unit of analysis often generalises the spatial configuration of poverty. Moreover, the emergent pattern suggests that some of the explanation of variance in the data can be explained by the presence of public sector housing. A range of recent qualitative studies has highlighted the complex nature of local poverty. In their study of Glenside, a housing estate in West Belfast, McAuley and Kremer (1990) recognised "all the hallmarks of a community on the periphery, a community which endeavours to sustain an alternative culture apart from the dominant grouping" (McAuley and Kremer, 1990, p. 258). Similarly, Evason and Woods (1991) underlined the sense of personal despair at the multi-dimensional nature of poverty in depressed housing estates in West Belfast. Moreover, some groups such as Community Development in Protestant Areas (CDPA) (1991) are critical of broad scale policies that fail to recognise the particular difficulties of deprivation in Protestant areas, where the tradition of self help and community cohesion is not as strong as in Catholic areas. Building on this, Sweeney urged the government to transcend the "nonsensical sectarian head counting in targeting social need". He said:

> What we really need is a vision of the targeting social need programme which concentrates on the real schism in the society which is the gap between the haves and have not's because that's the real gap and the government should be focusing on that with a great sense of urgency and precision (quoted in Haughey, 1993, p. 10).

The 1991 Northern Ireland Census of Population represented another opportunity to analyse deprivation in the city. In a recent paper, Hirschfield called for planners to map and describe the spatial dimension of deprivation based on "consistency, reliability and spatial focus which the census provides" (Hirschfield, 1994, p. 52). Townsend et al. (1987) provide an index of four indicators of material deprivation drawn from the census: unemployment; overcrowding; households without a car; and households not owner occupied, and these are analysed below.

In Northern Ireland as a whole, 106,000 people are currently without jobs, one in seven of the labour force. The Greater Belfast area has a slightly smaller, but still very serious, unemployment problem with one in eight out of work. In Falls (49.3 per cent), Whiterock (49 per cent), New Lodge (48.3 per cent) and Ardoyne (46.2 per cent) nearly half the economically active work force are unemployed. The figure for unemployment in the city is almost twice as high for males than for females. Map 6.1 shows that the highest concentrations of male unemployment are in the west and north of the city. Car ownership rates were also low in these wards. As map 6.2 shows, the lowest rates were in Falls (89 per cent without a car), Whiterock (84 per cent) and St. Annes (87 per cent). The success of the major housing redevelopment and renewal programme has helped to reduce overcrowding. There is, however, a correlation between wards with higher proportions of Catholics and overcrowding rates. For example in Whiterock in West Belfast 12.9 per cent of households experience overcrowding. In Upper Springfield the figure is 13.2 per cent and in Twinbrook 11 per cent. Map 6.3 shows that non-ownership of dwellings is concentrated in West and North Belfast, the inner east of the city and in parts of the outer city to the west and north. In Ballymacarrett in East Belfast 89 per cent of houses are not owned by occupants, in St Annes in the inner city 95 per cent are not owned and in the heartland of social deprivation, the Falls ward, 95 per cent of dwellings are also not owned by the occupants. Measured against these indicators the most deprived wards were concentrated in West Belfast (Falls, Whiterock, Upper Springfield), North Belfast (New Lodge and Ardoyne), inner city (St. Annes and Shaftesbury), East Belfast (Ballymacarett), and outer West Belfast

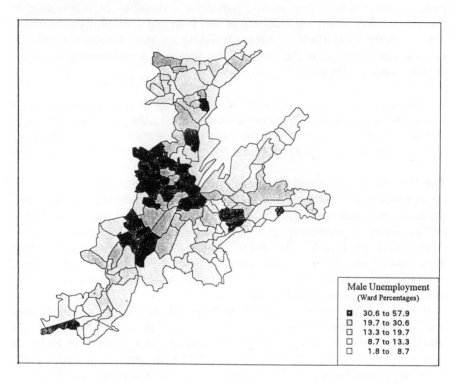

**Map 6.1 Male unemployment in the Belfast Urban Area
(1991 Census)**

(Collinglen and Twinbrook). The maps also show that the socially advantaged wards are concentrated in outer South and East Belfast. In Cultra, 4.7 per cent of dwellings are not owner occupied, 0.4 per cent are overcrowded and unemployment is 4.3 per cent for the ward. Only 5.5 per cent of households are without a car.

Policy initiatives and deprivation in the city

The first major policy for tackling urban deprivation in Belfast resulted from the 1976 ward analysis of social need. The resulting Belfast Areas of Need Programme (BAN) targeted expenditure on the 20 worst wards in the city. Nearly £4.5 million were spent on recreation and leisure centres and £700,000 on environmental improvement projects. The Eastern Health Board, responsible for health and social services in the city, received an additional £4.5 million and a programme of renovation and redecoration of schools in the

192

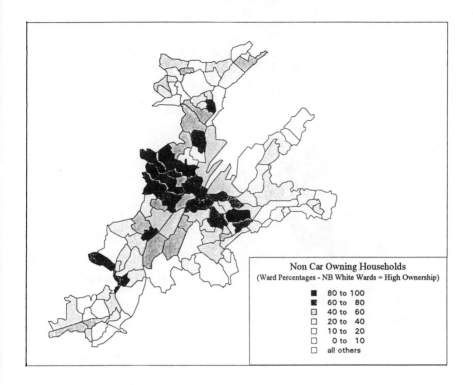

Non Car Owning Households
(Ward Percentages - NB White Wards = High Ownership)

- ■ 80 to 100
- ▨ 60 to 80
- ☐ 40 to 60
- ☐ 20 to 40
- ☐ 10 to 20
- ☐ 0 to 10
- ☐ all others

**Map 6.2   Non car owning households in the Belfast Urban Area
(1991 Census)**

BAN areas cost £1 million. Approximately £500,000 were spent on two neighbourhood business units between the Falls and the Shankill areas. However, the programme was widely criticised by community groups who were dissatisfied with the level and quality of consultation, the scale of the funding and emphasis on the leisure and recreation projects. In addition, they felt that "Communities were being forced to compete with each other over a pittance of money. This was splitting the working class and gave rise to sectarian rivalries" (Community Organisations of Northern Ireland, 1977, p. 3).

In 1979, the Conservative administration in Westminster brought an approach to land use planning that stressed the role of private finance and enterprise as the key to the regeneration of depressed urban areas and implicitly rejected direct intervention from the public sector (Sorenson, 1983). However, as Friedland et al. (1977) and others have recognised, there are constraints on the extent to which governments can withdraw from economic and societal management. In particular, they point to the damaging effects of

193

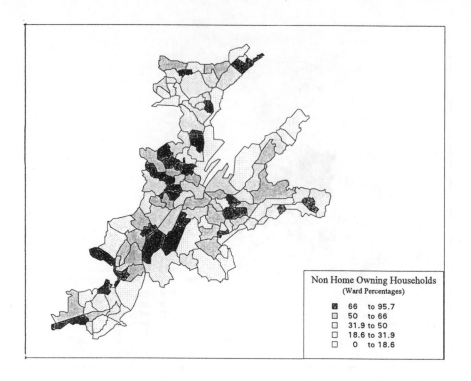

Map 6.3   Non house owning households in the Belfast Urban Area
           (1991 Census)

"urban crises" on the physical and social fabric of cities and show how
interventionist inner city and neighbourhood planning policies in some American cities in the mid seventies were a response forced by ethnic and class
tension. Some political commentators (Pyle, 1990; West Belfast Economic
Forum, 1990) have likewise suggested that the intensification of violence in
West Belfast in the late 1980s, persistent unemployment and visible poverty
challenged the government's reliance on private capital to lead recovery in
inner city areas. The policy response to this research was the Making Belfast
Work programme which aimed to "stimulate greater economic activity,
reinforce local enterprise, improve the quality of the environment and equip
the people of these areas to compete successfully for available employment"
(Northern Ireland Information Service, 1988, p. 1).

   The programme started in 1988 and was targeted on wards in North and
West Belfast and had an initial funding commitment of £10 million over one
year. This was later complemented by £35 million for the following two

financial years. Economic measures included the upgrading of training, particularly in information technology, and improvement in the literacy and numeracy skills of school leavers. New Action for Community Employment (ACE) posts, designed to enable the long term unemployed to return to work, were provided along with funding for the West Belfast Enterprise Board. Additional finance also supported improvements to school buildings, the provision of information technology suites and better facilities for adult and continuing education. The establishment of an Immunisation Task Force, the promotion of environmental health and the adoption of additional environmental improvement schemes were also included in the programme. Provision was also made for the establishment of Belfast Action Teams (BATs). These are small teams of civil servants set up "to improve the effectiveness with which Government expenditure in the targeted areas is used" (DOE(NI), 1988, p. 1). Nine teams have now been established, each with an initial budget of £500,000 per year, which is used mainly to support community projects linked to employment creation, improving employability, community development and environmental improvements.

The MBW initiative has been criticised because the level of committed finance was too low and because it ignored the scale and complexity of the deprivation problem. Gaffikin and Morrisey (1990) point out that the scale of the funding is small relative to Government support for the Laganside development project and to public disinvestment in West Belfast caused by benefit changes and reductions in the Belfast City Council community services budget. Similarly, Birrell and Wilson (1993) conclude that "In terms of its key objective MBW has not been very successful. The initiative has not made significant in-roads into the lack of jobs and long-term unemployment in disadvantaged areas" (Birrell and Wilson, 1993, p. 51). In particular, they point out that the majority of the jobs created by the initiative to date have been in social and community services rather than in commercial or business enterprises and are low paid or part-time. They also make the point that the objectives have become too wide and the initiative now lacks an overall focus. Formal evaluation of the BAT initiative showed that it, too, fell short of its original objective of creating new employment. Again, the number and quality of private sector jobs have been low but the evaluation did conclude that at least the initiative had a concentrated spatial focus that targeted specific disadvantaged groups in small local communities (PA Cambridge Economic Consultants, 1992).

MBW and the Belfast Action Teams were attempts to address the real social malaise in the city, and yet, even here, a preoccupation with reimaging is reflected in a strategy to improve Belfast's street frontages. By 1986 the government had become increasingly concerned that the significant improvement in the quality and appearance of Belfast's housing stock was hidden by poor arterial route frontages and consequently undervalued. Belfast is a city with main roads (arterial routes) radiating from the city centre to the suburbs.

These main roads were often characterised by dilapidated buildings, vacant blocks, poorly maintained property and low environmental quality. The Department of the Environment therefore commissioned a series of studies designed to upgrade the appearance of the poorest roads. In the depressed areas of North and West Belfast the Antrim, Falls, Springfield and Shankill roads were early targets for the initiative. Political murals, graffiti and kerb painting helped to reinforce the tribal and fractious nature of these areas and their prominent visibility on the road frontage added to their image as a 'place apart'. In an attempt to soften hard sectarian imagery, the Arterial Routes strategy used enhanced rates of the existing Urban Development Grant scheme to target the worst properties. Statutory owners were encouraged to upgrade the external appearance of their properties and environmental improvement money was used to create parking bays, provide planting boxes and re-pave footpaths. No formal evaluation of the initiative has been published and indeed its evolution and implementation were characterised by a closed and semi-corporatist strategy (Murtagh, 1992b). However, it did finance the improvement of some of the worst frontages in the city, some eyesores were removed and the colours that badged green and orange territory were toned down with an infusion of post modernist colour and architectural style.

The initiative represented a significant attempt to reimage the physical manifestations of poverty and ethnic division. Viewed in the context of the severity of social malaise it can be safely concluded that the target was not the local poor but an external audience of investors, tourists and key workers. These interests must not be alienated by symbols of urban decay and communal division. The policy perception underlying the strategy was that the rebirth of the city must embrace these interests, minimize their fears and exploit their potential.

Another approach

The presence of concentrated areas of social malaise and the association of an urban underclass with local authority housing has received popular attention in Britain (see Murray, 1994). Recent academic research and theory provide a framework for the exploration of the nature and scope of urban deprivation in Belfast. Peter Saunders lays down a specific theoretical foundation on which such an empirical analysis can be structured:

> Social and economic divisions arising out of the ownership of the key means of consumption such as housing are now coming to represent a new major fault line in British society, that privatisation of welfare provision is intensifying this cleavage to the point where sectoral alignments in regard to consumption may come to outweigh class alignments in respect to production, and that home tenure

196

remains the most important single aspect of such alignments because of the accumulative potential of house ownership and the significance of private housing as an expression of personal identity as a source of ontological security (Saunders, 1984, p. 203).

The process of "social restratification" has a number of causes including the growth of service occupations, the decline in employment in heavy manufacturing, the introduction of new technologies demanding a highly skilled and autonomous workforce, the rise in the number of dual earner households which creates a new division between "work rich" and "work poor" households, the expansion of managerial and administrative functions in both the public and private sectors, the collapse of Keynesian full employment strategies and the emergence of large scale unemployment among specific sections of the population and the attempts by government since 1976 to control the growth of social expenditure. According to Pahl (1984, 1988) the result of such developments has been the growth of what he calls the "middle mass" on the one hand and the underclass on the other. In Farewell to the Working Class, Gorz (1982) also argues that the period of fulltime waged work for all has ended. He suggests that increasingly the quality of individual life and life chances will be divorced from the formal world of work. In particular, the control that individuals exercise over the consumption of key services and facilities provided by the state will determine their quality of life. Pahl suggests that, in Britain, the class system is coming to correspond less to the familiar metaphor of a pyramid (that is, a small stratum at the top, a larger middle stratum and the mass of production at the base) and more to that of an "onion" (with the majority in the bulging and comfortable middle, while the smaller stratum remains anchored at the bottom). Seen in this way, familiar class cleavages are losing their significance. As Pahl puts it:

> The division between the more affluent home owning households of ordinary working people and the less advantaged underclass households is coming to be more significant than conventional division based in manual/non manual distribution... The new line of class change is now between the middle mass and the underclass beneath (Pahl, 1984, pp.314-324).

For Saunders (1989) four factors are pertinent in describing the features of the emerging underclass. First, it suffers multiple deprivations, an assimilation of social pathologies and disadvantages. Second, it is socially marginal in that its members do not generally belong to formal organisations such as trade unions, or find it easy to participate in mainstream society for they are often unemployed and lack everyday means of communication such as cars and telephones. Third, it is characterised by a culture of fatalism which is both a response to hopelessness and a factor which reproduces it. And finally, it is dependent. Its members are powerless clients of a patronage state, relying upon state provision not only for their health care and their children's schooling, but for virtually every aspect of their lives including their income and most significantly their housing.

Tenurial divisions do not coincide with this distinction between the middle mass and the underclass. Clearly, by no means all of the 34 per cent of Northern Ireland households living in public rented housing are members of the underclass. The point is that as owner occupation expands, "public housing is drifting solely towards a residual, welfare role – an ambulance service to carry off the wounded – catering largely for lower income and disadvantaged groups" (Yates, 1982, p. 218). Likewise Forest recognises the spatial implication of such a trend:

> Although marginal groups such as the long term unemployed, ethnic minorities, working class youth, single-parent families, are not concentrated exclusively in the state housing sector, the largest spatial concentrations are to be found in the council estates of the inner city or urban periphery (Forest, 1987, p. 1620).

This is not the place to engage in a detailed debate about production and consumption perspectives nor the analysis of trends in social structure. The specific spatial implications of that debate have been addressed comprehensively elsewhere (Murie, 1986). The purpose of the remainder of this chapter is to test the empirical significance of this analysis in the context of planning Belfast.

Estate based targeting

Thirty individual estate based household surveys carried out by Housing Executive researchers were analysed and showed that tenants identified a number of interrelated problems (Murtagh, 1991). These surveys were conducted between 1989 and 1991 and include both analysis of physical problems and household surveys of tenants. Figure 6.1 shows that physical problems include the condition of the environment (23 estates), non-traditional design (11) and lack of defensible space (7). Isolation, particularly on peripheral estates (9), poor community facilities (10) and an inadequate range, quality and number of shops (12) were also identified by tenants. There were also high rates of dissatisfaction with estate utilities (18), including the bus service, public telephones and street lighting. In addition, 22 of the estate household surveys identified problems with the dwelling maintenance and repair system reflecting the housing management dimension to depressed housing estates. However, many of the issues which appear, on the face of it, to be problems of design and maintenance or administration have to be understood in terms of a lack of resources. For example, shops and services tend to be limited because traders need to establish economic viability.

These problems have been compounded by the residualisation of the NIHE stock which was highlighted in a 1985 survey of NIHE house sales. The process of residualisation is illustrated by the fact that the dwellings that were most likely to be sold to tenants were semi-detached and built in the post-war period. Moreover, those who bought were more likely to be middle aged, in full time employment and on higher incomes than non-purchasers (NIHE, 1986). Spatially, the best located estates with the best dwellings and with households in relatively advantageous economic circumstances were most

Figure 6.1: **Self reported problems by more than 50 per cent of residents on 30 depressed NIHE estates in Northern Ireland**

Factor	Number
Isolation/Out of town	9
Poor environment	23
Large size of estate	4
Void dwellings	13
Car parking	10
Impersonal public space	7
Lack of play facilities	9
Lack of community facilities	10
Poor shopping facilities	12
Poor estate utilities (phone/bus etc.)	18
Poor dwelling conditions	10
Too much noise	2
Design unpopular	11
Heating problems	14
Electric wiring problems	12
Security problems	11
Inadequate repair and maintenance	22
Vandalism	20
Lack of community spirit	12
Crime	10
Sectarian problems	3

likely to have high sales rates leaving a growing proportion of unpopular estates with declining property in the public rented sector. The increasing residualisation of the public rented stock is also shown by Northern Ireland Family Expenditure Survey data on inter-tenure differences in household income between 1981 and 1989. When adjusted to allow for time the data show that the rate of increase of household income for mortgage holders was four times greater than for the Housing Executive tenants over the same period. By 1989, the gross average weekly income for a household with a mortgage was £380.94 compared to £151.86 for a household in the public rented stock (statistics supplied by PPRU).

Clearly, the problems of depressed estates are complex and intense and not easily treated with spatially based policies and physical plans. The ineffectiveness of large scale zone based programmes, such as the BAN initiative in the mid 1970s, clearly calls for fresh thinking on the nature of the problem and the potential of alternative policies. The previous analysis has highlighted the correlation between public sector housing estates and indicators of social need. The remainder of this chapter examines the NIHE concept of Estate Based Strategy and assesses the potential of this approach in planning for deprived urban areas.

Planning the pariah city: estate based planning?

The Estate Based Strategy (EBS) concept was articulated in a number of published and unpublished NIHE policy documents (NIHE, 1986). As the 1970s redevelopment programme in Belfast neared completion, the emphasis in housing planning shifted to rehabilitation and regenerating existing estates. Central to the strategic housing plan for Belfast is the role of estate plans which, "are used to evaluate the nature of local problems and the priorities for investment" (NIHE, 1988). It is, in essence, a procedure through which future plans and proposals affecting an estate are considered and prepared in a comprehensive manner. The methodology is based upon the use of multidisciplinary teams looking at the problems or issues affecting individual estates. Comprehensive surveys of social and economic conditions, tenant attitudes, residents' associations, housing management issues and dwelling environmental conditions form the basis of the strategy. The plan also identifies the potential role of other development agencies such as British Telecom, the public transport company, health and social services and economic development agencies. An action plan, usually lasting three to five years, contains cost based projects to be implemented by the Housing Executive and other identified agencies.

A central feature of EBS is a recognition of the need for effective community participation. "It is only through participation that we can design and build a new Belfast to reflect the aspirations of the citizens" (NIHE, 1988, p.

28). A recent EBS in Divis Flats in Belfast employed "design clinics" to give tenants an effective forum to discuss ideas about the future design and layout of their area. Personal attitude surveys informed the priorities to be addressed by the planning strategies while regular public meetings and detailed formal consultations guaranteed tenant access to the plan formulation and implementation process. This was supported by the establishment of Joint Consultative Committees that help to structure relations between tenants, planners, designers and housing managers more effectively. All of this recognised that solutions to the problems of depressed estates must be rooted in the concerns of local people. In this respect, there is a commitment to empowerment of local communities as the Housing Executive recognizes that the involvement of tenants must move beyond information dissemination and consultation to effective participation with "tenants becoming more actively involved in the implementation of plans and day-to-day management" (NIHE, 1986, p. 1). Estate plans have been prepared for more than 50 estates in Northern Ireland and a comprehensive evaluation is needed to test the effectiveness of the programme. However, case study evidence from strategies that have been in operation for some time suggest that there are signs that they are having some impact on residents' lives.

Suffolk estate is located in West Belfast and its problems owe much to the sectarian geography of this part of the city and, in particular, to the isolation experienced by the small Protestant community. The Housing Executive plan for the estate was based on a household census survey and detailed consultations with the estate's two residents' associations. These established tenants' priorities which informed the content and direction of the strategy. A five year action plan costing £5.9 million (1985 prices) proposed improvements to doors and windows, greater privacy for gardens and communal areas of flats and maisonettes and environmental improvements to open space. Local training and ACE schemes were developed and a row of vacant dwellings converted to small workshops. Improvements to the bus service, play facilities and response maintenance system were also recommended. Writing about the initiative after two years, a worker with one of the residents' associations commented that:

> The enthusiastic involvement of the NIHE District Management staff in responding to the needs expressed by the Residents' Association has resulted in positive steps such as the refurbishment of dwellings, the introduction of NIHE Repair Receipts, the entry of Suffolk Residents' Association into discussions with NIHE management and planners so that tenants can have a large influence on future improvement schemes planned for the estate and the extension of NIHE sub-office opening hours to three and a half days per week (O'Halloran, 1987, p. 16).

This endorsement of the planning approach was also reflected in the attitude of tenants. When tenants were re-surveyed, five years after the strategy started, 55 per cent of tenants thought that the sub-office performed well as opposed to 19 per cent who were dissatisfied. Nearly half of all tenants thought that maintenance had improved while only 12 per cent thought it had deteriorated. Further improvements were identified in physical dwelling conditions (81 per cent) and in the physical appearance of the estate (58 per cent). Significantly, two thirds of residents thought that the influence of tenants had increased in housing management matters.

The estate based approach to inner city deprivation in a 1970s urban environment is well illustrated in the Lower Shankill Estate Survey. The estate was constructed between 1971 and 1979 and consists of 1,229 dwellings. Some unpopular non-traditional dwellings had been demolished but the problems of vandalism, dereliction, under occupance and high rent arrears continued. A household survey, carried out in 1985, revealed high levels of head of household unemployment (67 per cent), single parent families (32 per cent) and elderly households (34 per cent) (Estate Action Project, 1985). The survey revealed that 75 per cent of tenants wanted improvements to external spaces, 75 per cent to play areas and 65 per cent to the maintenance system. A close working relationship was established between NIHE planners, housing management staff and tenants in identifying problems and the "scope for joint development of the estate" (NIHE, 1989, p. 48). The tenants' association drew up their own plan for the area separate from the NIHE plan and as Figure 6.2 shows there was a strong "level of consensus on the appropriate decisions to be taken in the future" (NIHE, 1989, p. 5). For example, both plans emphasized the need for elemental improvements to dwellings and for privacy in gardens and alleyways. Both plans stressed the need to break up the estate into smaller zones and both recognised the role that a formal joint management committee could play in plan implementation. Adult education classes were promoted and job clubs established to help improve the employability of the local labour force.

Built in the same period as the Shankill, Unity Flats were equally unpopular. In the plan to redevelop the flats individual tenants were "afforded primacy in the consultation process" (NIHE, 1988, p. 24) with the preparation of regular information circulars for all residents, house-to-house interviews to collect residents' views on the development and design clinics to allow a realistic discussion of the area's future. Running alongside these initiatives were consultations with the residents' associations, discussions with elected representatives and consultations with other statutory interests and neighbouring residents' associations. A formal Steering Group consisting of NIHE planners and designers, the residents' association and independent community planners was established to oversee implementation. A joint press release from the NIHE and the residents' association highlighted the level of agreement that had been reached on basic design concepts and concluded that "The present overall renewal is the result of these joint negotiations wherein the priorities of tenants dictated the agenda" (Carrick

Figure 6.2: A People's Plan? NIHE and Tenant Plans for the Lower Shankill Estate

Proposal	NIHE Plan	Tenant Plan
Demolition	103 Units	None
New Build	Special Needs Housing Association Private Sector	Conversion of Maisonettes only
Elemental Work	Re-wiring Plumbing Doors/Windows External Walls	Doors/Windows External Walls
Stock Occupancy	Allocate singles out of large property and attract family groups	Refuse new single person applicants
Tenant Consultation	Joint Working Agreement Joint Consultative Committee EMB Sub Office	Joint Working Agreement
Maintenance	Improve Speed	Improve Speed
Access Design	Close Roads Create new footpaths Privatize back alleys	None
Environmental Work	Creation of 5 sub-areas with individual identities	Create 'Smaller Zone' identities
Other Agency	Involve in Implementation	Involve in Implementation
Implementation	NIHE/Tenant only	Multi-Agency group with 4 Sub-committees: Housing/Maintenance/ Environment/Social
Promotion	None	Leaflet/Brochure aimed at waiting list applicants

Hill Residents' Association/NIHE, 1987, p. 1). It would be wrong to assume that the relationship between the Housing Executive and residents was always harmonious in these case studies. However, important themes drawn from the studies have important implications for planning practice and policy.

The need for a comprehensive approach

Graham Gudgin highlights the significant improvements made to Belfast's housing stock and city centre (Gudgin, 1994). The possibility of sustained peace has brought with it speculation about inward investment to reinforce that possibility. Gudgin points out that this financial support is likely to be modest. He writes that "Even though the new, extra, amounts may be small, they can have real value if targeted at the heart of Northern Ireland's social problem. This means a peace dividend chiefly, perhaps exclusively, for the long term unemployed – the people least likely to benefit from private sector expansion" (Gudgin, 1994, p. 9). He earlier identified the problems in Belfast with the "Housing Executive estates of West and North Belfast" (Gudgin, 1993, p. 10). If Gudgin's priorities are accepted, this research has implications for planning at three levels. The first relates to elements of estate planning that could help to inform the concepts on which local planning could be carried out in the city. The second concerns the relevance of the housing estate as a basis for a planning response. The third is the acceptance that at a broader level consumption sector cleavages have relevance for understanding other aspects of local society and for framing government policy.

At the first level, of estate based planning, there are a number of lessons for the way local land use plans are developed and implemented. The first relates to the way tenant interests were mediated by the Housing Executive. Forester (1989) draws a distinction between merely "hearing" and effective "listening" in the planning process and suggests that the latter should be a guiding principle in participatory planning. The emphasis on household survey research, backed up by broad ranging and extensive consultations, ensured that tenants' priorities were built into the planning process at an early stage. The Executive's strategies in each estate imply a change in the power relationship between landlord and tenant which is a necessary basis for effective "consumerism" in the public sector. The second lesson is that the case studies show the benefits of decentralised structures in planning. The use of formal structures such as sub-offices, steering groups and joint consultative committees guarantees tenants access to the planning process, builds trust between tenant and landlord and ensures that problems in plan implementation are resolved quickly. The third lesson is that the values of planners and designers are important determinants of planning outcomes. A commitment to understanding the needs of people, taking their position seriously and helping them to resolve problems with objectivity underpins effective partnership in planning. As McGivern noted:

> At both Divis and Unity and numerous other locations local people are being encouraged to work in partnership with the Executive's design teams. At Divis, the Executive's design team opened a special 'design clinic' on the estate to help complement a wider programme of consultation and participation with the local community... Housing renewal in Belfast has indeed become a business about and for people (McGivern, 1990, pp. 181-182).

At the second level, the EBS approach acknowledges the limitations of relying exclusively on housing measures in tackling the problems of depressed estates. The concept recognises the multi-dimensional nature of the problem and the need for concerned inter-agency action. In particular, the need to restructure depressed local labour markets is pressing. The tentative success of the programme highlights the potential of a not so "radical agenda" and it is important that, in the short term at least, the EBS approach to tackling urban deprivation is not restricted by continuing pressure on housing finance in Northern Ireland.

Crucially, at the third level, this chapter raises the issue of the housing estate as the local unit for ameliorative action and the significance of consumption sector politics for planning in Belfast. This is not to suggest that planning for urban deprivation can only be considered at the estate level but merely that programmes to deal with urban deprivation should begin where problems are severest and where resources can be coordinated and targeted with greatest effect. Why should the top thirty or so depressed estates not receive priority treatment instead of the top depressed wards as under the original Making Belfast Work programme? Where estates are contiguous or have functional relationships with other estates or present a significant spatial challenge, such as at the sectarian interface, they can form broader spatial alliances that have relevance to the nature of the problems and to the limitations of area based responses. The establishment of a peripatetic Outer Belfast Action Team emphasises the spatial dispersion of poverty. Many of these areas contain the dysfunctional populations that have little resemblance to the cohesive community which existing strategies seem to assume as a given starting point. With current levels of unemployment likely to be an enduring feature of the Northern Ireland economy (Northern Ireland Economic Council (NIEC), 1993), the need to rethink not only area deprivation and unemployment but also the nature of society itself, is pressing. The limited prospect for full time waged work for all and the reduction in the role of waged work as the centre of gravity in individual life experiences raise questions about the employment emphasis in deprivation strategies. With the Industrial Development Board, the Local Enterprise Development Unit, EU funding programmes and local councils all addressing the spatial dimension of the problem, the opportunity for programmes such as MBW to focus on a spatial unit more relevant to the nature of deprivation in the city is significant to policy makers.

Given the lack of community cohesiveness in some of these areas and the disaffected nature of the people who live there, one point of departure would be to develop individual autonomy and control outside the sphere of work. Some of the initiatives already explored have involved tenants in the re-design of their living environments; in providing better public transport links to their areas; in providing relevant and accessible education and in develop-ing the role of women in community organization and development. The shape and content of such an agenda and the role of initiatives such as estate planning and MBW clearly need further exploration. The role of consump-tion based initiatives in tackling deprivation or even consumption sector politics in realigning the local political framework are possibilities that remain underdeveloped. This chapter has questioned traditional analysis of deprivation and many of the assumptions underpinning current policy. Given the limited resources devoted to deprivation programmes, perhaps the time has come to concentrate less on the world of work and more on increasing control over collective consumption to improve the quality of individual and community life. Such an approach could also satisfy demands for greater accountability of key services provided by the public sector in Northern Ireland. This is a broad and multi-dimensional research agenda and, while much remains to be done to improve our understanding of the complexity of local society, the need for prescriptive comment on the best way to use scarce resources to tackle the problems of Belfast's dispossessed is crucial.

References

Bardon, J. (1982), Belfast: An Illustrated History, Blackstaff Press, Belfast.
Birrell, D. and Wilson, D. (1993), 'Making Belfast Work: An evaluation of urban strategy', Administration, vol. 41, no.1. pp. 40-56.
Boal, F. Doherty, P. and Pringle, D. (1974), The Spatial Distribution of some Social Problems in Belfast Urban Area, Northern Ireland Community Relations Com-mission, Belfast.
Boal, F., Doherty, P. and Pringle, D. (1978), Social problems in the Belfast Urban Area: an exploratory analysis, Occasional Paper no. 12, Department of Geogra-phy, Queen Mary College, University of London, London.
Carrick Hill Residents' Association/NIHE (1987), Joint Statement regarding Carrick Hill Renewal Strategy, CHRA, Belfast.
Community Development in Protestant Areas (1991), Report on two seminars held during 1991, CDPA, Belfast.
Community Organisations of Northern Ireland (1977), Poverty: The BAN Answer?, CONI, Belfast.
Department of the Environment (NI) (1988), Belfast Action Team Information Pack, Belfast.

Donnison, D. (1991), A Radical Agenda, Rivers Oram Press, London.

Estate Action Project (undated), Household Survey of the Lower Shankill, EAP, Ballymena.

Evason, E. and Woods, R. (1991), Qualitative Studies of Life in Disadvantaged Areas of Belfast, Part 1, Northern Ireland Voluntary Trust, Belfast.

Eversley, D. (1990), 'Inequality at the spatial level: the task for planners', The Planner, vol. 76, no.12, pp. 13-18.

Forest, R. (1987), 'Spatial mobility, tenure mobility and emerging social division in the United Kingdom housing market', Environment and Planning A, vol. 19, pp. 1611-30.

Forester, J. (1989), Planning in the Face of Power, University of California Press, California.

Friedland, R., Fox Piven, E. and Alford, R. (1977), 'Political conflict urban structure and fiscal crises', International Journal of Urban and Regional Research, vol.1, pp.447-71.

Gaffikin, F. and Morrisey, M. (1990), 'Dependency, decline and development: The case of West Belfast', Policy and Politics, vol.18, no.2, pp. 105-7.

Gorz, A. (1982), Farewell to the Working Class: An Essay on Post Industrial Socialism, Pluto Press, London.

Gudgin, G. (1993), 'Jobs: the shocking facts', Belfast Telegraph, 18 May.

Gudgin, G. (1994), 'The pampering of Belfast', Guardian, 6 October.

Haughey, N. (1993), 'Social Need', Fortnight, no.322, p. 10.

Hirschfield, A. (1994), 'Using the 1991 Population Census to Study Deprivation', Planning Practice and Research, vol.9, no.1.

Knox, P. (1978), 'Social differentiation in urban areas: Housing or occupational class at work?', Tidschrift voor Econ, en Soc. Geographie, vol. 77, no.3, pp. 345-357.

Murray, C. (1994), 'Underclass', Sunday Times, 10 July.

Murtagh, B. (1991), Depressed Estates and the Role of The Estate Action Project, NIHE, Belfast.

Murtagh, B. (1992a), 'Housing Statistics in Northern Ireland: Research Data in Northern Ireland', ESRC Data Archive Bulletin, Special Issue, pp. 13-14.

Murtagh, B. (1992b), 'A Comparative Analysis of Land Use Planning in two organisations in Belfast', unpublished PhD Thesis, Department of Architecture and Planning, Queen's University Belfast.

Murtagh, B. (1993), Public Sector Housing and Deprivation in Belfast, Centre for Policy Research, University of Ulster, Jordanstown.

McAuley, P. and Kremer, J. (1990), 'On the fringes of society; adults and children in a West Belfast community', New Community, vol. 16, no.2, pp. 247-259.

McGivern, W. (1990), 'Health of the inner cities and urban areas: a Belfast perspective', The Statistician, vol.39, pp. 173-184.

Northern Ireland Economic Council (1993), Annual Report, NIEC, Belfast.

Northern Ireland Housing Executive (1984), Northern Ireland House Condition Survey 1984, Computer Database, Belfast.

Northern Ireland Housing Executive (1985), Greater Belfast Household Survey 1985, Computer Database, Belfast.

Northern Ireland Housing Executive (1986), 'Estate Strategies and Tenant Participation', NIHE Board Paper, Unpublished.

Northern Ireland Housing Executive (1987), Shankill Estate Strategy, Belfast.

Northern Ireland Housing Executive (1988), Carrick Hill Renewal Strategy, Belfast.

Northern Ireland Housing Executive (1990), Household Survey of Suffolk, Unpublished.

Northern Ireland Information Service (1988), Making Belfast Work, NIIS, Belfast.

O'Halloran, C. (1987), Division of Labour, Oxford, Blackwell.

P.A. Cambridge Economic Consultants (1991), 'Evaluation of Belfast Action Teams', P.A. Consultants, Cambridge.

Pahl, R. (1988), 'Some remarks on informal work, social polarisation and the social structure', International Journal of Urban and Regional Research, vol 12, pp. 247-67.

Policy Planning Research Unit (1987), Belfast Areas of Relative Social Need: 1981 Update, PPRU, Belfast.

Project Team (1976), Areas of Special Social Need, HMSO, Belfast.

Pyle, S. (1990), 'Shankill problems rival those on the Falls', Irish Times, 14 March, p. 9.

Saunders, P. (1984), Social Theory and the Urban Question, 1st ed., Hutchinson, London.

Saunders, P. (1986), Social Theory and the Urban Question, 2nd ed., Hutchinson, London.

Saunders, P. (1989), Social Class and Stratification, Tavistock, London.

Sim, D. (1986), 'Beginning to tackle the outer city', The Planner, vol. 72, no.3, pp. 25-27.

Sorenson, D. (1983), 'Towards a market theory of planning', The Planner, vol. 62, no.4. pp. 78-80.

Townsend, P., Corrigan, P. and Kowarzik, U. (1987), Poverty and Labour in London, Low Pay Unit, London.

West Belfast Economic Forum (1990), Is West Belfast Working?, WBEF, Belfast.

Yates, D. (1982), 'The English housing experience: an overview', Urban Law and Policy, vol.5, pp. 203-33.

7 Image making versus reality: ethnic division and the planning challenge of Belfast's peace lines

Brendan Murtagh

Nobody could imagine the fear the residents had to live under. It was a fact of life in her area that everyone had to be on the constant look-out. The residents felt it was a potential killing field and were terrified for their lives – they desperately wanted a brick wall built *(Life on the Interface*, 1992, p. 24).

Introduction

This chapter outlines the spatial problems created by ethnic division in the Belfast urban area. The chapter begins by describing the context for the development of territorial division and the difficulties this has created for the design and development of land. These problems are at their most stark where Catholic and Protestant neighbourhoods interface in the city and using empirical survey data the chapter attempts to explain the severity and complexity of the challenge to land use planning.

The City's ethnic map has been well documented in terms of its evolution (Jones, 1960), socio-economic profile (Doherty, 1990) and the significance that both communities attach to land (Boal, 1982). However, that literature has spawned relatively little comment on the planning or policy options open to government. As a consequence debate has drifted into accusations that the territorial imperative has been high on the political, military and even international agenda (Murtagh, 1993). From this perspective planners in the Department of the Environment and the Northern Ireland Housing Executive are seen as dupes of an Orwellian political machine over which they have little or no control (Blackman, 1984). This view has enjoyed academic, pressure group and local political support. It is, however, founded on anecdotal evidence and has no basis in empirical analysis. Building on survey data the chapter suggests that planners and the methods and techniques of land use planning have much to offer the management of one of the most crucial spatial problems in the city.

At a time when a tentative and delicate peace could become a long term reality, public policy in Northern Ireland is confronted, more than ever, with a prescriptive challenge. Sustained violent conflict has infused decision makers in a range on policy sectors with a sense of hopelessness that has allowed them to draw limits on the impact of their brief. Academic research on spatial ethnicity has reinforced that sense of insurmountable difficulty in the delivery of planning and housing policy in particular (Brett, 1986). Spatial division and peace lines have always been part of Belfast's spatial fabric and even regardless of the wider political context planners have much to offer in tackling the reality of this situation.

Development of segregated space in Belfast

It is not the purpose of this chapter to describe in detail the physical development of Belfast. Rather, the focus is on the development of ethnic segregated space as a fundamental spatial feature of the city. Gordon describes an ethnic group as "any group which is defined or set off by race, religion or national origin or some combination of these categories" (Gordon, 1964, p. 27). Where these categories have a common social-psychological function, is that they serve to create a sense of peoplehood and where there is an assumption of common origin, real or imaginary (Greeley, 1969, p. 40), the result is the formation of a coherent ethnic group. In the case of this research, it is reasonable to describe Protestants and Catholics in Northern Ireland as forming two separate ethnic groups.

A number of American sociologists have suggested that there is an inverse relationship between the degree of assimilation of two ethnic groups and the degree of residential segregation that exists between them (Lieberson 1961). Thus, increasing assimilation will be accompanied by decreasing segregation. Residential segregation between two ethnic groups is likely to indicate some significant degree of difference between them. Indeed, the physical separation of residence may contribute to and reinforce division. Equally, however, segregation between groups may act as an integrating force within each group. Boal (1982) argues that common residence permits the maintenance of ethnic cultural attributes and reduces the likelihood of dilution due to outside contact. He concludes that, in Northern Ireland, residential segregation indicates that the two groups are relatively unassimilated and that segregation may indicate and contribute to significant levels of integration within each group.

Jones (1960) suggests that residential segregation of Protestants and Catholics may have been a characteristic of the city from its inception. He notes that relationships between the two groups during the latter part of the eighteenth century appear to have been fairly amicable. However, as the nineteenth century proceeded these relationships deteriorated. This was related to the rapid growth in the number of in-migrant Catholics in the city at the time of the industrial revolution. The deteriorating relationship was accentuated by outbursts of inter-ethnic rioting (Boal and Murray, 1977) and these sharpened the growing segregation, in that Protestants and Catholics living in situations where they perceived themselves to be vulnerable minorities moved house in search of greater security provided by the ethnic cluster (Boal, 1982, p. 252). Throughout the latter part of the nineteenth century and into the twentieth there was a sequence of periods of relative tranquillity punctuated by out-bursts of conflict, the latter triggered by the political agitation associated with the Home Rule campaign.

The first year for which it is possible to quantify ethnic residential distribution in Belfast is 1911. In 1911, 41 per cent of Catholics and 62 per cent of Protestants were residentially segregated (Boal, 1982, p. 252). Between 1911 and 1969 levels of segregation increased as by the latter year the proportion of Catholics living in segregated streets had risen to 59 per cent while the corresponding figure for Protestants had risen to 69 per cent. Boal concludes:

> Thus, overall, at an early phase of Protestant-Roman Catholic contact in Belfast quite high levels of segregation were established. More importantly it would appear that segregation since then has increased, suggesting a sharpening of differences between the two ethnic groups (Boal, 1982, p. 253).

Boal also points out that some degree of ethnic mixing had been a feature of the city for a very long time. At the end of 1972, within the area of Belfast County Borough, 23 per cent of households were resident in streets where there was a significant degree of ethnic mixing (i.e. Protestants and Catholics each formed at least 10 per cent of households). However, more recent research has tended to confirm increasing levels in segregation throughout the 1970s and 1980s (Doherty, 1990; Keane, 1990).

Developing this point, Boal (1982) suggests three underlying reasons for the pattern of segregation in Belfast. First, people like to live with others who belong to the same culture; share values, ideals and norms; understand and respond to symbols in the same way; and agree about child rearing, interaction and lifestyle. Working class areas have tighter knit networks of social interaction and in these localities the neighbourhood is an extension of the home (Weiner, 1980). A second factor contributing to segregation between working class households may be the greater degree of conflict between the two ethnic groups in the working class context. This conflict is generated by situations of scarcity and competition particularly in housing and jobs. The third factor is what Boal refers to as the reservoir hypothesis. This suggests that an ethnic group's reaction to the in-movement of a member of a different

211

group will be partly conditioned by how large they perceive the reservoir of followers of that in-mover to be. In Belfast, Catholics are perceived as the faster growing group producing a threat in particular pressure localities in the city. Goering noted that "future expectations about the fate of the neighbourhood have appeared to play an important role in determining the rate at which the neighbourhoods change" (Goering, 1978, p. 76).

The peace lines

The most dramatic period of population movement as a result of ethnic turmoil in the city came between 1969 and 1973 when it was estimated that 60,000 people left their homes. That movement tended to be concentrated in the working class areas of North, West and inner East Belfast. The particular ethnic patchwork of Catholic and Protestant neighbourhoods in North Belfast experienced the worst of the internecine conflict and population flight and the starkest division of territory. The consequence was thirteen peace lines, where physical barriers are used to separate respective communities (Map 7.1).

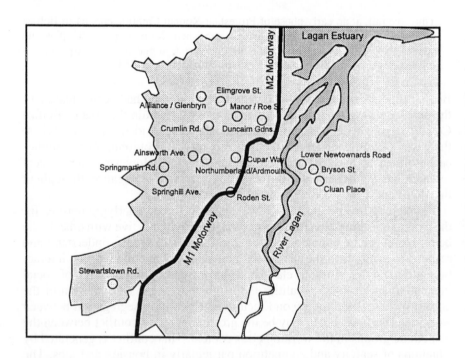

Map 7.1   Belfast's peace lines

The impact of the peace lines can be expressed in their cost to state and society. These can be described as actual financial costs, opportunity costs, social costs and image costs. The first two can be readily quantified. Figures supplied by the Belfast Development Office show that the cost of construction of the 13 peace fences was £1,927,000. In terms of overall public expenditure in Belfast this figure is not high. Costs for individual peace lines range from £16,000 in Bryson Street to £335,000 in Manor Street. When opportunity costs are estimated, however, the impact on the economic return from public sector housing is highlighted. For example, if all the 130 void properties identified in a physical survey conducted by the author of peace line interfaces were let, it would realise an annual rental income of £190,000 at current prices. Moreover, if all the surplus land was available for housing development this could realise an annual public sector rent of £400,000 on interface zones. Therefore, the government incurs a potential revenue cost from the peace lines of over £0.5 million per year. This ignores the multiplier effects that a re-established stable and viable community would have on local shops, services and facilities. However, the direct and indirect costs of the peace fences are minor when compared to the human costs to local residents. The report by community groups, *Life on the Interface*, shows that the peace lines affect nearly every aspect of daily life: going to the shops and work; getting access to play or recreation areas; supervising children; the threat to life itself and the psychological problems created by the constant pressure and fear of peace line living (*Life on the Interface*, 1991).

The broader image created by the peace lines among audiences outside Northern Ireland also incurs a significant cost. International press reporting of the peace lines helps to explain the central position that image and reimaging occupy in planning policy in the city. *The Guardian* has described one Belfast peaceline thus:

> Belfast's so called "peace line" is a barrier of concrete, brick and corrugated iron running some two miles in a forlorn attempt to protect the Protestant houses of the loyalist Shankill area and the Catholic houses of the Falls from each others attacks. It must be the only 30 foot high wall which neither side thinks is high enough (*The Guardian* 1986, p. 5).

Ever conscious of the divisive image projected by the peace lines planning policy has largely concentrated on a programme of softening the hard concrete and steel frames with coloured brick, pastel rendering and extensive use of greenery and planting. More recently, statutory planning instruments including Comprehensive Development Area status and compulsory acquisition powers have been used in an attempt to reimage interface zones. At the Duncairn interface in North Belfast the Comprehensive Development Area initiative introduced neutral light industrial and commercial land uses to provide a buffer between the two communities and at the same time dismantle the hard urban edge of the peace line. However, these are superficial responses to the complex problems of spatial division and the intense social problems that characterise life on Belfast's interfaces.

Life on the interface

This section profiles community life on the interface. It is based on household survey data on three interface areas representing different relationships be-

Photograph 7.1   Peace line: hard edge of sectarian division

tween Protestant and Catholic communities (Murtagh, 1994a). Suffolk in West Belfast represents a small Protestant community physically surrounded by a larger Catholic community. Conversely on the Short Strand in East Belfast the Catholics are outnumbered by the Protestants in the lower Newtownards Road. In Ardoyne in North Belfast, Protestant and Catholic communities are in roughly even numeric and spatial proportions. A total of 1350 households were surveyed across the three case study areas and the data are presented here in three parts. Firstly, the analysis addresses the issue of deprivation. It suggests that the peace line communities experience com-

Photograph 7.2   Peace line: soft edge of sectarian division

pounded deprivation. This is particularly so when the impact of the peace line on community movement patterns is taken into account. Cross community attitudes are then analyzed to explore the potential for building a local development agenda at the peace fence. This is supported by an examination of the level, type and purpose of contact across the peace line. The section closes with a profile of community substructures at the peace fence which attempts to draw together the main themes of the analysis.

Deprivation and peace line communities

The household research showed that deprivation is compounded by proximity to the sectarian interface. Three points emphasize this: firstly, key indicators of social malaise show that interface areas experience significantly higher levels of poverty than other parts of Northern Ireland; secondly, both communities are deprived because of the restricted access to services and facilities perceived as trapped in the territory of the out-group; thirdly, the image of these areas and the level of development of community infrastructure make it difficult for internal or external solutions to local economic development to have any real prospect of success. The recognised indicators of social deprivation illustrate graphically the extent of the problem (Fig. 7.1). For example, if the case study areas are considered as typical of peace line zones, then 69 per cent of those in work in the community earn less than £5,000 a year compared to only 45 per cent of Northern Ireland as a whole (Policy Planning Research Unit, 1992). Similarly, the unemployment rate for Northern Ireland as a whole in 1993 was 14 per cent but at the interface was 31 per cent, more than twice that figure. High benefit dependency underscores the nature of poverty at the peace line. A total of 41 per cent of households receive Income Support compared with 21 per cent in the province as a whole. Similarly, 2 per cent of the province's families received family credit compared to 5 per cent at the peace line.

Educational attainment levels complement the economic data in profiling peace line communities. Twelve percent of the economically active population of Northern Ireland achieved Advanced level standard as their highest qualification and the same percentage a university degree. The comparative figures for the peace line were 2 per cent and 1 per cent respectively.

The population mix of the peace line community is linked to the different demographic profile of Protestants and Catholics. This has implications for policy in these areas as the Catholic community is characterized by higher housing waiting lists, lower void rates and a better correspondence between household size and property size. For example, 27 per cent of the households in Protestant Suffolk were equal to the bedroom standard compared to 46 per cent on the Catholic side of the line, indicating that under-occupation is a major housing management problem in Protestant areas. In Ardoyne and

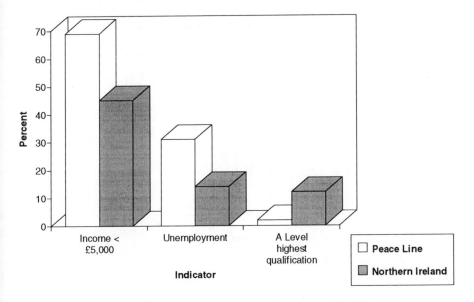

Figure 7.1   Three deprivation indicators on the peace line

Short Strand nearly half (43 per cent and 44 per cent respectively) of Protestant households are classified as elderly compared to 26 per cent of Catholic households in each area.

Also interesting about the data is the extent to which individual peace line communities share a common position in the social hierarchy of deprivation when some of the key indicators are considered. For example, figure 7.2 shows that low head of household income is a feature of all areas with almost identical statistics for each locality.

Impact on community movements

Peace line areas experience multi-dimensional problems. Some of these affect the way people move and interact. Ensuring the effective and efficient movement of pedestrian and vehicular traffic and the orderly management of resources, services and facilities have been at the core of planning practice and education. However, the survey showed that communities that are in a minority in their area experience significant problems in activities such as getting to work, visiting friends and relatives and gaining access to health services and to recreation facilities. For example, 28 per cent of Catholics in the Short Strand said that monthly shopping trips were a problem and 11 per cent of residents in Protestant Suffolk had a problem getting to a leisure centre. People generally in Protestant Ardoyne had a problem with daily

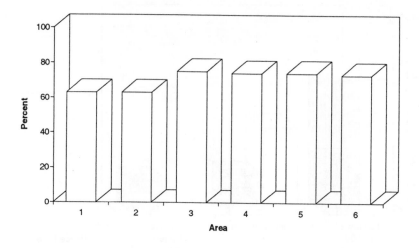

1.	Protestant Suffolk	2.	Roman Catholic Suffolk
3.	Protestant Ardoyne	4.	Roman Catholic Ardoyne
5.	Protestant Short Strand	6.	Roman Catholic Short Strand

Figure 7.2   Head of household income less than £5,000 on the peace line

shopping and 51 per cent experienced a problem doing weekly or monthly shopping.

Attitude to area

The survey highlighted negative attitudes to locality among peace line communities. For example, 27.3 per cent of those surveyed complained about the number of bricked up properties. Nearly one third (30.8 per cent) of all the sample complained about broken street lighting and 18.9 per cent about the condition and amount of vacant land. In terms of ideas to help reduce the problems of the peace line, 14 per cent thought that physical improvements were necessary while 13.5 per cent wanted to see local services and facilities developed. A total of 11.8 per cent wanted security improvements in the locality and, together with 4 per cent who wanted the peace fence strengthened, this reflects the immediacy of the problem to local people. Less than one quarter (22 per cent) thought that cross community projects had a role to play in addressing problems.

Figure 7.3 shows satisfaction with area expressed by each community. Overall 62.1 per cent were satisfied with their area. Lowest levels were experienced in Protestant Suffolk (42.6 per cent) and Protestant Ardoyne (48 per cent). However, only 50 per cent of Catholics in Ardoyne were in fact satisfied with their area. Highest rates of satisfaction were in the Short Strand. Protestant communities generally had the most pessimistic attitude toward the past and future of their areas. Nearly half of the residents of Protestant Suffolk thought that the area had deteriorated over the previous three years (49 per cent) while the same percentage thought it would deteriorate over the next three years. More than two thirds of Protestants in Ardoyne (67.7 per cent) thought that the area had deteriorated over the previous three years and a further 50 per cent thought that this would continue over the next three years. This contrasts with the 66.7 per cent of people in Catholic Short Strand who thought that their area had improved and the 42.5 per cent who thought it would improve in the future.

Inter community attitudes

This section explores the attitudes of the communities who live at peace fences to their own identity (the in group) and to the identity of those on the opposite side of the peace fence (the out group). The survey data, gathered thirteen months before the announcement of Republican and Loyalist para-military cease fires, will give an indication of the extent to which a cross community agenda is realistic or even desirable. In line with other social attitude surveys in Northern Ireland most Protestant communities were likely to describe themselves as British (57.9 per cent in Suffolk, for example). The next most common description for all three communities was Protestant. Conversely Catholics were most likely to call themselves Irish and secondly, Catholic. However, there was some degree of agreement on a Northern Irish identity as in Protestant Ardoyne 8 per cent identified themselves as Northern Irish while 9 per cent in Catholic Ardoyne used the same label. In fact, 8 per cent of Catholics in Suffolk thought of themselves as a "Belfast man/woman" while 7 per cent of Protestants used this description.

Indeed, when cross community attitudes are measured in a structured way it shows that positive opinions and attitudes are prevalent at the peace line. For example, 81 per cent would allow a member of the out group to join their clubs and societies. This figure progressively rises when entry into neighbourhood (90 per cent) and visiting rights to area (94 per cent) are considered. However, a constant theme across all case study areas is that Protestant communities judge Catholics less acceptable than Catholics do Protestants. In Suffolk, 87.7 per cent of Catholics would allow a member of the Protestant community to marry into their family compared to 60.2 per cent of Protestants. The differ-

219

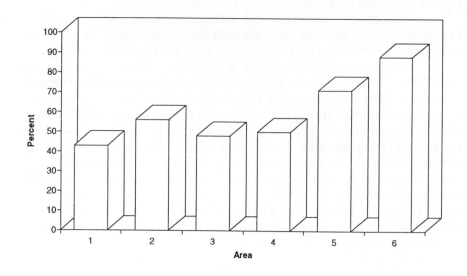

Figure 7.3   Satisfaction with area on the peace line

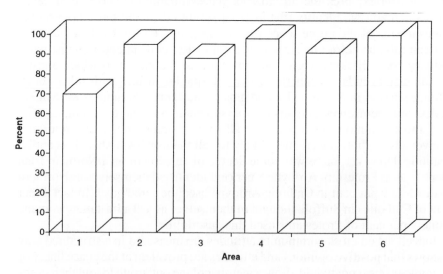

1.	Protestant Suffolk	2.	Roman Catholic Suffolk
3.	Protestant Ardoyne	4.	Roman Catholic Ardoyne
5.	Protestant Short Strand	6.	Roman Catholic Short Strand

Figure 7.4 Would you allow a member of the out group to visit your area?

ences in the other areas were 92 per cent versus 65 per cent in Ardoyne and 90 per cent versus 59 per cent in Short Strand. Pursuing this theme, while 90.2 per cent of Suffolk Catholics would allow the peace line Protestant community to "live in their street as neighbours" the comparative figure for Suffolk Protestants was 69.5 per cent. Similarly, 78.7 per cent of Ardoyne Protestants would allow Catholics to live in their street as neighbours compared to 97.1 per cent of Ardoyne Catholics. Figure 7.4 shows the same attitudinal trend at community level when visiting rights to area are considered. At the one extreme, 100 per cent of Catholics in Short Strand would allow entry to their area by Protestants compared to 69.5 per cent of Protestants in Suffolk who would reciprocate. It is arguable that this is the product of a community under a prolonged period of actual and perceived threat. As Catholic housing pressure grows and as void rates increase in the Protestant estate, any incursion would be perceived as the beginning of the end for the resident community. In these areas attitudes are a product not of an irrational historic bigotry but of very genuine fears for the future of territory and community stability. The implication is that before cross community initiatives can be realised, the communities themselves must feel confident about their own identity and future sustainability. The previous analysis highlighted pessimistic attitudes among the Protestants of Suffolk about their area in the next three years. At a broader level, if community relations in space are to be successful, then they must be based on the concept of a viable and positive "community". In this respect community development may be a necessary prerequisite in areas where dysfunctional communities make the prospect of improving cross community relations particularly unrealistic.

The majority of those sampled have only friends and relatives of their own denomination (75.7 per cent). However, 18.2 per cent have half and half, in terms of religious composition and 5 per cent have more of the opposite religion. While these figures are not large, they again reject the notion of a rigidly segregated environment where contact is shunned, regarded with suspicion and not easily engaged. This is supported by the view that Catholics have more in common with Protestants locally than they do with Catholics in the Republic of Ireland. For example, 58.2 per cent of Protestants in Short Strand felt this way as did 64.2 per cent of Catholics. A similar proportion of Protestants (58 per cent) felt that Protestants had more in common with Catholics than they do with British people. In Ardoyne 59 per cent of those on the Protestant side of the peace line felt this way compared to 66 per cent of Catholics. When asked about their preferred type of neighbourhood, 45 per cent of the total sample wanted to see integrated living but this varied between 52.5 per cent of Catholics who felt this way in the Short Strand compared to 32.2 per cent on the Protestant side of the peace fence. However, there are clear difficulties in using attitude measures to project ideal living environments and the very presence of the peace fence questions this instrument as a reliable guide to true attitudes and opinions.

Contact across the peace fence

Despite the physical and psychological impact of the peace line, this does not mean that there is little or no contact or interaction. In total, 28.2 per cent of respondents had friends or relatives on the opposite side of the peace fence and, of these, 27 per cent visited each other once a week or more. A total of 38 per cent never visited their friends or relatives on the opposite side of the peace line.

People crossing the peace fence felt that, to some extent, movement patterns and feelings of threat depended on the level of tension or violence locally. A total of 90 per cent of the total sample stated that the level of tension or violence increased at different times of the year. In particular, there was a feeling that traditional anniversaries (94 per cent) and marches and parades (62.7 per cent) were the main reasons for increases in tension. The implications are that this is where local community relations efforts should be targeted. Actual physical sectarian assaults such as rioting (7 per cent) stone throwing (7.5 per cent) sectarian graffiti (3.5 per cent) accounted for very little of the overall increase in tension.

There seems to have been little perception of change in community relations over time. A total of 14.7 per cent thought they were better now than they were in the past but 14.2 per cent felt they were worse. The majority (60 per cent) felt that relations had remained the same. Again there was relatively little difference between the two communities with regard to the future. Here, 13.4 per cent feel that relationships will improve in the future but 16.7 per cent feel that they will deteriorate. Again, the majority (51 per cent) feel that they will stay the same.

While the emphasis in terms of improving future conditions is on increasing employment opportunity (38.2 per cent), nevertheless 15.2 per cent felt that better local community relations would improve the quality of life of local people. Again this was evenly cited by Catholic and Protestant communities. Protestant communities thought that a priority should be to develop derelict land and re-use vacant buildings (39 per cent and 9.4 per cent respectively in Protestant Ardoyne).

Who lives at the peace line?

The quantitative analysis has explored some of the differences in community attitudes in peace line communities. While there are important differences between Protestants and Catholics, both sides contain identifiable sub-sets of people characterised by common attitudes to the out group. The following analysis draws on both quantitative and qualitative evidence but does not claim any particular scientific rigour. It is suggested that these groups are recognisable in similar proportions within each community. In short, cluster based techniques were used to define five significant groups.

Liberals are the largest group in the peace line community. They tend to have the most positive attitude to the out group, have regular contact with members of the out group locally and recognise the potential for cross community development. They tend to be in the middle income bracket, in the middle age range (or with a grown up family) and to have lived in their area for a relatively long period of time. Household survey data suggest that a disproportionate number of liberals are female. This group sees the causes of local problems as rooted in lack of opportunity for disaffected youth rather than in sectarian hostility. Liberals tend to vote for more moderate parties such as the Official Unionists or the Social Democratic and Labour Party and for neutral parties such as the Alliance Party. They provide the basis for significant cross community development along a number of fronts. Currently among this group positive contact has largely been based on recreation but they provide an important resource for inter community development.

Leaders. A small number of leadership people in both religious groups also display attitudes and behaviour on which sustainable cross community contact and development can be based. Recognised leaders have been involved in youth or church based activities, organised tenants associations or have represented their community group. Again they have positive attitudes to the out group and have often directly engaged in cross community projects in their area. They tend to be younger than the average local age, are in full time employment and have higher than average incomes. They tend to be among the better educated members of the community and also have a greater confidence about their own community identity and its prospects for the future. Often they have a strong political alignment such as with the democratic left or the Green Party. Together with the liberals, they provide some of the basic elements necessary for community development and the improvement of cross community relations.

Extremists. Cross community projects can be obstructed by a small number of radicals from the in group. These extremists have the most hostile attitudes to the out group and are the least likely to accommodate cross community initiatives. Despite their relatively small numbers, they wield significant local power and, often with the backing of the paramilitaries, can impose a degree of control over the local social structure. This control restricts independent action by leaders or liberals. Part of any prescriptive strategy for these areas must recognise and attempt to understand these restrictions (or the way the controlling frame is structured) in order to develop a realistic community development and community relations policy in peace line areas.

Young toughs have been identified as a key element of local society in Belfast's most violent areas. They are largely unemployed, experience high benefit dependency and achieve relatively low levels of educational attainment. They have little investment in their area or community and have often been directly involved in the violence and vandalism at the peace line. However, they often sit outside the control frame imposed by the extremists leading to punishment responses.

The apathetic. It would be wrong to assume that all members of the peace line community have an interest in or position on ethnic issues in Northern Ireland. The survey revealed that a small proportion of respondents had no allegiance to any religion, political party or ethnic code. They had little awareness of what was determined their out group and little interest in the future prospects for the in group. While not a particularly positive element of the population, this group does not obstruct local cross community development.

This analysis has highlighted the relative disadvantage of peace line communities and the need for a coordinated programme of action within the framework of a planning agenda. However, assessment of the community profile and inter community attitudes clarified the constraints on and opportunities for the development of such a programme. Three factors can be highlighted: first, the majority of people living in interface areas have a positive attitude to the out group and to the role of community relations in local development. In addition, leaders in each area provide an important point of reference for the development of any local initiative; second, any such initiative can be severely restricted by extremists in the community who can often determine the rules governing local community life and the scope for independent action; finally, if planning policy for these areas is to have any prospect of success, then it must recognise the rules governing them, the way they are imposed and their effect on local initiative.

Implications for policy

This section examines the implications of the survey findings for planning and housing policy. In developing recommendations, the analysis is based on an explicit acknowledgement of three principles. In particular, the need is to develop a prescriptive approach that relies neither on imported ideology nor on a concept of planning driven by imagery. Planners need to apply their skills and methods to a serious and deeply structural spatial problem and come up with imaginative policy responses. The principles are as follows: firstly, that an agenda on planning policy should not start with the assumption that segregated housing is totally negative and that integration is the only possible or logical programme response. Strong ontological factors underpin the need for segregated living and to force or pursue solutions that ignore these factors will result in a fruitless and ultimately unsuccessful search;

secondly, that the development of an effective policy must rely on an understanding of the opportunities and constraints created by local conditions and that the existing legislative and policy framework should not determine the content and scope of the recommendations resulting from necessary research; thirdly, that there is a legitimate link between community relations and urban planning. The cost of the peace lines, their impact on the image of Belfast, the effect they have on vehicular and pedestrian movement, on where services and facilities are located and how they are used and, crucially, the impact they have on the life experiences and chances of the people who live in these areas, all highlight the need for planners to address this issue at a strategic and operational level. With these principles in mind it is possible to project a series of options for development. These could range from doing nothing at one end of the spectrum to ambitious residential integration strategies at the other. Neither of these extreme responses is practicable. The urban scar of sharp ethnic division demands a serious response that must move significantly away from the surface bandaid approach that has characterized much of the image based planning in the city.

The role for land use planning

The potential role for land use planning described here details the elements of an alternative approach to defining spatial problems and to applying planning methodology to generate an applied response to the reality of urban fracture.

Spatial coverage

Different spatial units of analysis form the focus of land use planning responses and these are determined by the nature of the issue under investigation. Housing Action Areas, Local Area Plans, Structure Plans, Comprehensive Development Areas, Redevelopment Areas and Estate Based Strategies all represent different approaches to the problems created by urban change. It is argued that there is a 'zone' or area affected by the presence of peace lines. It has been shown, using physical analysis and social surveys, that definable areas and communities experience problems directly created by the peace line. These areas can themselves be sub-divided into inner and outer zones, in which the experiences and attitudes of people differ significantly. In Protestant Suffolk the main problems of the community at the peace line (inner zone) related to the direct threat and occurrence of physical damage and intimidation. In the outer zone, the main problems related to the way the peace fence impacted on movement and access to key services and facilities. Thus, for each area, socio-economic, demographic and physical land use surveys should be used to establish the exact extent of the territory affected. However, the specific dimensions of the relevant spatial unit can only be determined on a site by site basis. Clearly a necessary requirement before defining community boundaries is therefore a well founded idea of what constitutes a community. In interface areas these are localities, shaped largely through the interaction of people and particular tracts of land or territory. Through time, and particularly since the early 1970s, this interaction has created a form of local society. Coombes et al. (1993) suggested that heritage, culture, demography, landscape, infrastructure and economy help to define a local community as distinct. It has been shown in the various local surveys that informed this analysis, that all of these factors are present in helping to define the communities that live on either side of Belfast's 13 peace lines.

The point is, that the people affected by the peace line represent communities living in distinctive spatial units that present a significant challenge to the discipline of urban planning. As has been stressed, the scope of each unit can only be established by locally relevant survey work. This highlights the need for a qualitatively different approach to planning for ethnic space. This is discussed under the headings of strategy, skills, policy systems and planning style.

Strategy

In order to develop a conceptual approach to peace line planning it is necessary to return to the basic principles of planning methodology. Expressing it in its most simple form, Patrick Geddes (1949) suggested that the process of plan making could be set out in a three stage framework: survey, analysis, plan. The way that this could be applied to interface planning is illustrated in Figure 7.5.

Stage	Content
Survey	Ethnic Audit should complement traditional land use planning surveys
Analysis	Qualitative analysis should balance traditional reliance on technical projection techniques in land use planning
Plan	Community relations strategies and methods of approach should be central to the development of area based proposals

Figure 7.5 Strategic framework for interface plan

The nature of the problem calls for a significantly different approach to survey work. An ethnic audit should complement traditional land use, retail, labour force, demographic and industrial surveys upon which development planning is based. This audit could be reported on separately, but would define the scope, opportunities and constraints for community relations initiatives in the plan. The review should be an explicit account of the ethnic profile of the area built on several dimensions:

- An analysis of the population balance between the two religious groups in the area.
- An assessment of the physical relationships and points of contact between the groups including the impact of and implications for pedestrian and vehicular movements.
- An assessment of the area's history in terms of the development, extent and causes of violence and inter community tension.
- A description of inter group contact and the potential for the development of cross community initiatives.
- An assessment of attitudes to the out community and an identification of the issues or priorities that local people feel might form the basis of a programme for mutual development.

This list is not exhaustive, but indicates the need explicitly to survey ethnic problems, which will necessitate the use of a range of research instruments including household surveys, analysis of secondary census data and qualitative interviews. The use of newspaper archive material to trace the development of local problems should not be excluded. This all implies a move away from the quantitative methodologies that inform much of traditional development planning. In analysing the data, planners should not over rely on rational projective techniques to predetermine spatial responses. Value judgements on the potential for a community relations strategy should be central to the interpretation of the data.

All of this should lead to a plan of action that addresses the physical, economic and social development of interface areas. It has already been shown that some of the more recent initiatives by the Department of the Environment for Northern Ireland do just that. What is called for here is the infusion of an explicit community relations agenda into the development of such initiatives. If these issues are addressed through survey at the start of the plan making process, community relations concerns will become integral, rather than being bolted on to traditional proposals for local development. Specifically, such a plan should include proposals for the treatment of the peace fence and surrounding land and also contain a local community relations strategy that would embrace prejudice reduction, as well as dispute and conflict negotiation and resolution.

Skills

The approach suggested requires the development of a different range of skills from those normally associated with land use planning. The starting point for such a development must rest with the accredited professional institution responsible for planning education. The role of planners as mediators of conflicting interests in land is a recurrent theme in the planning literature (see for example Healey, 1989). One of the major conflicts in the use of land in Belfast revolves around the issue of territoriality. Yet this issue and how planners should respond to it do not seem to inform the range of skills or specific techniques that planners are taught at university. Part of the explanation for this is that the Royal Town Planning Institute validates course content based on a value set that emphasizes the relevance of planning to British urban experience. Given that the role of managing ethnic division in space is as relevant to Belfast as it is to Tower Hamlets, Brixton or St. Pauls in Bristol the local branch of the Institute should take a closer interest in developing a more locally relevant programme of Continuing Professional Development that would help to equip planners with an understanding of the community relations skills that are suited to the tasks of land use planning. The traditional skills of town planning also have a significant contribution to make to the development of such an agenda. These include the conduct of valid and reliable surveys and crucially the ability to interpret and analyze complex data sets leading to a structured programme of activity. It is in the combination of all these skills and techniques that the success of the proposed strategy rests.

Policy Systems

The development of a planning approach for interface areas cannot proceed in isolation. Any such development sits within a broader policy system and must be complementary to the programmes and policies pursued. One of the key relationships is that between community relations issues and development control. While a development plan can proactively develop community relations issues, it is important that these are not undermined by decisions taken by development control officers or other statutory agencies responsible for the provision of local services and facilities. Glendinning (1993) has pointed out how the closure of a state primary school has destabilised the Protestant community in the religiously mixed Ballynafeigh area of South Belfast, while Murtagh (1994b) showed how the provision of an improved bus service and part time children's clinic helped to stabilise the Protestant community in Suffolk. Interface areas are sensitively balanced ethnic areas. Major statutory decisions and planning applications should be subjected to an ethnic impact assessment in the same way as sensitive environmental areas often enjoy the protection of mandatory environmental impact assessments.

A further issue for consideration here is the need for monitoring and evaluation data. If any such initiative were to proceed, then the inputs in terms of financial, human and capital resources need to be evaluated with regard to outputs (particularly changes in cross community contact and attitudes). It is acknowledged that these are nebulous concepts and it will be difficult to validate real changes in circumstances. However, the design of a monitoring system that builds in qualitative measures could give some perspective on the effectiveness and efficiency of the initiative.

Style

Stylistically then, this is a very different type of plan from that normally associated with land use planning. The concept plan explicitly acknowledges that land use issues on their own ignore the complex reality of problems at the interface. The plan must be multi-dimensional in nature and draw together skills in planning, community relations, public participation, anti deprivation policies and environmental design. In addition, ethnographic survey and analysis are neglected by planners but can offer much in understanding conflict in space and how to address it. In this respect, the concept plan proposed calls for a new way of thinking about, and planning for, one of the most serious land use and social problems facing contemporary Belfast.

Conclusion

As the analysis opening this chapter emphasized, ethnic division has always been a feature of Belfast. At times of internecine conflict segregation has become more acute and during relative peace there has been some blurring of hard ethnic boundaries. The potential for lasting peace provides important opportunities to address the sustained increase in segregation since 1969. Land use planning has a role to play in creating a more successful urban environment. However, as has been argued, a redefinition of the content, scope and style of local planning strategies is an essential pre-requisite for this. Given the context of the problem and the opportunity for policy development, a strategy dominated by a philosophy of reimaging has limited relevance as a point of departure for such a project.

References

Blackman, T. (1984), 'Planning in Northern Ireland – the shape of things to come', *The Planner*, vol. 76, no. 30, pp. 13–15.
Boal, F. (1982), 'Segregation and Mixing: space and residence in Belfast', in Boal, F. and Douglas, N. (eds) *Integration and Division – Geographical Perspectives on the Northern Ireland Problem*, Academic Press, London.

Boal, F. and Murray, R. (1977), A city in conflict, *Geographical Magazine*, vol. 44, pp. 364–371.

Brett, C. (1986), *Housing a Divided Community*, Gill and Macmillan, Dublin.

Coombes, M., Openshaw, C., Wong, C. and Raybould, S. (1993) 'Community Boundary Definition: A GIS design specification', *Regional Studies*, vol. 27, no. 3, pp. 280–286.

Doherty, P. (1990), 'Social contrasts in a divided city', in Doherty P., Geographical Perspectives on the Belfast Region, Geographical Society of Ireland, Dublin.

Geddes, Sir Patrick (1949), 'Cities in Evolution', Williams and Northgate, London.

Glendinning, W. (1993), 'Planning and mixed housing, The Community Relations Perspective', in Murtagh, B. (ed.), *Planning and Ethnic Space in Belfast*, Centre for Policy Research, Occasional Paper no. 5, University of Ulster, Belfast.

Goering, J. (1978), 'Neighbourhood tipping in and racial transition, A review of social science evidence', *Journal of the American Institute of Planners*, vol. 44, pp. 68–78.

Gordon, M. (1964), *Assimilation in American Life*, Oxford University Press, New York, .

Greely, A. (1969), *Why Can't They Be More Like Us?* Dutton, New York.

The Guardian (1986), 'The soft ... divide', 6 August, London.

Hirschman, A. (1970), *Exit, Voice and Locality*, Harvard University Press, Cambridge, Massachusetts.

Healey, P. (1989), *Planning for the 1990s*, Working Paper no.7, Department of Town and Country Planning, University of Newcastle.

Keane, M. (1990), 'Segregation processes in public sector housing', in Doherty, P., Geographical Perspectives on the Belfast Region, Geographical Society of Ireland, Dublin.

Jones, E. (1960), *A Social Geography of Belfast*, Oxford University Press, London.

Life on the Interface (1991), 'Report on a Community Group Conference', *Island Publications*, Belfast.

Murtagh, B. (1993), 'The role of the security forces and peace line planning', in Murtagh, B. (ed.) *Planning and Ethnic Space in Belfast*, Centre for Policy Research, Occasional Paper no. 5, University of Ulster.

Murtagh, B. (1994a), *Ethnic space and the challenge to Land Use Planning: a study of Belfast's Peacelines*, Centre for Policy Research, Research Paper no. 7, University of Ulster.

Murtagh, B. (1994b), *Public Sector Housing and Deprivation in Belfast*, Centre for Policy Research, Occasional Paper no. 6, University of Ulster.

Policy Planning Research Unit (1992), *Continuous Household Survey*, Bulletin, Department of Finance and Personnel, Belfast.

Shuttleworth, I. (1993) The Census of population as a measure of segregation in Northern Ireland, Paper presented to Economic and Social Research Council Seminar on Violent Conflict, Queen's University Belfast.

Weiner, R. (1980), *Rape and Plunder of the Shankill*, Farsett Co-operative Press, Belfast.

8 Concluding Comments: Reclaiming the Pariah City

William J.V. Neill

As stated in the preface, the intention of this book is to highlight some of the issues involved in the reimaging of cities, especially the role of city centre development in such agendas. A focus on pariah cities places some of the matters raised in particularly sharp relief. The gap between image and reality is greater, the opportunity costs are higher, the tension between imaging for outsiders and residents is more problematic and the cosmetic aspects are especially striking. At times, in such contexts, the ideas of the image makers reach new lows of insensitivity. None is more crass, for example, than the following comments by James Rouse, the developer behind Boston's Quincy Market and Baltimore's Harbor Place, on the tourist potential of Belfast where a voyeuristic thrill is to be had from visiting the sites of terrorist carnage:

> Cities are beginning to understand the new potential of their waterfronts ... strong impressions are irresistible and one such was the impression that the waterfront at the foot of High Street constituted a huge potential opportunity for Belfast ... in a perverse way the present image of Belfast might even be made a plus in attracting people to this dramatic new waterfront. There is excitement in finding things different than expected, in finding good where there is supposed to be bad, in a spirit of venture into what may seem a little dangerous. (Rouse, 1985)

The remainder of these concluding comments suggest what is needed for the cities of Belfast and Detroit to reimagine more agreeable urban futures. Risking the charge of academic naïveté and even at times conflicting with notes of pessimism sounded in other chapters, these concluding reflections emphasize the basis for hope that Detroit and Belfast can substantially improve the urban product to be imaged. Both places in 1994 face the opportunity of a fresh start; Detroit with a new mayor and a policy of rapprochement with the city's suburbs and Belfast with the prospect of an end to political violence. Both cities will not reimage themselves with any subtle application of the advertisers' air brush. Rather, their futures depend on the degree to which local proactivity can be mobilized to tackle difficult, almost overwhelming circumstances. The seemingly anonymous forces behind an increasingly globalized economy do not make this an easy task. The temptation is to find personal rather than social answers to problems. Nevertheless, on the assumption that local progressive civic reflexivity (Lash and Urry, 1994) can be mobilized in Belfast and Detroit it will have to take on board the issues of social justice, an economic development path based more on substance than hype, and the need to foster a more inclusive urban future which respects differences while acknowledging the history which has generated them. However, such a concluding concentration on the real problems of Detroit and Belfast does not imply that they should have refrained from playing in the image game altogether. It is rather the particular reimaging strategies which have engendered critique. When a popular commercial proto-virtual reality motor cycle ride invites vicarious thrill seekers to accompany Robocop on the murderous streets of Detroit, it would be surprising indeed if urban image was not a matter of concern in the real city. Likewise when the main German travel and tourist journal *Merian* (1993) produces a special edition on Ireland with the North represented only by pictures of conflict, pressures to emphasize more positive aspects of life in Belfast are understandable.

In terms of product development, however, the hope must remain that Detroit and Belfast will banish pariah status in the eyes of outsiders in the future, with the city reclaimed not least on the basis of greater social justice. The problems engendered by poverty and inequality remain in Belfast as a fragile peace struggles to take hold. In Greater Detroit the most extreme affluence exists cheek-by-jowl with Third World-like deprivation. Image based urban development flagship projects in both cities have been unable to deliver more than the dual city of "haves" and "have nots". Alongside racial and ethnic antagonism this remains an explosive urban brew. In the more affluent suburbs of both Detroit and Belfast the indifference towards the real city is comparable. Residents of Belfast's "Gold Coast" suburbs along the shores of Belfast Lough have been able to seek comfort at a safe distance in the promoted image by the Belfast Development Office of a fantasy city whose "normality" has been propped up by a massive outside subvention. In Detroit's "Gold Coast" Grosse Point and other suburbs the impulse is increasingly to rebuild the city elsewhere leaving the more undesirable aspects behind. This has stretched the projected image and reality of "old Detroit" to breaking point.

Nevertheless, while acknowledging an "epistemic conservatism" accepted by much of the political left about the limits of what is possible by way of social renewal (Miliband, 1994, p. 5) there is, it is to be hoped, some possibility for urban planning to attenuate the social division accentuated by capitalist uneven development in both pariah cities. In Detroit, area-wide property tax base sharing must remain the cornerstone of any plan based on fairer regional resource distribution. Regional investments in public transportation, financial support for City of Detroit cultural institutions, for example, rather than creating them anew in the suburbs, and effective control of urban sprawl require attention if reimaging hype is not again to ring hollow. In Belfast, the social disadvantage described in Chapter Six on which grievance and alienation thrive, unless tackled with vigour, will threaten to undermine any peaceful political settlement. It is to be hoped that the upbeat image expressed on tours of the city led by officials from the Belfast Development Office, describing "pockets of unemployment", and the "unfortunate Troubles" intruding irritatingly into the life of a generally normal city with its new shopping centres, waterfront developments and so forth (Greenslade, 1993), does not shield policy makers and elements of the Belfast populace itself from the grimmer reality which remains to be tackled.

Economic development policy based less on image laden property developments must become central to any future plans for rebuilding the urban economies of Detroit and Belfast. The difficulties in formulating a proactive policy which seeks to bolster the manufacturing base of the Detroit region were discussed in Chapter Five. While the actual impact of Michigan industrial policy is open to debate, the problem of the City of Detroit is economic exclusion from what remains a prosperous core industrial agglomeration. The City of Detroit now boasts a collection of image conscious physical capital projects surreally floating free amidst a human capital wasteland. Recent commentators have argued that an embryonic corporate supported human capital investment strategy is taking root in Detroit. In particular attention is drawn to the institution in 1989 of the Detroit Compact, an agreement between the Detroit Public School system, the city's business community, the City of Detroit and the State of Michigan which offers pupils guaranteed "certainty of opportunity in the form of college tuition or employment, for meeting stringent academic and attendance standards" (Orr and Stoker, 1992, pp. 7–8). While this is clearly a move in the right direction and has resulted in measurable educational improvements (Detroit Compact, 1992), with only $3.5 million per annum in additional resources modestly topping up a $1 billion Detroit Public Schools budget, even the Executive Director of the programme admits it is a form of educational triage which helps those who have the best chance of survival in a school system still fraught with problems (Vollman, 1993).

The Detroit Compact idea, itself based on a similar programme in Boston, deserves consideration in Belfast even though it would presently fall foul of fair employment legislation. However, a more radical rethink of urban economic policy in Belfast and Northern Ireland would involve engagement with ideas such as the Detroit industrial policy discussed in Chapter Five. Indeed such an engagement with post-Fordist debates has recently been suggested

(Teague, 1994). The Michigan experience demonstrates that there is no simple policy model to be transferred since Belfast is as economically distinct from Detroit as the latter is from the Third Italy. Nevertheless, the possible return of some devolved economic development powers to Northern Ireland might enable debate and even application of ideas drawn from a fertile industrial policy literature with a degree of freedom from the less interventionist economic nostrums of the British Conservative government. It would be naïve to assume that peace in Belfast and Northern Ireland will sweep peripherality aside and that a tourist revival and injections of economic aid from the United States and the European Union would be enough to overcome what has been described as a "mendicant entrepreneurial culture" (Teague, 1994, p. 289).

Last but not least, Belfast and Detroit need to be reclaimed in the interests of equality of esteem for racial and ethnic identities. It is difficult to see this emerge other than on the basis of respect for difference and compromise. Here the difficulties expressed in the observation that people in Belfast and Northern Ireland generally are "much better wired for transmission than they are for reception" (Hayes, 1994) could equally well apply to the recent history of relations between the City of Detroit and its white suburbs. Whether Detroit's new mayor can overcome the tension between creating a representation of place comfortable to black Detroiters and presenting an image which does not alienate outsiders will depend on compromise decisions on hard issues discussed in Chapter Four, such as regional resource redistribution, but also on an overcoming of a lack of empowerment based, at least partly, on an over acceptance of victim status (West, 1993). In Belfast, equality of esteem for ethnic identities would enable a reclaiming of the city by the populace at large as local democracy returned to physical planning. While the heart of Belfast has been rebuilt over the last ten to fifteen years with residents as passive bystanders, important issues remain. These include the need for a more sustainable transportation policy for the city, a sound cultural and arts policy, urban design matters, the nature of special events in Belfast and, most importantly, the impact of peace on physical integration and division. Resolving the matter of the expression of ethnic identity might also open up space in an urban planning debate about other marginalized identities in the city. Consideration of the ideas that urban landscapes could be gendered or that sexual orientation could be a basis for identity thus requiring expression in urban planning terms, remains relegated to the fringes of discussion. Here urban design may well be a barometer of change. One looks forward to a situation where design is turned to expressing difference less contentiously rather than cosmetically masking it by decorating peace walls and security installations and where developers of new private housing in Belfast feel less need to ape the aesthetics of provincial Britishness.

In conclusion, reference is necessary to the role of urban planners in the reimaging agendas in Detroit and Belfast. In both cities professional urban planners have suffered from a degree of marginalization in policy formation. In Detroit the City Planning Department was always, under Mayor Young, subordinate to the Community and Economic Development Department which was less likely to clutter debate with consideration of options, alternatives and longer term planning. In a situation where it was possible for a strong mayor to dominate the policy agenda of the city because his office was empowered at the expense of the city council and operated with few institutional checks and balances (Rich, 1989, p. 278), planners in Detroit faced severe restraints on the ability to "talk truth to power" (Benveniste, 1989). However, the recent merger of these departments under Major Archer signifies new opportunities to do so in the future. Likewise in Belfast, most planners fit the characterization by Benveniste of planners generally as centrally preoccupied with the technical dimension of their activities and "quite unaware of, or unwilling to discuss, the managerial and political implications of their role and their work" (Benveniste, 1989, p. 52). This does not prevent a certain degree of frustration as planners are accountable upwards through a buffer layer of politically attuned administrators to government ministers. Here the alarming gulf between theory and practice in planning (Yiftachel, 1989, p. 23) looms large for those practising in Belfast. Forester characterises planners as "selective organisers of attention to real possibilities of action" (Forester, 1989, p. 4) and exhorts planners to endeavour to ensure a "political democratisation of daily practice" (ibid. p. 21). Healey proposes a view of "planning as debate" which "recognises the diversity of legitimate interests in environmental change and the role of discussion and negotiation as the media through which knowledge is translated into action" (Healey, 1989, p. 1). In Belfast, at least at the strategic level, the heavy hand of the state has acted to thwart such possibilities. Perhaps owing to a professional education which does not equip planners to understand how the organisations that employ them use power, planners in Belfast have been sidelined in policy formulation. As pointed out over ten years ago, "the physical planning of Belfast is in the hands of a small élite of professional civil servants, none of whom have necessarily any training relevant to town planning or urban problems" (Alcorn, quoted Cowan, 1982). Out of this frustration has come an apparent need by planners in some quarters to break out of narrow technical role conceptions which others have rightly discerned (Benvenisti, quoted Boal, 1993; Bollens, 1994), to identify professionally with the political planning agenda in order to massage professional self image. This is evidenced in a local Royal Town Planning Institute (RTPI) publication on planning in Belfast:

> We are all justifiably proud of the way Belfast has been developing over the past decade – and this despite all "The Troubles". This happier state of affairs is due, not just to the careful planning that has been proceeding quietly for several years now, but to the realisation by the public, politicians, and planners alike that a

successful future for Belfast depends on the fullest co-operation on the part of all her citizens, inspired by an optimistic vision of the shape of things to come and a common sense of purpose (RTPI, 1988, p. 13).

In a situation where the "public interest" has been orchestrated from above, this virtual endorsement of official policy seems misplaced. Government, of course, is unlikely to object to policy being presented in such a depoliticized consensual way. The advice of Reade here seems relevant:

> In the continuing debate between expertise and political ideas on which democracy depends, it surely ought not to be the role of the expert merely to 'respond', to go along with whatever vague equivocal and ambivalent catchwords and phrases government is currently hiding behind, but to confront slogans with facts – and preferably with inconvenient facts (Reade, 1989, p. 7).

However, without the return of some form of local democracy in Northern Ireland and the break-up of the present monolithic structure of the local state, Reade's exhortation is unlikely to be acted upon. In the event that peace does take root in Northern Ireland planners should transform their self image from being bearers, implementors and fine tuners of policy determined elsewhere to being more active facilitators and catalysts in policy and programme generation.

References

Benveniste, Guy (1989), *Mastering the Politics of Planning*, Jossey-Bass Publishers, San Francisco.

Benvenisti, M (1983), quoted F.W. Boal (1993) in 'Encapsulation: Urban Dimensions of National Conflict', paper presented at the Fulbright Colloquium on Managing Divided Cities, Magee College, University of Ulster, 6–8 September, p. 7.

Bollens, Scott A. (1994), 'Urban policy in ethnically polarized cities', paper presented at an international seminar jointly organized by the Urban Affairs Association, the School for Advanced Urban Studies, University of Bristol and the Department of City and Regional Planning, University of Wales College of Cardiff, 10–13 July.

Cowan, Robert (1982), 'Belfast's hidden planners', *Town and Country Planning*, June.

Detroit Compact (1992), 'Report 1989–1992', Detroit.

Forester, John (1989), *Planning in the Face of Power*, University of California Press, California.

Greenslade, Roy (1993), 'Belfast, beautiful Belfast', *Guardian*, 6 December.

Hayes, Maurice (1994), quoted by Hugh Hebert in 'Blame it on the box', *Guardian*, 7 July.

Healey, Patsy (1989), 'Planning for the 1990s', Working Paper no. 7, Department of Town and Country Planning, University of Newcastle-Upon-Tyne.

Lash, Scott and Urry, John (1994), *Economies of Signs and Space*, Sage, London.

Merian (1993) 'Ireland', Hamburg.

Miliband, Ralph (1994), 'The Plausibility of Socialism', *New Left Review*, no. 206.

Orr, Marion and Stoker, Gerry (1992), 'Urban Leadership and Regimes in Detroit', Special Research Series Report for the Center for Urban Studies, Wayne State University, Detroit.

Reade, Eric (1989), 'A Critical View of British Planning Education', paper presented to conference on Planning Education, Birmingham Polytechnic, 12–15 September.

Rich, Wilbur C. (1989), *Coleman Young and Detroit Politics*, Wayne State University Press, Detroit.

Rouse, James (1985), 'Belfast's Waterfront ... One Man's Vision', *Civic Trust Newsletter*, Belfast.

Royal Town Planning Institute (NI) (1988), *Belfast Arising*, Municipal Publicity Ltd., Belfast.

Teague, Paul (1994), 'Governance Structures and Economic Performance: The Case of Northern Ireland', *International Journal of Urban and Regional Research*, vol. 18, no. 2, pp. 275–292.

West, Cornell (1993), *Race Matters*, Beacon Press, Boston.

Vollman, James W. (1993), interview with the author, June.

Yiftachel, O. (1989), 'Towards a new typology of urban planning theories', *Environment and Planning B: Planning and Design*, vol. 16, pp. 23–39.